DEMOCRATIC LAW IN CLASSICAL ATHENS

The Fordyce W. Mitchel Memorial Lecture Series, sponsored by the Department of History at the University of Missouri-Columbia, began in October 2000. Fordyce Mitchel was professor of Greek history at the University of Missouri-Columbia until his death in 1986. In addition to his work on fourth-century Greek history and epigraphy, including his much-cited *Lykourgan Athens: 338–322*, Semple Lectures 2 (Cincinnati: 1970), Mitchel helped elevate the ancient history program in the Department of History and build the extensive library resources in that field. The lecture series was made possible by a generous endowment from his widow, Mrs. Marguerite Mitchel. It provides for a biennial series of lectures on original aspects of Greek history and society, given by a scholar of high international standing. The lectures are then revised and are currently published by the University of Texas Press.

PREVIOUS MITCHEL PUBLICATIONS:

Carol G. Thomas, *Finding People in Early Greece* (University of Missouri Press, 2005)
Mogens Herman Hansen, *The Shotgun Method: The Demography of the Ancient Greek City-State Culture* (University of Missouri Press, 2006)
Mark Golden, *Greek Sport and Social Status* (University of Texas Press, 2009)
Joseph Roisman, *Alexander's Veterans and the Early Wars of the Successors* (University of Texas Press, 2012)
Christopher Pelling, *Herodotus and the Question Why* (University of Texas Press, 2019)

DEMOCRATIC LAW IN CLASSICAL ATHENS

Michael Gagarin

UNIVERSITY OF TEXAS PRESS, AUSTIN

Printed in the United States of America
First edition, 2020

This book has been supported by an endowment dedicated to classics and the ancient world and funded by the Areté Foundation; the Gladys Krieble Delmas Foundation; the Dougherty Foundation; the James R. Dougherty, Jr. Foundation; the Rachael and Ben Vaughan Foundation; and the National Endowment for the Humanities.

♾ The paper used in this book meets the minimum requirements of ANSI/NISO Z39.48-1992 (R1997) (Permanence of Paper).

LIBRARY OF CONGRESS CATALOGING-IN-PUBLICATION DATA

Names: Gagarin, Michael, author.
Title: Democratic law in classical Athens / Michael Gagarin.
Description: Austin : University of Texas Press, 2020. | Series: Fordyce W. Mitchel Memorial Lecture Series | Includes bibliographical references and index.
Identifiers: LCCN 2019030029 | ISBN 978-1-4773-2037-2 (cloth) | ISBN 978-1-4773-2039-6 (nonlibrary ebook) | ISBN 978-1-4773-2038-9 (library ebook)
Subjects: LCSH: Public law (Greek law) | Justice, Administration of (Greek law) | Democracy—Greece—Athens—History—To 1500. | Athens (Greece)—Politics and government.
Classification: LCC KL4358 .G34 2020 | DDC 340.5/385—dc23
LC record available at https://lccn.loc.gov/2019030029

doi:10.7560/320372

For Daniel and Alexandra

CONTENTS

PREFACE

This book draws together a number of ideas about Athenian law that I have been thinking and writing about during the last two decades. These ideas have focused on aspects of Athenian law (and in some cases of Greek law more generally) that are generally considered marginal to the law. These included most importantly the close connection between Athenian law and democracy, as well as the role of "challenges" in litigation (which I analyze in the broader categories of proposals and negotiation), law as performance, the place of rhetoric in law, the connection between law and justice, and the role in litigation of factors such as public interest that are today considered irrelevant or only marginally relevant. These features have all been noted by others and have sometimes given rise to strong criticism of the Athenian legal system (see the introduction and chapter 1). This book is an attempt to understand how these marginal features affected Athenian law in practice.[1]

I argue that, when properly understood, these features can be seen to be fully consistent with the rule of law, with justice, and with the democratic insistence on public benefit. I argue that although Athenian law was indeed democratic, in the sense that it was truly in the hands of the people, as the Athenians wished it to be, it nonetheless succeeded to a large degree in observing the rule of law. Athenian law is not immune from criticism, for example, that the amount of litigation was excessive, but in general most Athenians seem to have had a favorable opinion of their legal system, so that it underwent relatively little structural change between ca. 460 and 323.

Some of the issues I deal with in the following pages have been controversial. My experience is that in even the most heated debates, both sides usually have something valuable to contribute. I have tried to draw on the

---

1. I have been much influenced by law and literature approaches to modern law and follow Goodrich (1998:115) in believing that "the study of Law and Literature draws attention to certain marginal features of law and makes that marginality central to a critical understanding of law."

contributions of these studies without getting bogged down in the controversies and disagreements. In the notes, I have tried to acknowledge my indebtedness to the many studies that have influenced me in this work, though I have undoubtedly neglected to mention some, for which I apologize. In the end, of course, the views expressed are my own.

DATES

All dates in this book are BCE unless the contrary is either stated or obvious.

TRANSLATIONS

The translations in the text are my own, but for the forensic speeches, they are usually based on the translations in the Texas series The Oratory of Classical Greece (Gagarin, ed., 1998–2017).

CITATIONS OF THE ORATORS

I refer to passages from Attic oratory by the name of the author or the standard abbreviation for it—Aes. (Aeschines), And. (Andocides), Ant. (Antiphon), Dem. (Demosthenes), Din. (Dinarchus), Hyp. (Hyperides), Is. (Isaeus), Isoc. (Isocrates), Lyc. (Lycurgus), and Lys. (Lysias)—followed by the speech's number and section number. For Hyperides, I also add the speech's title. For the most part, I ignore the question of authorship, since most of the speeches are evidence of fifth- and fourth-century forensic oratory, regardless of who wrote them, and thus provide evidence for how law operated in this period.

ABBREVIATIONS

IG = *Inscriptiones Graecae*
SEG = *Supplementum Epigraphicum Graecum*

MODERN LAW

Throughout the book I refer from time to time to "modern legal systems" or "our own legal system" or something similar, though the precise wording may vary. By the former, I mean to designate in general the common-law and civil-law systems of Europe, the United States, and many other parts of the world; other current non-Western legal systems, such as Islamic law, may not fit my picture of modern law. By "our own," I mean the common-law system as it has evolved in the United States, ignoring for the most part differences between the states.

ACKNOWLEDGMENTS

Many people helped bring this book into being and improve it along the way. My first and most important debt is to Ian Worthington and the History Department of the University of Missouri, who invited me to give the Fordyce Mitchel lectures there in October 2015. I am grateful to them not only for the invitation but for the abundant hospitality they accorded me during my visit. The preparation of these lectures and the discussions that followed them gave me new ideas and helped me refine, or in some cases discard, my previous ideas. The road from lectures to book has involved not just revision, but a large amount of rethinking and reorganizing. An obvious change is that the original four lectures—on democracy, performance, justice, and the rule of law—have become an introduction and nine chapters. But my main goal, a better understanding of Athens's extraordinary, truly democratic legal system, has remained unchanged.

At a late stage, the entire work was read by Adriaan Lanni and Bob Wallace, both of whom gave me extensive comments that have greatly improved the book. I also benefited greatly from the careful criticism and advice provided by Adele Scafuro, who read the book for UT Press; her comments and criticism saved me from many errors and forced me to rethink, and in some cases alter, my views on several matters. A second, anonymous reader also had some helpful comments.

As always, it has been a pleasure to work with Jim Burr and the rest of the staff at UT Press, in particular copyeditor Nancy Warrington.

DEDICATION

My two children, to whom I have dedicated this book, taught me a great deal about the study of classical Athenian law. As anyone who spends time with children knows, they are regularly involved in disputes with one another. We are all familiar with the "he hit me," "she hit me first" scenario, and with the more sophisticated rhetorical moves children often make as they get older. Anyone who tries to settle such disputes knows that they always have a history. Skillful parents and teachers take that history into account in resolving disputes, but even the most skillful cannot always succeed in satisfying both sides, and we have all experienced the inevitable complaint that "it's not fair." Just what is fair is rarely an easy question—an equal division may be the answer in many cases, but sometimes it is not.[2] The experience of working through the complexities of such situations when my children were young (and even occasionally after they were grown) has, I think, helped me better understand classical Athenian litigation as a process of dispute resolution, in which litigants in court regularly ask for and expect to receive "justice," and appreciate that the contextualization of the dispute is essential to anyone seeking to achieve a just result.

---

2. Recent scientific research has shown that even monkeys apparently care about fairness. A group of monkeys were trained to hand over a pebble for slices of cucumber (a desirable food). Then, in sight of the others, one monkey was offered a grape (an even more desirable food) in exchange for a pebble. Other monkeys were then offered a cucumber slice for the pebble but now they wouldn't take it. Some even threw the cucumber slice back at the researcher. It seems that they thought it was not fair (*New York Times*, Sunday Review for Sunday, June 4, 2017, p. 8).

DEMOCRATIC LAW IN CLASSICAL ATHENS

INTRODUCTION

I began studying Athenian law in the mid-1970s. My work to that point had been in philosophy (my dissertation and first article were on Plato and Protagoras) and literature (my first book was on Aeschylus). I had had no legal training but was interested in "intellectual history," an interest that appears quite old-fashioned today. In particular, I was interested in justice, and justice led me to law and to several questions and problems that I felt had not received satisfactory discussion in the existing literature. So I began investigating for myself.

At that time, Athenian law was little studied.[1] The two great legal systems of the ancient world in terms of area of influence were Roman and Chinese, both of which were the products of authoritarian political regimes that ruled empires. Each of these legal systems also influenced (and continues to influence) modern legal systems in many parts of the world. By contrast, Athenian law applied only to the inhabitants of the Athenian polis ("city-state," or better, "citizen-state"). It, and Greek law more generally, had almost no influence on other legal systems, though its ideological influence began to be felt in the mid-nineteenth century. In addition, Greek law produced no systematic scholarly analyses like the works of the Roman jurists and no systematic codes of law like the codes of successive Chinese dynasties. Indeed, it could be questioned whether Greek law was a "system" in any sense.[2] Most legal historians, therefore, took little interest in it.

The great advantage of this state of affairs for a young scholar like me was that I did not have to cope with enormous amounts of previous scholarship before formulating my own views. My initial interest was homicide

1. For personal reflections on the state of the study of Greek law in the 1970s, see Cohen 2005b:1–3; Lanni and Wallace 2018:1–3.

2. This was already noted by Cicero (*De Oratore* I.44 [197]), who claims that compared with Roman law, all other *ius civile*, especially that of the Greeks, is "disordered and almost ridiculous" (*inconditum ac paene ridiculum*).

law, including Draco's law and the speeches of Antiphon, but I also developed an interest in the Gortyn law code and other Cretan laws, and in early Greek law in general. During all this time, however, I maintained an interest in classical (late fifth- and fourth-century) Athenian law, and especially in two of the continuing controversies over the fundamental nature of Athenian law.

The first (and less important) of these concerns is the degree of formalism in Athenian law. To some extent (though not entirely) this reflects the division between scholars, primarily those in the civil-law countries of continental Europe, who have been trained in Roman law, and those in common-law countries, especially the United States and United Kingdom, who have generally been trained in history, philosophy, or literature. The former are more likely to find formalist elements in Athenian law and to use concepts derived from the more formalist system of Roman law in interpreting elements of Athenian law.[3] I readily acknowledge my sympathy with the latter group of scholars; in my view, the search for formalist elements in Athenian law only distracts one from many far more important features.

The second controversy provides the background for this book. It arose as scholars began to reassess the effectiveness of Athenian law, which had been almost universally criticized by historians since Roman times.[4] One of the most negative judgments came from the most distinguished scholar of Athenian institutions in the late nineteenth century, Gustav Gilbert:[5]

> The plan of entrusting the administration of justice to the common people proved a failure in the form in which it was tried in the Athenian Heliaia. The Heliasts, led away by their irresponsibility, too often disregarded the laws and acted on the mere impulse of the moment. More than this, bribery and interested motives not unfrequently determined the decisions of the courts. Further, the Heliasts' ignorance of the laws demoralized the speakers, who, not unfrequently, trading on this ignorance, misinterpreted and misrepresented the laws to suit their case. The system of allowing the people to administer justice produced a crop of

---

3. One small sign of this division is the paper I delivered at the 2017 meeting of the Symposion in Tel Aviv entitled "Challenges in Athenian Law: Going beyond Oaths and *Basanos* to Proposals" (Gagarin 2018b, whose ideas are largely reflected in chapter 3). My respondent, Gerhard Thür, confined his response to formal proposals in Athenian law (Thür 2018), implicitly rejecting my thesis of a basic similarity among all proposals, whether formal or informal. Thür's view is characteristic of those who see Athenian law as a science (see the end of chapter 2).

4. See note 2 to this introduction. Before Cicero, Plato had criticized Athenian law, but he did not have the comparandum of Roman law.

5. Gilbert 1895:415–416 (translated from the German original of 1893).

> sycophants at Athens, who made their living by false accusations, and by levying blackmail, which their victims were afraid to refuse owing to the vagaries of the Dicasteries. The result of this state of things was a general uncertainty in the administration of justice, which made it impossible even for the most upright citizen to live in peace at Athens, if this did not suit the caprice of some malicious neighbour.[6]

A similarly negative view was expressed by the English historian J. B. Bury, whose *History of Greece*, first published in 1900, was for many years the standard English text for Greek history:[7]

> It was a matter of course that in cases of a political character the judges of the *heliaia* should be swayed by their own political opinions and by the eloquence of the pleaders working upon their emotions. It was inevitable that the legal aspect of such cases should be lost to sight, and the facts often misjudged. It was an essential part of the democratic intention that the sovereign people should make its anger felt; and if its anger were sometimes, like a king's anger, unfair, that could not be helped. But it was far more serious that in private cases the ends of justice were liable to be defeated, not through intention but through ignorance. . . . They [the speakers] make a large use of arguments which are perfectly irrelevant to the case; a plaintiff, for example, will try to demonstrate at great length that he has rendered services to the state and that his opponent has performed none. There was thus no question of simply administering the law. The judges heard each party interpreting the law in its own sense; but they had themselves no knowledge of the law, and therefore, however impartial they sought to be, their decision was unduly influenced by the dexterity of an eloquent pleader, and affected by considerations which had nothing to do with the matter at issue. And there was no appeal from their judgment.[8]

Views such as these are still held by some scholars. In a study of law and rhetoric, for example, Yunis writes, "There was no presiding legal officer to impose rules of evidence or relevance, to require litigants to address any

6. The Heliaia was the traditional name for the Athenian popular court, which was later called the Dicastery (*dikastērion*). The term *sykophantēs* designated a person who maliciously prosecuted or threatened to prosecute someone in the hope of being paid to drop the suit (discussed below in chapter 1). I will designate such a person a "sykophant" to distinguish him from the "sycophant" in English, who has completely different attributes.

7. Bury's work was thoroughly revised by Russell Meiggs in 1975, but the section entitled "The Working of the Law-Courts," from which I quote, was retained verbatim.

8. Bury 1900:350 (= 1975:217).

matter of fact or law, or to question or limit the litigants in the presentation of their cases. . . . The only effective constraint was rhetorical; that is, litigants would constrain themselves from saying anything that might alienate their audience, the *dikastai*." From this Yunis concludes that "a litigant seeking only his own advantage could use rhetorical skill unimpeded to manipulate the *dikastai* into deciding a case contrary to their true wishes or best judgment."[9]

These scholars all note that the jury, ordinary citizens with no knowledge of the law, operated without restraint and thus (in their view) could be swayed by emotional appeals and misleading arguments crafted by skilled speakers or speechwriters. There is some truth to this judgment, for one of the most prominent features of Athenian law and Athenian government in general was that the jurors (as I prefer to call them) had no special training in law.[10] They were ordinary Athenian citizens, and they were free to decide cases as they wished, without oversight by any higher authority. There was no presiding official or judge (in our sense) who might instruct the jurors or impose any control on the arguments of the litigants. Under such conditions, it is easy to imagine that ignorance, emotion, and prejudice decided many cases. But was this in fact the case?

One response to this traditional criticism has been to reassess the purpose of Athenian litigation. Osborne, for example, in his often-cited article "Law in Action in Classical Athens," notes that several different procedures were available for prosecuting certain offenses. In such cases, Osborne argues, "the Athenian law courts were a public stage upon which private enmities were played out" (52), and thus "which type of procedure is used seems far more to be determined by the relative and absolute social positions of prosecutor and defendant" than by the legal differences between different procedures.[11] David Cohen argues that "litigation at Athens has as much to do with pursuing conflict as it does with resolving disputes" and that in Demosthenes' prosecution of Meidias, "each party . . . used the legal system as one means of harassing, attacking, or intimidating his opponent in a series of challenges and responses whose dynamic is driven by an ago-

---

9. Yunis 2005:194–195, 197.

10. Because members of the Athenian jury filled the roles of both judge and juror in modern legal systems that have juries, some scholars prefer to call them judges. Each English term renders part of the sense of Greek *dikastēs* but fails to render other parts. In my view, the large size of Athenian juries (up to five hundred members and more) makes "juror" the more appropriate translation, as the notion of a jury of five hundred judges sounds odd today. In the United States, at least, when a number of judges decide a case as a group, they constitute an appeals court. But either translation is acceptable.

11. Osborne 1985:52–53.

nistic ethos which aims at the enhancement of honor, status, and power."[12] For those who adopt this view, some of the factors identified by Gilbert and Bury as weaknesses, far from deterring the courts from their mission, actually helped the jurors assess the two litigants' cases according to criteria they judged appropriate.

Other scholars, rejecting this approach, have insisted that Athenian courts sought to judge cases according to the rule of law—that is, among other things, to decide whether or not the facts of the case showed that the accused had committed the offense specified in the law. Harris, for example, argues that "the Athenians held the rule of law in deep respect and adhered to a form of government that attempted to put that ideal into practice. Nor should we underestimate the ability of the average Athenian to understand the rudimentary law-code of his native community and to distinguish sound arguments from legal sophistries."[13]

I have long felt that each of these perspectives on Athenian law was valid up to a point and was applicable to some cases, but that neither could fully explain the arguments and outcomes of most cases, nor could either provide a full understanding of how Athenian law actually worked. My own view, in brief, is that Athenian courts did try to enforce the laws as written but that they deliberately allowed litigants to present a broad range of arguments, including arguments about relative social and political worth, which modern scholars generally see as conflicting with the strict enforcement of the law but which the Athenians saw as not only compatible with the rule of law but as essential to it. The following chapters are an attempt to elaborate this view by exploring some of the features of Athenian law in the classical period (fifth and fourth centuries) that seem most at odds with the modern concept of a properly autonomous legal system. It is essential, in my view, to examine these features if we are to understand classical Athenian law.

The first feature I examine is democracy (chapter 1), which is perhaps the most important factor influencing the unusual character of Athenian law.

---

12. Cohen 1991:164. Todd shares this view to some extent ("Punishment at Athens was designed neither to fit the crime nor to fit the criminal, but rather to reorder the relative position of the two litigants" [Todd 1993:162]), but overall his view is more complex and nuanced. See also Cartledge 2016:169–181, for example: "In major political trials—in a sense all trials were political, of course—the overriding consideration for a juror was not necessarily the guilt or innocence of the defendant as charged, but rather what verdict and (where relevant) punishment would most likely further Athens' best interests as a democratic *polis*" (170). Cf.: "Punishments were fitted to the criminal rather than to the crime" (ibid.: 118).

13. Harris 1994:132. Harris's views are further elaborated in many more recent publications (see the bibliography).

I have made "democratic law" part of this book's title because democracy, in its full Athenian sense of a government controlled at every level by the *dēmos*, the ordinary citizens, lies at the heart of Athenian law.[14] Not only did Athenian democracy differ from democracy today in being fully participatory, but the Athenians' conviction that law should be similarly democratic led them to create a legal system that was also fully participatory, controlled by ordinary citizens, not trained experts or legal professionals. I describe the basic components of Athenian democracy and its legal system, as well as the methods of litigation that were available, and make a preliminary assessment of some of the strengths and weaknesses of the system.

After democracy, I turn to performance (chapter 2) and examine the implications of viewing the trial process as a set of performances. Most good trial lawyers today are to some extent performers, but performance in general is not supposed to have a significant effect on judges or jurors. In Athens, however, the litigation process, and the large size of juries in particular, encouraged performances by both parties. I examine how the litigants' performance, often in combination with other factors, may have affected their pleadings and the outcome of the trial. The most important conclusion I reach is that performance involves an audience, and this audience exercises significant control over the performance. This gave the trial audience the ability to influence litigants' pleadings while litigants were also seeking to influence their audience. I also argue that performance made the litigants' pleadings more prominent and required them to have greater rhetorical ability than is required of advocates today.

Next I take up the subject of negotiation (chapter 3), which I analyze as consisting of proposals (some of which have traditionally been called "challenges") and responses or counterproposals. Negotiation with a view to settling disputes, both those that are in their early stages and those that are at the stage of litigation, is common in all human communities and all legal systems whether or not it is formally recognized as such. People resolve most disputes by themselves, or with the help of family or friends, or sometimes with the help of special mediation resources. In most legal systems, it is probably only a minority of disputes that reach the litigation stage, and many of these are settled before going to trial. Athens was no different. But Athens developed three special types of proposals—concerning the testimony of a witness, the swearing of an oath, and the interrogation of slaves under torture (*basanos*)—each with its own special rules that made it almost

14. Both Gilbert and Bury seem to recognize this: the former speaks of "the plan of entrusting the administration of justice to the common people"; the latter speaks of the "democratic intention" of the "sovereign people."

impossible in practice for the negotiation to succeed. The main, and almost only, purpose of these types of proposals, therefore, was rhetorical. They almost never succeeded in resolving the dispute, but they allowed a speaker to argue, for example, that his opponent was admitting his guilt by rejecting negotiation.

Because both performance and negotiation encourage litigants to develop their rhetorical abilities (or hire someone with rhetorical ability to write a speech for them), chapter 4 examines the role of rhetoric in Athenian law. Like performance, rhetoric is a feature of litigation today, especially in jury trials, but it is not supposed to have a significant effect on judges or jurors. This was not the case in Athens, and indeed at some trials, large crowds of onlookers gathered to observe the proceedings and enjoy the rhetorical performances of the litigants. However, without anyone present like a modern judge to restrain or control the pleadings, a litigant striving for rhetorical impact could theoretically introduce whatever arguments he wished, regardless of their relevance to the case.

This leads me in chapter 5 to examine means of restraining the litigants' rhetoric, beginning with the laws and the jurors' oath, which required them, among other things, to judge according to the laws of the city. I then examine the so-called rule of relevance. In the Athenian legal system, the relevant issues were determined by the formal, often quite detailed, accusation filed by the plaintiff, which was posted at the entrance to the court and read out at the beginning of the trial. Most litigants, I argue, largely confined their pleading to matters that were relevant by this criterion, and if they seemed to be straying from what was relevant (speaking "outside the issue"), they often explained why what they were about to say or had said was, in their view, relevant. Two factors helped ensure that litigants observe the rule of relevance: first, their obligation to do so in accordance with the rule of relevance, and second, their regard for the reactions of their audience, both the jurors and the onlookers, who could and would raise a *thorybos* ("hub-bub" or "uproar") if they were not pleased with a litigant's pleading.

In chapter 6, I examine the role of justice, a factor whose relevance the Athenians never question. Litigants often introduce arguments about justice but apparently never feel the need to explain or justify these arguments. Justice, to be sure, is in general the ultimate objective of every legal system, but justice in the specific sense of a just outcome in every case is rarely considered a goal. In most cases in the United States, at least, justice carries no weight in arguments in court. I argue that this is in part because in modern pluralistic societies there are few clear, universally accepted rules of justice. Thus, if the litigants in a case claim that they want justice or that justice is on their side, there is usually no way to decide between competing claims according to the kind of objective criteria that are desired in modern law. In Athens, however, litigants frequently appeal to justice in their pleadings and often seem to equate justice and law. It seems that the Athenians felt that their procedure for enacting laws was just, and that as a result, any law enacted according to this procedure would be just. A just outcome to a case was thus considered a lawful outcome and vice versa, and the appeal to justice was seen as fully consistent with the appeal to law.

Like justice, public interest is not directly relevant to the issue in most cases, but it was apparently considered acceptable nonetheless. The reasons for this are considered in chapter 7, in which I examine the relationship between the polis, public interest, and Athenian law. Because the Athenians considered their democratic legal system to be an integral part of their democratic political system, they saw law and public benefit as intrinsically related. Probably every legal system is thought to benefit the community in a general way, by providing orderly rules and procedures promoting peace and prosperity. But in Athens, the law was seen as providing more specific benefits than this. The Athenians thought that all laws should benefit the polis, and every judgment should take into account the public benefit it provided. This did not invalidate the need to punish those who had violated the law, and arguments addressing the main issues in a case were always necessary, but litigants seem to have expected that their public service could provide additional support for their case. The influence of public benefits on a verdict was not thought to conflict with the jury's obligation to judge according to the law; rather, it was seen as supplementary to other aspects of the rule of law. Thus, the mention of public interest may have been (according to our view of relevance) "outside the issue" in the case, but since public interest was inherent in the law, the Athenians did not treat it as a violation of the rule of relevance.

In chapter 8, I turn to an analysis of the rule of law, trying to determine if and how it might have coexisted with all the features analyzed in the previous chapters. I examine first the wide range of principles that have at one time or another been included in discussions of the rule of law and single out three that, in my view, are fundamental: the orderly and peaceful regulation of society according to a set of authoritative rules, the principle that no person is above the law, and the exclusion of "nonlegal" or irrelevant considerations from legal decision making. I conclude that the Athenians certainly observed the first two principles, and their observance of the second, in particular, was especially noteworthy. I am not aware of any other legal system before the end of the nineteenth century that did not make special provision for at least some officials or political leaders. The Athenians also observed the third principle to a large extent, inasmuch as, if we allow for their broader and more flexible understanding of relevance, most litigants observed the rule of relevance most of the time.

Finally, in chapter 9, I conclude that the Athenian legal system largely satisfied the Athenians' desire to provide a democratic legal process—one completely controlled by the *dēmos*—that nonetheless operated in accordance with the rule of law as they understood it. Most Athenians thought that the system worked well to ensure justice and public benefit together with the rule of law, and thus supported their democratic political system. Indeed, their legal system was viewed as one of the pillars of their democracy. Thus, democratic law worked well for the Athenians both as a legal system and as a democratic political institution.

CHAPTER I

DEMOCRACY

The Athenians deliberately shaped their law to be democratic—to be a fundamental pillar of their democratic political system (*politeia*). The study of Athenian law must, therefore, be grounded in an understanding of Athenian democracy, and I so begin this study with a brief overview of the major features of that democracy. Today, Athens is hailed as the birthplace of democracy, and democracy is so widely considered a good, if not the best, form of government that it is easy to forget that until the nineteenth century democracy was generally seen as the antithesis of good government—a system leading only to disorder and chaos, as exemplified in antiquity by classical Athens and in modern times by the French Revolution and its aftermath.[1] The American founding fathers very deliberately created a republic, not a democracy. Only as more liberal views of government began to spread in Europe and the United States did democracy become more respectable.[2] Abraham Lincoln's "government of the people, by the people, and for the people" captures the essence of Athenian democracy, but the word "democracy" did not appear in his Gettysburg Address, and our representative democracy is a far cry from the ideal described by that expression.

In the twenty-first century, most nations have some form of democratic government, but virtually all are representative democracies in which a relatively small number of people make almost all the decisions. If the ancient Athenians could see what people around the world today call democracy, they would be wondering how their word *dēmokratia* could come to be applied to so many different forms of government, none of which they would consider democratic. *Dēmo-kratia* means power (*kratos*) for the peo-

1. See Finley 1973:9–11 on the current universal approval of democracy.

2. See Roberts 1994. The most influential work leading to the reevaluation of Athenian democracy was Grote's *History of Greece* (1846–1856). Suspicion of democracy, however, continues to exist in the United States and elsewhere, and even today, undemocratic features such as the Electoral College remain in our constitution.

ple (*dēmos*),[3] roughly equivalent to the 1960s slogan "power to the people."[4] From the Athenian perspective, none of the governments that claim to be democracies today actually do give power to the people—not the United States, not the parliamentary democracies of Europe, and not the communist systems of Cuba or China. The people in these countries may participate in elections to select their leaders, but in none of them is the government actually run by the people, nor does it always work primarily for the benefit of the common people.

It is difficult for us today to appreciate how extraordinary classical Athenian democracy was. From today's perspective, it was marred by the exclusion of women and slaves from the class of politically active citizens. Today, such exclusion would be roundly condemned, but we must remember that in the United States and most of the rest of the world, the exclusion of slaves from the franchise endured until the nineteenth century and the exclusion of women until the twentieth. In the ancient world outside of Greece and Rome, giving even a small degree of political power to ordinary citizens was almost unheard of, but (with the limitation just mentioned) Athens managed to create a fully participatory democratic government not experienced anywhere else at any time.[5]

The most thorough ancient account of how Athenian democracy worked is contained in the second part of the *Athenaiōn Politeia* (*Ath. Pol.* for short) or *The Constitution of the Athenians* (chapters 42–69), a work traditionally attributed to Aristotle.[6] This is essentially a description of the Athenian government in the second half of the fourth century.[7] It begins with the citizen body and the Assembly (*Ath. Pol.* 42); continues with the officials, including the Council, who managed the business of government (43–62); and ends with the courts (63–69).[8] This description foreshadows to some extent the

3. *Dēmos* can designate the citizen population as a whole, but it is often used to designate the common people as opposed to the rich and powerful.

4. This sense of *dēmokratia* is also reflected in Lenin's "dictatorship of the proletariat" (Cartledge 2016:1), though the Soviet Union that Lenin helped create never came close to giving actual power to the common people.

5. For similarities and differences among ancient and modern democracies, see Finley 1973; Hansen 2010:xix–xvi and passim.

6. See Rhodes 1981, 2017. I will refer to its author as Aristotle, even though it was most likely written by one or more of his students in the Lyceum and published not long before his death in 322, or perhaps shortly thereafter.

7. Hansen 1991 provides a very good modern overview of the Athenian democracy with full references to the primary sources; see also Cartledge 2016. For a good brief account, see Carey 2000.

8. My discussion that follows, like that in the second half of the *Ath. Pol.*, assumes little change in the democracy between ca. 462 and 322. We know that changes oc-

modern division of government into three branches—legislative, executive, judicial—but the Athenians never developed any theory of the separation of powers. The Council, moreover, fits a bit uncomfortably in the category of officials; like officials, Councilors were selected by lot for one-year terms, but as a body, they had both legislative and executive functions.[9]

Because government by the people required the participation of a large majority of the citizenry, the Athenians structured their government in ways that would achieve this goal. Five features are notable in this regard. First, an Assembly, open to all citizens, approved all legislation and decided all major policy issues. Any Athenian citizen over the age of eighteen who had been duly registered in his deme[10] could attend and vote at an Assembly meeting. A quorum was six thousand, and evidence indicates that at least that many usually attended.[11] Anyone who wished could speak on the matter under consideration, but by tradition it seems that the more senior members usually spoke first.[12]

During most of the fifth century, the Assembly could pass almost any legislation it wanted, as long as the Council had put the proposed legisla-

---

curred, but the government nonetheless retained its basic democratic features throughout the period. Cartledge (2016:219–227 and passim) struggles with the question of whether the period saw one type of democracy or two—or three or even more. For a good review and discussion of the changes, see Rhodes 1995, 2016. One change, which became necessary after the Peloponnesian War because fewer citizens were available to serve, allowed the *thētes* (the poorest class of citizens) to hold office; this helped maintain the principle that no one should repeat in an office.

9. See Rhodes 2018:25–26. The *Ath. Pol.* treats the Council as a large board of officials (43–49), as do some of our other sources, but other ancient sources distinguish the Council from the officials; the Council also acted in a judicial capacity in some cases. See Hansen 1991:226–227 and 246–265 for details.

10. In 508/7, Cleisthenes divided the population of Athens into 139 demes, small political subdivisions comparable to neighborhood precincts today. Initially, deme membership was determined by a person's residence, but once a person had been assigned to a deme, he and his descendants retained the same deme membership even if they changed residence. An Athenian was commonly identified by his name, his patronymic, and his demotic (deme name); for example, Socrates son of Sophroniscus of Alopece. The demes were grouped into ten tribes, which were used for selecting candidates for public office, among other things (see below).

11. Modern estimates of the Athenian population vary so widely that it is pointless to give a firm figure for the number of Athenian citizens (and, of course, the population itself fluctuated over time). But it is perhaps likely that a quorum represented 15–25 percent of the eligible population. See further Hansen 1986, 2006:19–60.

12. The vast majority of attendees must have remained silent in Assembly meetings. A few apparently spoke regularly and were referred to as *rhētores* (speakers), a term that thus came to be roughly equivalent to "politician" (Hansen 1983).

tion on the agenda for that meeting. At the end of the century, however, the Athenians enacted a number of reforms.[13] These included reform of the legislative process so as to prohibit the enactment of any law that had not first been approved by a group of Nomothetai (Lawgivers). This group would post a copy of any proposed new law in the agora, the central community meeting- and marketplace, where anyone could read and comment on it. The Nomothetai would also examine the proposed new law to see whether it conflicted with any existing law. After this period of examination, the Nomothetai could approve the proposed law without further action by the Council or the Assembly. Thus, the enactment of new laws was more controlled in the fourth century than in the fifth.

The Nomothetai were selected from members of the jury pool (see below); thus, like those attending the Assembly, they were also ordinary citizens, though with a minimum age of thirty (as opposed to eighteen for members of the Assembly).[14] As Cohen observes, from a modern perspective, the creation of the Nomothetai as a way to curb the perceived faults of the fifth-century Assembly in enacting legislation "would have been the occasion to create a small specialized body of people with expert knowledge or training to undertake the mandated continuing oversight that was to ensure uniformity and eliminate contradictory laws."[15] The Athenians' commitment to the democratic participatory process, however, precluded any thought of requiring special training or expertise in this body. Legislative power thus remained entirely in the hands of ordinary citizens.

The second notable feature of Athenian participatory democracy is that almost all administrative offices, including the five-hundred-member Council, were chosen by lot and were limited to a single one-year term. In the fourth century, a second (nonconsecutive) term on the Council was allowed, probably because after the losses in the Peloponnesian War, there would not otherwise have been enough new citizens to fill the five hundred positions every year. The selection process began with each of the ten tribes proposing a list of available members for that year, and lots would then be drawn to determine who would serve in the coming year.

The Council was responsible for the overall supervision of all civic activities. Its five hundred members were divided by tribe into ten groups called prytaneis, each with fifty members, and each of these prytaneis served for

13. The exact nature of these reforms and possible changes during the course of the fourth century is disputed. See, for example, MacDowell 1975; Hansen 1985; Robertson 1990; Rhodes 1991; Canevaro 2013b.

14. See Hansen 1991:167–168.

15. Cohen 2015:169–171.

one-tenth of the year as a kind of executive committee. In the fifth century, on each day during this period of about thirty-six days, one member of the prytany, selected by lot, would be the head of government for that day; he would keep the keys to public money, organize a meeting of the prytany if one were needed, and generally have charge of the administration of the city. In the fourth century, however, these duties were carried out by nine *proedroi*, selected by lot, one each from the nine tribes who were not holding the prytany in that period. At some point in their lives, therefore, most Athenians would spend one day as head of the government, though with very limited power.[16]

Executive duties were also entrusted to several hundred officials.[17] Together with their assistants (many of whom were public slaves), these officials ran the day-to-day operation of public institutions and handled their finances. Most Athenians, in addition to a term on the Council, would also have served as one of the other officials at least once during their lifetime.[18] In addition, many would have held a position in their deme or tribe.[19] Thus, almost all Athenians had the experience of serving in public office, but no citizen developed expertise or amassed any significant power through such service.[20]

Free elections, which today are often a path to power and which we consider an essential feature of democratic government, were generally seen as elitist and were used only to select men for a few positions that required special expertise, such as military commanders and certain financial officials. As the Athenians saw it, most positions in government did not require special expertise but could be held by any citizen. As a result, whereas we think of the state as an entity separate from the people, for the Athenians, the

16. In Plato's *Apology* (32b–c), Socrates describes his service on the Council while his tribe held the prytany.

17. Hansen (1991:230) suggests about six hundred officials, not including the five hundred Councilors.

18. There were, however, an unknown number of "quiet Athenians," who chose to avoid public service entirely; see Carter 1986.

19. There were only a few officials in each deme and tribe (see Hansen 1991:104–106), but together they may have added a few hundred more persons with executive duties to the Athenian government. There were also deme assemblies that decided matters of purely local interest.

20. On the other hand, as Ismard notes, "public slaves held the same post for several years and in that sense embodied the permanence of a civic knowledge or competence that was beyond the purview of the magistrates, who were usually selected by lot and replaced every year" (2017:40). For details, see Hansen 1991:244–245. Todd refers to these public slaves as "the nearest equivalent to a permanent civil service" (1996:131). Of course, no matter how much expertise they may have acquired, because slaves ipso facto could not gain power in the city, their expertise was not normally seen as a threat.

state was the *dēmos*—the people of Athens.[21] An indication of this is that the Athenians always referred to the political entity we call "Athens" as "the Athenians" (*hoi Athēnaioi*). Like all other Greeks, they used the name "Athens" only for the geographical place they inhabited.

Besides the Council, the most important officials were the nine Archons. These included the Archon, sometimes called the Eponymous Archon because his name was assigned to the year as a means of dating it ("in the archonship of X"), the Basileus or "King" (usually referred to today as the King Archon), the Polemarch, and a group of six Thesmothetai.[22] These nine Archons had various duties, including supervising lawsuits. Each was in charge of certain kinds of cases. A case involving orphans, for example, would go before the Archon; a homicide case, before the Basileus, and so on. Besides the Archons, other groups of officials were charged with managing public finances, overseeing building projects, supervising markets, and many other public tasks (*Ath. Pol.* 50–62).

The third notable feature was accountability, which was accomplished by means of a scrutiny (*dokimasia*) of all officials, including candidates for the Council, before they began their term in office, and an accounting (*euthynai*) of their performance at the end of the term.[23] In the *dokimasia*, after candidates had shown that they were citizens of the right age, they could be challenged as being unfit for office. Most must have been confirmed without objection, but when there was an objection, a trial could be held to determine the candidate's fitness. We have speeches from four such trials, all by Lysias (16, 25, 26, 31) and all raising the same objection that the candidate had oligarchic sympathies as shown by his conduct during the oligarchic regime of the Thirty in 404–403.

Euthynai hearings primarily examined the financial accounts that officials had to submit at the end of their term in office concerning any funds that they had been given charge of. Embezzlement and bribery were the main offenses in question, but even if an official's accounts were in order, he could still be accused of other sorts of malfeasance during his term in office.[24]

---

21. In recent years, scholars have begun referring to Athens and other Greek poleis as "citizen-states" rather than the traditional "city-states." This appellation is surely more accurate.

22. In addition, a secretary to the Thesmothetai was selected; he and the nine Archons then represented the ten tribes.

23. See Roberts 1982. There were also various opportunities to challenge an official's performance during his term in office; see Hansen 1991:220–222.

24. See Antiphon 6.43, where the speaker argues that a procedural ruling by the Basileus, about which his opponent complained vehemently, was correct. To prove this he notes that his opponent, despite complaining about the Basileus's ruling, did not

The fourth feature was popular control of the legal process. Most legal cases were tried in the popular courts (*dikastēria*) and were decided by large groups of two hundred or more jurors, all of whom were ordinary citizens with no special training. These jurors had nearly complete control over the case. Officials and their assistants oversaw the process, timing the speeches and generally keeping order, but they had no authority to make significant decisions except to decide whether to accept a case, and even here their authority seems to have been quite limited.

Jurors for the popular courts were selected (by lot) from an annual pool of six thousand, who also were selected by lot from those who applied. Jurors could apply for this pool every year if they wished. Many undoubtedly served more than once, though evidence indicates that there was also a fair amount of turnover each year.[25] Members of the jury pool could present themselves for jury duty on any day that the courts were in session and hope to be picked to serve on a jury that day. No trial lasted more than a day, and the process of assigning jurors thus began anew each day. For each day of service, jurors received a small sum of three obols (equivalent to one-half drachma), enabling even the poorest to serve.[26]

Jurors had to be citizens over thirty, but they were not otherwise examined at the beginning of their term nor were they held accountable at the end of the year; because they cast their votes in secret, it would have been impossible to hold them accountable for any verdict. In his play *Wasps*, the comic poet Aristophanes parodies the popular juries by presenting one poor, cantankerous, and biased old man as typical. Other evidence, however, suggests that jurors more closely represented a cross-section of the population, though the very rich and those living far from the city center were probably underrepresented.[27]

In addition to the popular courts, a group of officials called the Forty—

---

challenge him at his *euthynai* hearing, even though he challenged many other officials at that time.

25. Hansen 1991:181–182.

26. A payment of two obols for jury duty was first instituted in the mid-fifth century. Later in the century this was increased to three obols. In the fourth century, attendance at Assembly meetings was similarly compensated. It is impossible to give meaningful modern equivalents to ancient monetary amounts, but it may help to note that the basic welfare payment for a poor disabled person was two obols per day and that most workmen made one to three obols per day. Of course, jury payment would have been irregular and thus was not enough to support a single person living alone (which was fairly rare), but it would have been a helpful contribution to a family's total income.

27. See Kroll 1972:261–267. I discuss the composition of the jury at greater length in chapter 2 (text at notes 26–28).

four men selected by lot from each tribe—decided private suits up to a value of ten drachmas. Public suits or private suits valued at more than ten drachmas were tried by the popular courts or by one of the more specialized courts. The latter included the Council of the Areopagus, which judged homicides and certain religious offenses;[28] because this body consisted of all former Archons, its membership varied, but it must always have consisted of more than a hundred members. The juries in the popular courts were even larger—201 or 401 in private cases and up to 2,501 in cases of great public importance.[29] After listening to the pleadings, they decided the case by majority vote. No authoritative official comparable to a modern judge oversaw the proceedings or made any significant decisions about legal matters, leaving it up to the jury to decide the entire case themselves.

The fifth notable feature of the Athenian democracy is its egalitarianism. Certainly there were differences in wealth, but the system of taxation and wealth distribution went some way toward lessening these differences (see below). Political power, moreover, was unstable. Because it was acquired not by holding office but by gaining approval for one's policies in the Assembly and winning court cases if necessary, it could come and go quickly. And—most important—everyone, no matter how rich or powerful, was subject to the law, and not just in theory.[30] Leading politicians, generals, and others were not infrequently tried, convicted, and sentenced, sometimes to death or exile.[31] As far as we know, this was a common feature of law everywhere in Greece. The earliest surviving law, enacted around 650 for the city of Dreros in Crete, prohibits the highest official in the city (the *kosmos*) from holding office more often than once every ten years and penalizes him if he violates this rule;[32] similar laws are found all over the Greek world.[33]

Financially, so that ordinary citizens could participate in running the government, they were paid for attending meetings of the Assembly, for serving on a jury, and for holding an administrative office (including serv-

---

28. In the fourth century, there may have been separate maritime courts for maritime commerce cases, which often involved foreigners or metics (resident aliens) together with Athenian citizens; see Lanni 2006:152–153.

29. The odd number was intended to prevent tie votes.

30. *Ath. Pol.* reports (16.8) that when Pisistratus, the sixth-century *tyrannos* (sole ruler) of Athens, was accused of homicide, he appeared in court to face the charge, but his accuser did not show up.

31. The career of Demosthenes, the leading politician in the city for two decades, ended abruptly in 323 when he was convicted of financial irregularities in the Harpalus affair and fined the enormous amount of fifty talents (300,000 drachmas).

32. *SEG* 27.620; Gagarin and Perlman 2016:200–207.

33. See Harris 2006d.

ing on the Council).[34] These payments required revenue, of course, which came from a variety of sources, mostly in the form of taxes and fees on various market transactions and on imports to Athens, or fees for leasing of mining operations and other public lands—together with fines for public offenses and court fees. Two special sources of public financing also existed: "liturgies" (*leitourgiai*)[35] and special levies (*eisphorai*) for an unusual expense, usually involving war.

The liturgies were a uniquely Athenian means of having the richest citizens fund special public needs. The main liturgies were the *chorēgia* (choral production), in which a *chorēgos* (choral producer) funded a choral production, and the *triērarchia*, in which a trierarch paid the expenses of maintaining a trireme (the main Athenian warship) for a year. The choral productions ranged from choruses of small boys to choruses for the annual productions of tragedies and comedies at the City Dionysia. The *chorēgos* would undertake the expense of assembling and training a chorus and providing room and board for the chorus members during their training. The trierarch would equip and provision a trireme for a year. The trierarch himself often also served as captain of the ship, though he could pay someone else to serve in his place. A trierarchy could be shared by two wealthy citizens.

Liturgies were assigned to the richest citizens in rotation. If someone thought that it was not his turn to perform an assigned liturgy, he could challenge an allegedly richer citizen to perform the liturgy in his stead in a procedure called *antidosis* (exchange).[36] When necessary, the *eisphora* was assessed on the richest citizens as a specific percentage of each one's total property, depending on how much revenue needed to be raised. Taken together, the liturgies and special assessments meant that the richest citizens in Athens contributed a much larger share of public funding than any other group.

The poorest citizens paid nothing in direct taxes (though they may have paid some fees) and received several benefits in addition to pay for attending the Assembly, serving on a jury, or serving as an official. Athens was

34. Hansen argues that most officials were not paid in the fourth century (1991:240–242), but recent scholars have disputed this (see Rhodes 1995:307–308; and especially Pritchard 2015:66–68). Tandy 2015:362 conveniently summarizes the amounts of pay for different kinds of service. Scafuro 2015 examines the economics of the Athenian courts. Burke 2019 provides details of Athenian state finances in the fourth century.

35. In this context, the Athenian "liturgy" is quite different from an English "liturgy."

36. The *antidosis* procedure is not well understood. For further discussion, see Gabrielsen 1987; Christ 1990; and Scafuro 2011:104–109.

known for the large number of public festivals it held each year,[37] at which free entertainment was often provided (paid for by the liturgies) and attendees were usually also provided a portion of meat from the many animal sacrifices that took place. Taking all these factors together, it is clear that the city had one of the most progressive financial systems ever created. Some rich citizens complained about being assigned a liturgy, but the system as a whole survived (with some modifications) for more than a century, even in times of severe financial stress.

In sum, the two bodies in Athens with significant decision-making authority were the Assembly for legislation and policy decisions and the jury for judicial decisions. Both bodies were large enough and their membership diverse enough that they could be seen as broadly representative of the Athenian citizen body. The Council and other officials had less power, but they, too, were broadly representative of the citizen body.[38] This meant that not only did ordinary citizens make virtually all significant decisions in the city, but most citizens participated in the running of the city in various ways during their lifetimes. Thus, on the one hand, everyone involved in running the Athenian government was an amateur, but on the other hand, almost all of these amateurs had some experience serving in the different parts of the government. An Athenian panel of two hundred jurors, therefore, would have had more experience and knowledge of the government and the law than a similar group of ordinary citizens chosen at random would have today, but less experience and knowledge, of course, than a panel of modern judges.[39]

I turn now to the legal system, which for the Athenians was an integral part of their democratic government and was, as noted above, entirely controlled by the people. The legal systems of modern democracies vary widely, but none is democratic in the sense of being directly controlled by ordinary citizens. Even in cases in which juries composed of laymen decide the fi-

37. See the "Old Oligarch" ([Xenophon] *Ath. Pol.*) 3.2, 3.8.

38. Taylor examines the sociological composition of Assembly members, elected officials, and officials selected by lot and concludes (2007:340) that "a wide range of citizens both attended and participated actively in the Assembly, and the Athenian democracy was not merely the concern of a privileged few. Elected offices . . . were held primarily by the wealthier members of demes near the city. . . . The selection of officials by lot, on the other hand, . . . allowed more citizens from other parts of Attica to participate in the political process."

39. In my view, both Calhoun (1944:35–37) and Harris (e.g., 2013c:11) overstate the jurors' experience in legal matters. No matter how many cases jurors heard—and the number would have varied widely from juror to juror—their learning by experience was significantly different from the specialized training and experience of judges today.

nal verdict, virtually all positions of authority are filled by trained legal experts—lawyers, judges, and other legal scholars—who may limit the evidence presented to the jury and restrict the range of issues that litigants are allowed to discuss and the jury is allowed to decide. Not so in Athens.

Such a close relation between a community's political ideology and its legal system, with the former determining or heavily influencing the form of the latter, is unusual. In the modern Western world, the separation of powers, and in particular the separation of law from politics, is (in theory) a basic tenet of most governments. The common law system that the United States inherited from England, for example, is not inherently monarchic or democratic. It was created and developed under a monarchy primarily for the benefit of the landed aristocracy, but because it has no particular connection with any specific form of government, it underwent no dramatic change in the move from monarchic England to democratic United States, even though legislative authority shifted from a king with a parliament to the state and federal governments. The same is true of the civil law system derived ultimately from Roman law, which has been adapted over the centuries by countries with a variety of political systems. This is in keeping with the widespread modern assumption that law should be autonomous, independent of whatever political regime may be in power.

The Athenians had no concept of an autonomous legal system. On the contrary, they intentionally created a legal system that would be an integral part of their democratic political system. Separation of law from government made no sense to them. In describing Solon's sixth-century reforms, Aristotle concludes that "the reform which is said to have given the most power to the common people was the transfer [of legal cases] to the popular court; for when the people (*dēmos*) are in charge of the vote [i.e., the verdict], they are in charge of the government (*politeia*)."[40] Before Solon, all legal cases had apparently been decided either by officials on their own or by the aristocratic Areopagus council. The Areopagus retained considerable power after Solon, but officials no longer judged private cases themselves, except for those valued at less than ten drachmas; all others were transferred to the popular courts, a major step, in Aristotle's view, toward the achievement of a fully democratic, participatory government in Athens.

In general, Athenian judicial procedure was simple and straightforward.[41] All litigation was brought by men, so that if a woman or a slave had

40. *Ath. Pol.* 9.1; see Rhodes 1981:160–162. Even if this observation misrepresents Solon's intentions, it is indicative of fourth-century thinking about democracy and law.

41. In the following overview, I will assume a case involving only two litigants, a plaintiff and a defendant, each speaking for himself. In some cases, one or more "co-

a grievance, the woman's *kyrios*[42] or the slave's master would bring suit on their behalf, or would defend them in court if they were accused. Most ordinary complaints—someone assaulted me, cheated me, damaged my property, and so on—were tried by a simple procedure called a *dikē*.[43] Someone who wanted to bring suit first had to file his complaint with the official in charge of that type of case. The complaint described the alleged wrong in some detail. A clerk would write down the complaint and schedule an appearance before the official in charge. The plaintiff then had to issue a (verbal) summons to the accused to appear on the assigned date. In issuing the summons, he would take along one or more witnesses in case the accused did not show up at the hearing. In that event, the accused could be convicted in absentia, unless he had a good excuse.

On the appointed day, the plaintiff repeated his complaint before the official, the accused presumably denied the charge, and the official would schedule a preliminary hearing. In most private cases, the preliminary hearing was before an arbitrator, who was selected by lot.[44] Every Athenian was eligible to serve as an arbitrator in his sixtieth year. Thus, like everyone else involved in the legal process, the arbitrator would be a citizen with no special training but presumably a good amount of wisdom and judgment. At this hearing, the two litigants would present their arguments; the arbitrator might question the litigants, and they could question one another. Litigants also had to present all of the written evidence they planned to use in the trial, such as the text of a law, contract, or will, or the testimony of a witness. The arbitrator would try to reconcile the two sides; failing that, he would issue his ruling, but either side could reject the ruling, and the case would then automatically go to trial. In that event, all the written evidence

---

pleaders" (*synēgoroi*) presented part or all of the case. In the *diadikasia* procedure, which was often used in inheritance cases, two or more claimants competed for the deceased's estate, and there was no plaintiff or defendant. For a more detailed account of legal procedure, see Lipsius 1905–1915; Harrison 1971; MacDowell 1978; Todd 1993; and Gagarin 2019.

42. The *kyrios* ("authority," often translated "lord") was normally a woman's father, husband, brother, or son. He represented her in all legal proceedings and major financial transactions.

43. *Dikē* has many different meanings, including "trial," "justice," "punishment," and others, but in the context of Athenian law, it usually means either a "suit" of any kind or more specifically a particular type of suit, which could only be brought by the victim himself, the victim's representative, or in some cases (notably homicide) by the victim's family.

44. Homicide cases were considered private in the Athenian system, but they had their own rules, among them that three preliminary hearings were required, one month apart, before the Basileus.

presented at the arbitration hearing would be sealed in jars and kept until the trial, and no other documents could be presented in court. Because the witness testimony and other evidence had been presented earlier at the arbitration hearing, when preparing for the trial, each litigant would have a fairly good idea what his opponent's evidence and arguments amounted to.

At the trial, each litigant presented his entire case in one speech;[45] in some cases, a second, shorter rebuttal speech was allowed. After hearing the speeches, the jury voted immediately for one side or the other. The speeches were timed by a water clock so that each party had equal time. The speaker would pause whenever he wanted to have the court clerk read out a document to the jury, and in private cases the clock was stopped while the clerk was reading. The most common type of evidence was witness testimony: in early days, the witness would read his statement in court, but beginning in the early fourth century, the clerk would read the witness's statement to the court, and the witness himself would simply affirm it. No cross-examination of witnesses occurred, but a litigant could sometimes question his opponent in court.[46]

When the pleadings ended, the jury voted immediately; there was no deliberation beyond whatever discussions jurors might have as they waited to cast their vote. A majority vote won. The jury's verdict was final; no appeal was allowed. However, the losing litigant could, if he wished, bring suit against one of his opponent's witnesses for false testimony (*pseudomartyria*) based on his deposition at the trial. In the absence of an appeal process, suits for false testimony were, in effect, a way to retry a case. Another way for the losing litigant to (in effect) reopen the case was to bring suit, or have a friend bring suit, against his opponent or a close associate of his opponent in a different but related matter.[47]

The traditional *dikē* procedure described above bore some resemblance to our civil procedure, in which one person sues another for damages, but it was also used in many cases when someone was the victim of an offense that today we would prosecute as a criminal offense, such as fraud, assault, or homicide. Victims of such crimes today, however, can also bring a civil

---

45. Our knowledge of individual cases comes primarily from about one hundred speeches that survive from actual Athenian trials. All these speeches are translated into English in volumes of the Loeb Classical Library (with facing Greek text) and in a series from the University of Texas Press (Gagarin 1998–2017).

46. On the process of questioning one's opponent in court (*erōtēsis*), see Carawan 1983. It seems that in the fifth century, litigants were allowed to question their own witnesses (And. 1.14) but not to cross-examine an opponent's witness.

47. For an example of the series of suits and countersuits that might result, see the account in Dem. 59.1–13.

suit against the offender, instead of or in addition to criminal proceedings, and such suits would resemble Athenian *dikē* suits. It was also possible (as it is today) for the two sides to negotiate a settlement. In our system, negotiations usually involve the two parties and their lawyers; in Athens, family and friends would often bring the parties together and try to resolve their differences.[48]

In cases where someone was accused of a public offense, the procedure was similar in many ways, but there were some differences. Because the Athenians never created a position of public prosecutor, the prosecution of public offenses was left to ordinary citizens. The main procedure for such prosecutions, the *graphē* (lit. "writing"), or "indictment" (as it is usually translated), was created by the lawgiver Solon (ca. 594).[49] Although a *graphē* could be used for certain offenses against individuals, it was more often used for prosecuting offenses for which no individual victim existed, such as treason, military desertion, or embezzlement of public funds.[50] A *graphē* could be brought by "anyone who wished" who was eligible—meaning by any citizen who was in full possession of his civil rights. Where there was an individual victim, as in a *graphē* against *hybris*, the suit was often brought by the victim himself or by a family member. When there was no victim, the case would be brought by a third party, often by a personal enemy of the accused, but at times by an ambitious public figure seeking to advance his career (who might also be an enemy of the accused), or perhaps even by a disinterested public servant. The *Ath. Pol.* (9.1) calls the *graphē* procedure another one of Solon's three most democratic reforms.

In a *graphē*, the prosecutor presented his indictment in writing and then summoned the accused to appear before the official in charge. A preliminary hearing was scheduled, not before an arbitrator but before the official in charge, but the hearing was probably similar to an arbitration hearing in allowing the litigants to question each other and in requiring them to present any evidence they would later want to use at the trial at this preliminary hearing.[51] The trial, too, was similar, with each litigant presenting his case in one speech and the jury voting immediately on the verdict.

---

48. The role of negotiation will be discussed in chapter 3.

49. Solon also instituted several other procedures that could be used for specific offenses for which the traditional *dikē* procedure was unsuitable, such as *eisangelia* (impeachment) for treason, but most of these were less commonly used, and I will not discuss them here.

50. Public offenses also included those in which the victim himself would probably be unable to bring suit, such as offenses against orphans, and a few offenses against individuals that involved a significant public interest, such as *hybris* (insolent assault).

51. See Thür 2008:51–66.

If the jury voted for conviction, the penalty was sometimes fixed by statute (for example, death or exile for intentional homicide). In many private suits, the penalty was the amount claimed by the plaintiff, and in many public cases, it was a fine. In some public cases, the penalty was "assessable" (*timētos*). If the jury voted for conviction, there would then be a shorter punishment phase during which each litigant gave a short speech and proposed a specific penalty; the jury would then decide between the two.[52] In a private case, the plaintiff himself had to collect any amount owed to him. In some cases, this was not easy, but with the backing of a favorable verdict, a litigant had several procedures available to him, including seizing property. In public cases, the fine was usually owed to the public treasury; sometimes a portion of this fine went to the prosecutor. To aid in the collection of public fines, the convicted person would be officially declared a public debtor; his name would be inscribed on a registry of public debtors for all to see, and he would lose his political and legal rights until he paid the fine.

The ease of litigation was in keeping with democratic ideology, but it also rendered the system open to abuse, especially in public cases that anyone could prosecute. Those who frequently brought cases for personal gain were commonly referred to as "sykophants" (*sykophantai*),[53] and a law against sykophancy was enacted, though it is uncertain whether anyone was ever prosecuted under this law. The charge of being a sykophant is mostly used by litigants against their opponents in court and is rarely supported by any clear evidence.[54] The most important measure to prevent abuse was the rule that if the prosecutor in a public case dropped his suit or did not receive one-fifth of the jury's votes, he was fined one thousand drachmas and in some cases lost his right to bring similar cases in the future.[55] In private cases, the losing party was required to pay the winner's court fee, but this was a much smaller amount and would have been less of a deterrent to prosecution.

In sum, it seems clear that with regard to judicial procedure, the Athenians accomplished what they set out to do. They created a procedure that

52. This kind of separate procedure for assessing the penalty (*timēsis*) was necessary because a large jury can only decide between two alternatives (guilty or innocent). It cannot easily reach consensus on a penalty if none is specified by the plaintiff or fixed by law.

53. This Greek "sykophant" is quite different from our English "sycophant."

54. Osborne 1990 questions the existence of a procedure against sykophancy, arguing that "sykophant" is simply a rhetorical accusation of "vexatious litigation," *contra* Harvey 1990.

55. One could drop the case before the preliminary hearing but not afterward. Scholars disagree about the additional penalty of losing the right to bring future cases; see Harris 1999; Wallace 2006b; Harris 2006b.

was truly democratic, with ordinary citizens in charge at every stage: as litigants, they prosecuted and defended cases by themselves; as arbitrators, they helped prepare cases for trial and sought to resolve cases before trial; as jurors, they decided the outcome of all litigation; and if a litigant won a conviction, he enforced the verdict himself. Officials oversaw the process and handled administrative details but made no significant decisions; these officials, moreover, were themselves ordinary citizens serving one-year terms, not trained experts. The entire system, in short, was in the hands of amateurs. A litigant, however, had to do almost everything himself (with the help of family and friends)—investigate the case, gather any evidence, find witnesses and prepare and write down their testimony, and enforce the penalty if he won.

The only help available that might be considered professional was that of a logographer (speechwriter), who for a fee would write a speech for the litigant, who would then memorize it and deliver it in court. A few logographers (like Lysias and Isaeus) seem to have made a profession of it, earning their livelihood from logography. Others (like Andocides and Aeschines) wrote only a few speeches and only for their own cases. And still others (like Antiphon and Demosthenes) wrote speeches for others and also for their own cases. Logographers who wrote many speeches undoubtedly acquired considerable knowledge of the law, but their talent, acquired primarily from experience, was more rhetorical than legal (though they had no formal training in either law or rhetoric).[56] Their goal was to help the litigant deliver a speech that would win the case, and they must have learned from experience what sorts of arguments were most helpful for winning in court.

Because forensic science was essentially unknown in Athens, very little hard evidence was available in most cases. The main evidence came from witness testimony, which then (as now) could be problematic and may often have been presented by both sides in support of conflicting accounts. As a result, a litigant's speech in court was by far the most important factor in his case, and an effective rhetorical performance was crucial for the success of his case. It is easy to see why a litigant who could afford it would often seek the help of a logographer. Just how much good a logographer did is uncertain, but presumably he gave his client an advantage, just as a skillful (and usually expensive) lawyer almost certainly provides an advantage today.

56. Reports that the young Demosthenes, for example, sought advice from Isaeus (Plutarch, *Demosthenes* 5) do not refer to formal training. The only true school at the time in which public speaking was taught was that of Isocrates (Isoc. 15.162), and he certainly did not teach students how to litigate private cases, a task he denounced as belonging to the sophists (Isoc. 13.19–20)

Litigants who hired a logographer must on average have been significantly richer than most Athenians, and as far as we can tell, their opponents appear to have been quite rich, too. Litigants' wealth is evident in the speeches that survive today, most (if not all) of which were written by logographers.

Thus far I have been focusing primarily on legal procedure, but Athenian substantive law was also democratic in that the legislative process was entirely in the hands of the people. The earliest laws in Athens were written by individual "lawgivers," beginning in the late seventh century (ca. 621) with Draco, whose homicide law was still in effect in the classical period. Fragments of a late fifth-century copy of this law survive today (*IG* I³ 104).[57] It appears that Draco may also have written other laws, but if he did, these have perished, because a generation later (ca. 594), a second lawgiver, Solon, wrote an extensive set of laws, overriding all earlier laws except for Draco's homicide law. Solon's laws covered a wide range of subjects, and even in the fourth century, Athenians would often speak of all their laws, even laws that certainly were passed at a later time, as "the laws of Solon" or "the laws of Solon and Draco." These early laws were not enacted directly by the people, but the people, or some part of the people, in some way appointed or authorized Solon to enact laws,[58] and because he was considered the founder of the democracy, his laws (which included Draco's homicide law) were treated as ipso facto democratic. After Solon, subsequent legislation was enacted by the *dēmos* in the Assembly, with the participation of the Council, and in the fourth century by the Nomothetai.

It is more difficult to make an argument that the substance of Athenian laws was democratic (relative to other societies' laws), since we know the wording of only a small number of laws. Only ten inscribed statutes survive, in whole or in part, from the classical period,[59] and although many more are cited by the orators, and in some of these cases the text of the law is given in our manuscripts, the orators' words may often be inaccurate or misleading, and many of the preserved texts are, or may be, later creations. Even if genuine, moreover, these citations in the speeches rarely include more than a part of the law.

Despite these difficulties, we can identify at least one Athenian law that provides unusual protection for the lower ranks of the society, the law against

57. For the first ten lines of this law, see chapter 5.

58. Draco also probably had an appointment that gave him the authority to enact laws.

59. Stroud 1998:15–16 lists the eight inscribed laws preserved from the fourth century in addition to the grain-tax law (which he publishes in this work); we must also include the fifth-century copy of Draco's homicide law.

hybris (insolent assault). Even if the text of this law that is preserved in Dem. 21.47 is not entirely authentic,[60] discussions of the law in this speech (21.46–48) and elsewhere confirm that the law explicitly prohibited *hybris* against any man, woman, or child, free or slave.[61] Since *hybris* was generally seen as characteristic of the upper class, one purpose of the law seems clearly to have been the protection of the common people, including (remarkably) their slaves. Also democratic were the various laws punishing officials for not performing their work as required.[62]

Other democratic or egalitarian aspects of Athenian substantive laws include the writing down of all laws on relatively permanent materials[63] and displaying them in public spaces where everyone could see them and many could read them.[64] In early times, inscribed laws were scattered around the city, and thus it may have been difficult for an ordinary citizen to find those that pertained to his own situation, but at the end of the fifth century, all valid laws were collected together and displayed in the agora. At about the same time, a public archive was created where copies of laws were stored on papyrus,[65] and those who wished may have found it more convenient to read these copies than the stone originals. Some litigants speak of having read laws (e.g., Dem. 47.71), sometimes of having studied them (e.g., Dem. 54.17).[66] And because Athenian laws tended to be written in everyday lan-

60. Harris (in Canevaro 2013a:224–231) questions the authenticity of the text, though his arguments in my view are not conclusive.

61. The law may have made an exception for masters who beat their own slaves, though it seems to me not impossible that a particularly violent and arrogant beating in the absence of any good reason could be prosecuted.

62. The law on silver coinage, for example, has the following clause: "If one of the officials does not act according to what is written (in this law), let any Athenian who wishes and is eligible bring him to the Council; and if he is convicted, let him cease being an official and let the Council fine him up to 500 drachmas" (*SEG* 26.72 lines 32–36; Stroud 1974).

63. Draco's homicide law may have been written on bronze. Solon's laws were written on wood and displayed, probably in the agora. Later Athenian laws, like most laws in other Greek cities, were inscribed on stone.

64. Scholars disagree on the degree of literacy in classical Athens. Harris (1989) made the case for relatively limited literacy, which many scholars accepted, but more recently Pébarthe (2006) and Missiou (2011) have argued convincingly that a relatively high degree of literacy was necessary for the classical Athenian democracy to function. See Gagarin 2008:67–71, 176–180; Gagarin and Perlman 2016:53–55. Langdon (2015) has now published some sixth-century graffiti scratched on rocks around Attica by shepherds and goatherds, suggesting at least a rudimentary level of literacy among many ordinary Athenians (cf. *SEG* 50.101–103).

65. Sickinger 1999:114–122.

66. Gagarin 2008:179–181.

guage, most Athenians with a grievance could find the relevant statute and read it, perhaps with a little help from their friends, and then initiate proceedings if they wished. Today, it is nearly impossible for an individual to bring suit in court without professional help, except perhaps in small-claims court.[67]

The Athenians, moreover, had great respect for their laws and considered them the heart of their legal system. Litigants regularly praise a law or all Athenian laws, and no litigant ever criticizes the laws in general. Litigants may criticize their opponents' explanation of a law's meaning, or dismiss a law as irrelevant to the case at hand, but except when accusing someone of enacting a law that is "inexpedient" (Dem. 20 and 24), a litigant never says that an existing law is wrong or unjust.[68] On the contrary, litigants often remind the jurors of their obligation to follow the law and vote according to it. This obligation stems in part from the jurors' oath, which committed jurors to judge "according to the laws and decrees of the Athenian people." It is possible, of course, that some jurors ignored their oath, but because no one could know why a juror voted the way he did, nothing could be done about this unless it could be shown that a juror had been bribed, and jury selection at Athens was guided by a complex set of rules that made bribing a juror very difficult, if not impossible (*Ath. Pol.* 63–65).

Most scholars today have a rather favorable view of Athenian democracy, but in the past it has often been criticized as little more than mob rule. The Assembly could vote for something one day and then reverse itself the next, as it did after Athens suppressed the revolt of Mytilene in 428.[69] Popular rule could also mean rule according to popular prejudices, and although the Athenians were generally quite tolerant of dissent, they could be very severe about dissent if they felt that it caused or threatened political harm. The trial and execution of Socrates has commonly been cited as the primary illustration of the majority's suppression of dissent, though we should remember that until he was seventy, Socrates was tolerated as a well-known public gadfly, who often challenged traditional views. Only after Athens had suffered a disastrous defeat in the Peloponnesian War and had endured the rule of the Thirty was Socrates finally accused (of corrupting the youth),

67. Today, moreover, professional legal organizations sometimes work hard to prevent people from using simple self-help guides, thereby avoiding the need (and expense) of a lawyer. In light of this, it is hard to disagree with cynics like Charles Dickens, who observes in *Bleak House* that "the one great principle of the English law is to make business for itself."

68. For the close connection between law and justice, see chapter 8.

69. The episode is famously described by the historian Thucydides (3.36–50).

and the prosecutors may have been motivated more by the participation of some of Socrates' students in the brutal reign of the Thirty than by his own outspoken conduct. His death sentence, moreover, appears to have been a reaction against his defense speech (if Plato's version of the speech in the *Apology* is fairly close to the original). Although his accusers proposed death, they probably expected the sentence to be exile. But when Socrates' counter-proposal was not exile but a small fine, the jury, which had to decide between these alternatives, chose death.[70]

All in all, Athens's government seems to have worked well and been quite popular. In almost two hundred years, its democracy was more stable than the governments of many other Greek cities. It suffered two takeovers by oligarchs, both of them short-lived and both coming during a period of severe stress caused by the Peloponnesian War. And although it could not withstand the attack of Philip of Macedon in the late fourth century, neither could any other Greek city (or foreign empire), no matter what its form of government.

The same charges of arbitrariness and political bias that have been leveled at the Athenian political system have also been leveled against its legal system. Such criticism can be traced back as far as Plato, whose views were probably shaped in part by the fate of his teacher Socrates. Plato preferred a form of limited oligarchy to the democratic form of government in which he lived and worked. Along with democracy, he also rejected some core features of its culture, notably drama (in the *Republic*) and rhetoric (in *Gorgias*), and in his last work, *Laws*, he proposed a radically different legal process in which rhetoric was banned and judges were accountable for their verdicts.[71] Criticism of Athenian law continued in Roman times,[72]

---

70. By law, the jury could only decide between the penalties proposed by each side. Even after sentencing him to death, many jurors probably expected Socrates to go into exile, as his friend Crito urged him to do (in Plato's *Crito*); see Cartledge 2016:179–180.

71. See *Laws* 937d–38c, where rhetoric is not mentioned by name but is obviously the knack (*empeiria*) that is being condemned, and 766d–68c for the accountability of judges and the organization of the many different courts; in capital cases, moreover, Plato specified that judges had to deliberate over a period of days before reaching a verdict (855c-56a).

72. For example, Cicero *De Oratore* I.44–45, cited in the introduction, note 2. I owe the Cicero reference to Beauchet (1897, 1:ix), who provides many specific criticisms of Athenian law and concludes, "Au point de vue scientifique, l'infériorité du droit attique vis-à-vis du droit romain est indéniable" (xiv; "From a scientific viewpoint, Attic law's inferiority to Roman law is undeniable"). He attributes the superiority of Roman law in part to its longer period of development (six hundred years vs. less than three hundred from Solon's laws to the death of Demosthenes).

and these views have dominated the modern understanding of Athenian law until quite recently.

In the introduction, I cited two modern historians critical of Athenian law. A similar view was expressed by the highly regarded legal scholar William Wyse, in the section on law in *A Companion to Greek Studies*, a basic reference work for much of the twentieth century:[73]

> The amount of injustice cannot now be estimated, but it is sufficient condemnation of the courts that appeals to passion and political prejudice, insinuating sophistry, and outrageous misrepresentations of law were judged by shrewd and experienced observers suitable means to win a verdict. . . . The conclusions of a court were bare affirmations or negations, not discriminating between law and fact, applicable only to a particular case, and based on reasons, which were known only to the individual voters, and perhaps not always to them.

There is some basis for this judgment, for the jurors and court officials were ordinary Athenian citizens without special training, and they had total authority in deciding the case. Some of these amateur participants must have gained considerable experience in the law by serving on a jury in previous cases, by being involved in past litigation, or by observing trials as spectators, but they were otherwise untrained, and the Athenians could be quite suspicious of someone who had too much knowledge of the laws.[74] Under such conditions, it is easy to conclude that ignorance, emotion, and prejudice decided most cases.

These criticisms will be addressed in later chapters, but although Athenians sometimes criticize specific verdicts in past cases, they seem for the most part to have been satisfied that their system worked well to produce just results while at the same time ensuring easy access for all and satisfying the democratic principle of popular control. Athens is mocked by Aristophanes for its abundance of courts and trials, but the *dēmos* was never inclined to change the system. More pointed criticism was mostly confined to certain intellectuals, beginning with Plato. But for most Athenians, their legal system seems to have worked pretty well. The remainder of this book

73. William Wyse in Whibley 1905:388–389. The excerpt is from the paragraph on "the character of the courts." For the fourth edition, published in 1963, the section on law was revised by F. E. Adcock, but the paragraph on "the character of the courts" was unchanged (476–477 of the 1963 edition).

74. Litigants could criticize an opponent for knowing the laws too well (e.g., Dem. 57.5); see Carey 1994b:180 with note 25. Expertise in general was the province of slaves (Todd 1996:131).

is an attempt to better understand just how that system worked and why it was, as it appears, a success.

The Athenian legal system should be especially interesting for us in the United States today, because despite obvious differences, our American version of the common law is probably more similar to the Athenian legal system than any other legal system is, ancient or modern.[75] As in common law, the procedure in Athenian litigation was adversarial. Moreover, despite very different material circumstances, the issues and arguments in actual cases are familiar ones: one man claims he was assaulted after having done nothing to provoke it, another was victimized by a fraudulent contract, another was cheated out of his inheritance by an unscrupulous relative, and so on. And in presenting their cases, litigants often use arguments very much like those we might use in similar circumstances today.

The most important similarity, however, is that many cases in the United States are tried before juries, as they were in Athens. The United States is almost alone today in still using juries in a large number of civil cases, and we make more use of juries in criminal cases than most other countries. In part, this results from the strong populist streak in our cultural heritage. In many states, for example, judges are chosen by popular election, and even where they are appointed, they often must be approved by some political process. Similarly, a "jury of our peers" continues to be ideologically important for most Americans. To be sure, jury decisions are often criticized as biased or uninformed, but few people want to relinquish the right to trial by jury if they are accused of wrongdoing.[76] Thus, despite much discussion, there have been no serious attempts to eliminate juries from our legal system.

Of course, the Athenian legal system also differs from our own in important ways. The involvement of trained professionals today undoubtedly helps avoid some of the potential arbitrariness of the Athenian system. But the Athenian system also had several clear advantages. An ordinary citizen could bring his complaint directly to the court in a timely manner, at relatively little cost,[77] and without having to make his way through complex

---

75. The recent movement to "democratize" criminal law in the United States would bring our law even closer to Athenian law (Kleinfeld et al. 2017).

76. Despite much evidence to the contrary, many defendants believe that a jury will be more sympathetic to their case, and thus more likely to acquit, than a judge.

77. No fee was charged for public cases or for private cases valued at less than one hundred drachmas; for those valued between one hundred and one thousand drachmas, the fee was three drachmas; for more than one thousand drachmas, it was thirty drachmas. The fee was paid by both litigants, but the loser had to reimburse the winner after the trial was over. See further Thür 2015. He speculates at the end of his article that the

rules and procedures. Athenian laws tended to be written in clear, everyday language with little technical terminology, and legal procedures, for which some technical language was necessary, were clearly laid out so that an accuser could know how to proceed. It appears that although literacy was not so widespread as it is today, it was common enough that most citizens who wished to bring suit could read what they needed to.[78] And since the laws were much simpler to understand and less complex than our laws are, they were undoubtedly more accessible to the average citizen than are laws today, when most laws contain considerable detail and complex syntax, and almost no one other than a trained legal professional actually reads a law.[79] The question remains, however, whether these advantages brought with them the kind of arbitrary verdicts largely influenced by prejudice and emotion that critics have charged.

As a framework for the following investigation it may help to think in terms of a tension between "science" and "rhetoric." Following the example of the Roman jurists, scholars have tended to view law as science, in which rules of conduct are combined with procedures for adjudicating these rules and institutions that implement these procedures. A legal system can be said to be scientific to the extent that rules, procedures, and institutions derive from a coherent set of basic principles that (with training) can be understood and objectively applied to cases in court.[80] The obvious difficulty with the theory of law as science is that each case ought to result in a single solution agreed on by all, but this is obviously not always the case today when, for example, members of the US Supreme Court, supposedly the best judicial minds in our country, regularly disagree among themselves about the cases they decide. This makes the whole notion of an objectively correct verdict questionable.

---

fees for logographers (see below) may have added significantly to the cost of litigation, but a logographer was not required. We have no information about what percentage of litigants used a logographer or how large the logographers' fees were.

78. On literacy, see note 64 to this chapter.

79. Perjury, for example, is defined in the US civil code as "when a person, having taken an oath before a competent tribunal, officer, or person, in any case in which a law of the United States authorizes an oath to be administered, that he will testify, declare, depose, or certify truly, or that any written testimony, declaration, deposition, or certificate by him subscribed, is true, willfully and contrary to such oath states or subscribes any material matter which he does not believe to be true; or in any declaration, certificate, verification, or statement under penalty of perjury, willfully subscribes as true any material matter which he does not believe to be true" (18 USC). We do not know the wording of the Athenian law on false testimony (*pseudomartyria*), but it probably included little more detail than "if someone testifies falsely."

80. For a brief history of legal science and its alternatives, see Simpson 1995:4–9. For a brief treatment of Athenian law as legal science, see Calhoun 1944:30–49.

Law viewed as rhetoric, on the other hand, is an institution in which human beings with different experiences, beliefs, and values, guided by a set of rules, debate their conflicting claims before a disinterested third party, either an individual or a group, in which each side hopes to secure a favorable decision. The main difficulty with law as rhetoric is that rules, even when enforced by a trained judge, can only imperfectly control the litigants' arguments, resulting in decisions that are necessarily subjective and may to some degree be arbitrary.

In reality, no legal system is purely scientific or purely rhetorical; rather, these are points on a continuum: at one pole, rules objectively and conclusively determine the outcome of every case; at the other pole, only the litigants' unrestrained rhetoric and their relative ability to speak persuasively determines the outcome. Most modern legal systems try to be as scientific as possible, but the US legal system is more rhetorical than most of them. Athenian law, on the other hand, lies closer to the rhetorical pole but has scientific elements as well. The extent to which Athenian law (or any other legal system) achieved justice is an unanswerable question, but to help us understand how a legal system can be highly rhetorical and still function effectively, there is no better place to look than classical Athens. And because many of the marginal features I will be discussing in this book also can be found in the US legal system, Athenian law provides a case study that I believe can help us better understand our own law.

CHAPTER 2

PERFORMANCE

In recent years, a number of scholars, largely inspired by Edith Hall's groundbreaking paper,[1] have examined the performance of forensic speeches and, more specifically, the similarities between Athenian dramatic performances, in which actors performed previously written texts before a large audience, and Athenian litigation, in which the litigants, like actors, performed their (often) previously written pleadings before a large audience of jurors and other observers.[2] Hall argued that

> the conventions and content of the fictional worlds created in the theatre . . . came to affect the conventions and content of the more "real"—but nevertheless highly performative—world of the Athenian law-courts. . . . From the physical layout of the courtroom space, to style of vocal delivery, orchestration of "cast" members, attention given to costume, deportment, and gesture, mythical analogies, and emotional reactions, the experience of the juror witnessing the speeches of litigants at an Athenian trial was in manifold ways similar to his experience as a spectator at the theatre.[3]

Other similarities noted by Hall include that protagonists in court and in the theater were from the same upper social group, and that character portrayal was a crucial part of both. Moreover, drama's cast of characters provided the stock characters for forensic storytelling, and the audiences in both settings regularly responded to the performance vocally.[4] The dra-

---

1. Hall 1995, revised and updated in Hall 2006:353–392.

2. Serafim 2017:17–20 provides an overview of the scholarship.

3. Hall 2006:399. Unlike Hall, most scholars who followed her have used the comparison between law and drama to shed light on drama, not law, but there are exceptions, such as MacDowell 2010.

4. Hall 2006:363–366; she draws on the standard study of audience "uproar" (*thorybos*) by Bers 1985.

matic performances were popular and entertaining; they were also a setting for public discussion of social, political, and ethical values. Athenian forensic litigation, it is argued, shared these features and many more. Trials were a form of popular entertainment; most appear to have attracted onlookers, and some attracted large crowds of observers. In pleading their cases, moreover, litigants often engaged in discussion of social, political, and ethical values.

The comparison between law and drama must be drawn with caution, however, as there are also obvious differences between Athenian theatrical and forensic performances. Perhaps most important was the difference between the consequences in each area. Although both types of performance were competitions, dramatists and actors competed for prizes, which could bring honor and prestige. These were important but qualitatively different from the consequences for forensic litigants, especially for defendants, for whom an inferior performance could even result in death. A less important difference was that even though dramatists and actors were competing, a theatrical audience could enjoy a single performance without giving much thought to other competing performances. A forensic jury, however, had to attend to both of the opposing performances, because it could only assess them relative to one another.[5] Despite the differences, however, we must grant the importance of performance in Athenian litigation, even if we do not entirely agree with Hall that "the manner in which forensic speeches were *performed* was as important to their success as their intellectual content and their literary merit."[6] Thus, we need to consider what role performance played in Athenian litigation and how it may have affected the outcome of a trial.

To begin with, Hall's claim that performance features of drama influenced the performance features of forensic oratory ignores the long history of Greek litigation, an essential element of which from its earliest representation in Homer was performance. Thus, Athenian forensic oratory acquired most of its performative features through a long process of self-development, not through the influence of dramatic performances. Accordingly, we must begin by examining the earliest Greek accounts of litigation.[7] These accounts begin around 700 BCE, not long after alphabetic writing was introduced to Greece. Because of its portrayal in the poems of

5. Even observers who were not members of the jury probably listened to both speeches in a trial.

6. Hall 2006:355.

7. If there was any litigation in the Greek Bronze Age (ca. 3000–1150), we know nothing about it.

Homer and Hesiod, Greek law is one of the few, perhaps the only, legal system whose transition from an oral to a written stage we can trace, and which was not influenced by outside forces in making this transition. The main legal systems of the ancient world, in Asia, the ancient Near East, or Rome, have left us virtually no evidence for their operation in preliterate periods. And almost all the other legal systems whose transition from oral to written is visible to us made the change under the influence of another legal system that already used writing.[8]

As far as we can tell, in Greece, this transition was indigenous, shaped by no outside influence. Homer provides the most and the best evidence for the formulations of rules of conduct, the procedures for adjudicating these rules, and the still informal institutions that helped implement these procedures. In particular, evidence of the procedures for settling disputes is extensive and includes one scene of particular interest, a trial depicted on the shield made by the god Hephaestus for Achilles in Book 18 of the *Iliad*.[9] Homer describes the god's work with a fair amount of detail (18.478–607), beginning with the entire natural world and proceeding to the two cities that are depicted in it, one at peace and one at war.

In the city at peace, Hephaestus portrayed just two scenes, a wedding and a trial, both key events for the maintenance and perpetuation of a peaceful community. The trial is described as follows (18.497–508):

> The people were assembled in the agora, where a dispute
> had arisen: two men contended over the blood-price
> for a man who had been killed. One pledged he would pay everything,
> demonstrating this to the people. The other refused to accept anything.
> Both were eager to find a conclusion at the hands of a wise man (*istōr*).
> The people were shouting out on both sides, supporting both litigants;
> but the heralds restrained the crowd. The old men
> were seated on polished stones in a sacred circle;
> they held in their hands the scepters of loud-voiced heralds.
> Then the two men rushed forth before them, and one after the other they gave their judgments (*dikazein*).

---

8. For example, except for the brief account of Tacitus in the first century CE (*Germania* 12.20–21), our earliest knowledge of Germanic law is provided by the compilations of rules written in Latin in the late middle ages, which are clearly influenced by Roman and canon law. And traditional legal systems in Africa and Asia evolved only under the influence of colonial powers.

9. On these early scenes of dispute settlement, see Gagarin 1986:19–50; 2008:13–38. The evolution from oral to written of rules of conduct in Greece will be discussed in chapter 5.

In the middle lay two talents of gold,
to be given to the one among them who would speak the straightest judgment (*dikē*).

This well-known scene contains much of interest for legal historians and has occasioned considerable debate concerning several matters, but the broad features of a ritual and performance scene are clear.[10] First, the setting for the trial is the agora, a communal gathering place in both war and peace. Within this space there is a sacred area in the shape of a circle, formed of polished stones on which the old men sit.[11] Evidently, the circle of polished stones marks a formal civic space where figures of authority may speak and deliberate and around which the community may gather to observe and participate, and in some cases make its views known.

The trial itself is a competition—a double competition, in fact, since not only do the two disputants compete, each seeking a judgment in his favor, but the elders, too, apparently compete, each seeking the prize for proposing the best judgment. The competitions follow a set order: the litigants speak in turn, first the plaintiff (who is ready to pay the blood price and apparently has it with him and displays it) then the defendant (who apparently refuses to accept any amount). The elders, too, speak in turn (*amoibēdis*), perhaps according to age, as the heralds hand each one the scepter that signifies the authority to speak.

The poet emphasizes the performers' voices: the litigants plead their cases orally, with one "pledging" and the other "refusing"; the people "shout out" (*epēpuon*) their support; the heralds who keep order are "loud-voiced"; and the elders "give judgments" (*dikazein*), each seeking to "speak" the straight-

10. The main disagreements are: What is the subject of the dispute? Is it about the amount of the blood price, whether or not it has been paid, whether the victim's relative is required to accept it, or something else? (For a suggestion about the subject of the dispute, see chapter 5, note 9.) Who is the "wise man" (*istōr*, lit. "one who knows")? Is he one of the elders or a separate official, and if the latter, what is his role? Does the judgment or settlement that each elder gives have to follow a prescribed form, such as a directive that one or the other litigant swear an oath? And are the two talents of gold awarded to an elder, as most scholars think, and if so, how is it determined which elder receives it? Homer, of course, is a poet and thus is not interested in clarifying every detail that might interest legal scholars, but the importance of the scene, as indicated by the large crowd that attends, suggests that the issues are complex. For further discussion, see Wolff 1946; Gagarin 1986:26–33; Thür 1996 (cf. Thür 1970); Cantarella 2002, 2005; Gagarin 2008:13–19.

11. We find similar polished stone seats elsewhere in Homer, at *Odyssey* 3.405–416 (where King Nestor and his sons honor their guest Telemachus with a sacrifice and a feast) and *Odyssey* 8.6 (where King Alcinous and the other Phaiacian leaders prepare to escort Odysseus home).

est judgment (*dikē*).[12] This is a performance in which each participant's role is marked by a different kind of speech act. And eloquence—speaking well—is clearly important for the litigants, for the elders, and probably even for the members of the community who voice their various opinions.

In addition to the various sounds, the poet also notes the motion of the two litigants, who "rush forth" to plead their cases, and of the crowd, which has to be restrained by the heralds. Other features that mark the scene as a ritual performance include the fact that when the judges speak, and probably also when the two litigants speak, each one takes hold of a scepter, signifying authority. It is standard practice in Homer that the speaker in an Assembly holds the scepter, which confers on him the authority to speak; here the heralds apparently give the scepter in turn to the elder who will speak, creating the proper context for each declaration of a judgment. Moreover, the first disputant does not just speak but demonstrates his case to the people, perhaps actually displaying the amount that he is swearing he will pay or has paid. And after the litigants speak, one by one each elder probably rises, with a scepter in his hand, and speaks his judgment.

The performative features of the trial scene are particularly interesting in relation to the other scene in the city at peace, a wedding celebration (18.491–496):

> In it [the city at peace] there were weddings and wedding feasts,
> and accompanied by blazing torches they led the brides from their
> chambers
> through the city, and the wedding song arose everywhere.
> And young men twirled in dance and among them
> the pipes and lyres added their cries. And the married women
> stood, each in her own doorway, and marveled.

The poet fills this scene, too, with sound and movement, as well as light from blazing torches. The spectacle is observed by the older married women, representing the community, whose approval is apparently being sought. They are not part of a large crowd, as in the judicial scenes, but as is appro-

12. *Dikazein* is a speech act, cognate with Latin *dico*, but it is not a formula (as Benveniste 1973:385–388 argues). Rather, it is also cognate with Greek *deiknumi* (show) and may have originally meant to point out a boundary mark (Palmer 1950). *Dikazein* is thus the performative speech act of designating or showing that is embodied in proposing a settlement. Elsewhere in the epics, the context either requires or suggests or allows that *dikazein* be an act of speaking, and the final line in this passage, "the elder who speaks (*eipoi*) the straightest settlement (*dikē*)," confirms that *dikazein* here designates an act of speaking (see also Talamanca 1979).

priate for them, each stands sedately in her own doorway. Here, too, we are observing a ritual performance, in which light, sound, and movement are joined; and by means of this performance, the central performers, the brides and grooms, enter into and obtain approval for their new roles in the community, watched over by an audience of elders, here women who have already performed this ritual themselves. In the same way, the performances in the trial scene, accompanied by sound and movement, will presumably make it possible for the disputants in the case to be reintegrated into the community.

Returning to the trial scene, we should note the central role played by the people, the *laoi* (emphatically the first word in Homer's description) assembled in the agora. The people crowd around the two disputants, shouting out their support for one or the other, so that the heralds have to hold them back. Judging from similar scenes of dispute settlement in other small communities, the people's voice will play a significant role in determining the final outcome and ensuring that both disputants accept the final settlement and abide by its terms.[13] In these smaller communities, even if the final judgment is determined by a judge or village elder, the audience's views always influence the judgment, and their support is necessary for the well-being and even the survival of the community.

In the Homeric scene, we are first told that the *laoi* include supporters of each side; but judging from similar procedures elsewhere, during the course of the trial support is likely to shift toward one side or the other, or toward a compromise between them. In this process, the audience influences both the performances of the litigants and those of the elders, who must render their decisions. In the end, it is probably audience approval that determines which judgment is the straightest (i.e., which prevails) and thus which elder wins the prize. Finally, after a judgment is rendered in early Greece, as in other small communities, the community's approval would play a crucial role in bringing the litigants to accept the final settlement.

Much scholarly debate has focused on whether the procedure depicted

---

13. In an earlier discussion of this scene (Gagarin 2008:13–19), I cited examples from medieval Europe ("No one in Europe lived only among kin; one needed support from neighbours, dependents, lords, and this was available above all in the public arena . . . Going to court was the only way that much of one's reserve of support could be brought into play at all," Wickham in Davies and Fouracre 1986:235), and from the Tiv, a preliterate African society ("Concurrence of the litigants never occurs without concurrence of the entire community: no one is ready to make concessions while any portion of public opinion still supports him. It is the opinion of the community which forces concurrence. Judging, like all other activities of Tiv leaders, consists largely in the timely suggestion of what the majority thinks is right or desirable," Bohannan 1957:65).

on Achilles' shield is voluntary or compulsory,[14] but in small communities like early Greece, this distinction would to a large extent have been blurred. As examples from other small communities show (see above, note 13), when a dispute is settled by the kind of process depicted on Achilles' shield, the judgment will necessarily meet with the general approval of the crowd and will have to be accepted by both litigants, since it would be impossible for them to continue to live in their community without the support of family, friends, and neighbors. The only alternative to accepting the proposed settlement would be to leave the community and go into exile. For this reason, neither this scene nor any of the other scenes of dispute settlement in early poetry say anything about enforcement of the settlement. It goes without saying that once the community has found a settlement to be acceptable, the disputants will have to abide by it (or at least appear to do so). Specific enforcement is not needed.

The relationship between the performers and their audience, therefore, is crucial in any dispute settlement, as it is to any performance. Litigants seek to influence their audience through their pleadings, but they must also be sensitive to the moods and feelings of the audience and must adjust their performances accordingly. Thus, each performer seeks to achieve a kind of partnership with the audience. As Richard Bauman, a leading scholar of oral performance, has observed, "it is part of the essence of performance that it offers to the participants a special enhancement of experience, bringing with it a heightened intensity of communicative interaction which binds the audience to the performer in a way that is specific to performance as a mode of communication."[15] Or, to put it differently, "performance involves on the part of the performer an assumption of accountability to an audience."[16]

Bauman, like most scholars who write about performance in small communities, is thinking primarily about poetic performance, but as Hesiod tells us in the preface to the *Theogony* (80–92), the "king" (*basileus*)[17] who is skilled at settling disputes in the agora must have the same gift of the Muses as the poet:

---

14. See Wolff 1946: esp. 36–49; *contra* Gagarin 2008:15–16.

15. Bauman 1977:43.

16. Bauman 1986:11. Any good performer, including stage actors, political speakers, classroom lecturers, and many others, will acknowledge the importance of the audience's response.

17. Since there were apparently several *basileis* even in the small communities in Hesiod's Boeotia, these must be thought of as lords or nobles, not kings in the usual sense. However, I retain the traditional English translation.

For she [the Muse Calliope] accompanies honored kings.
Whichever of the divinely nourished kings
the daughters of great Zeus [the Muses] honor and look upon at birth,
on his tongue they pour sweet honey
and soothing words flow from his mouth. And the people (*laoi*)
all behold him, distinguishing the rules (*themistes*)[18]
with straight settlements (*dikai*). And he, speaking surely,
quickly and skillfully puts a stop to even a large dispute.
This is why there are intelligent kings, so that when the people (*laoi*)
have been harmed, they may restore matters in the agora,
easily, persuading them with gentle words.
And as he comes to the gathering, they honor him as a god
with gentle reverence, and he stands out among those assembled.

This description of the king is followed immediately by a similar tribute to the poet (93–103), from whose mouth flow sweet words that soothe the minds of his audience so that they forget their cares.

Hesiod's comparison of kings to poets makes clear that those who settled disputes in early Greece did not simply declare a judgment; rather, like poets, they had to perform with eloquence so as to persuade not only the litigants but also the *laoi*, the community, to accept their judgment. And a wise king would make sure that his judgment was guided by the response he was receiving from the community. The king who could do this was justly revered. And although those who judged cases in classical Athens three centuries later were no longer kings or elders delivering verdicts intended to persuade, the ability to communicate with their audience remained just as important for the litigants who delivered their pleas. Their ability to communicate depended on their ability to shape their pleading in accord with the response of their audience.

These early Greek scenes of forensic performance also show that to communicate effectively, the litigants' performances must follow rules and traditions that require that they take place in a particular space, designate specific roles for the different performers, and regulate the ways in which they all perform their roles. This does not mean that there is no room for creativity or spontaneity, but these occur within the prescribed limits of the forensic competition, at fixed times and places. And the normative function of these early poems meant that they carried the implicit message that a per-

18. *Themistes* (sing. *themis*) are the traditional (oral) rules and customs of a community. They are often said to have come from Zeus.

formance that does not accord with these rules will not achieve its desired effect.

Finally, although it may be wrong to speak of professionals in a community at this early stage of social development, I simply note that no one in the scene on Achilles' shield is a professional; there are no trained advocates and the judges are either "kings" or simply the elders of the community. Some of these kings or elders may be particularly wise because of their age and experience, but there is no sign that any of them had special training.

There are many other scenes of dispute settlement in early poetry, most of them only briefly described or alluded to, and the details often vary;[19] judging, for example, may be in the hands of a single person, such as Hesiod's king, or a group, as on the shield. But all the scenes are consistent with the basic set of features found on the shield. Even when a single judge settles disputes, as in Hesiod's *Theogony*, it is clear from some of the descriptions that there were usually several judges in the community from whom disputants could choose to settle their disputes, so that even a single judge would be competing with other potential judges to gain the best reputation for good judgments so that more disputants would bring their cases to him, which would increase his stature in the community and for each of which he may have received a small gift or payment.

After Homer and Hesiod, this legal proceeding evolved into a more formal process, though it remained a performance, with many of the features we noted in Homer and other new features noted by Hall and others. Trials continued to be held in public, either in the agora or in some other public space, and continued to feature litigants competing directly with one another by means of oral pleadings, each side seeking the approval of the community, which by the fifth century was represented in Athens by a large jury together with other members of the community who attended the proceedings.[20]

The earliest portrayal we have of this process in Athenian literature comes in Aeschylus's *Eumenides*, first performed in 458. This play, the third in a trilogy, dramatizes the creation of the court of the Areopagus by Athena, patron goddess of Athens. The court was so named because it met on the Areopagus hill overlooking the agora. The action of the *Eumenides* takes place in the mythical past, several years after the Trojan War, and shows the court being created to try Orestes on the charge of murdering his mother, Clytemnestra, an act that took place in the second play of the trilogy (*Libation*

19. Gagarin 1986:19–50.

20. Lanni (1997:189) suggests that the bystanders in classical Athens are the descendants of the crowds listening to dispute settlement in Homer and Hesiod.

Bearers). Orestes' defense is that he was punishing Clytemnestra for killing his father, Agamemnon, when he returned from the war, as was dramatized in the first play of the trilogy (*Agamemnon*). Orestes further claims that he was ordered by Apollo to avenge his father's death.

In the *Eumenides*, Orestes is prosecuted by the chorus, a group of Furies, who are Clytemnestra's avenging spirits. They demand, quite logically, that if Clytemnestra deserved punishment for killing Agamemnon, then Orestes, too, should be punished for his act of murder. At first, the Furies and Orestes confront one another directly, the Furies insisting that he pay for his crime and Orestes responding that his act was fully justified. Each side adds further arguments, but when they are unable to resolve their dispute, the Furies ask Athena to deliver a "straight judgment" (*eutheian dikēn*, 433), just as in the Homeric trial. She decides to convene a court to help her judge the case (470–489), and then presides over the trial (566–753). The two sides continue to plead their case before the court in orderly fashion, with roughly equal time for each; but after a while, Orestes calls on the god Apollo to plead for him (609–613), since it was at his urging that Orestes did what he did. When the pleadings are finished, Athena calls on the members of the Areopagus to vote, after which she announces her own vote in favor of Orestes. She then proclaims that because the votes are equal, Orestes is acquitted, thereby establishing the historical rule in Athenian law that a tie vote favors the defendant.[21]

The trial on stage differs in several ways from an actual fifth-century trial: in an actual trial, each side would give only one main speech followed by a rebuttal rather than the series of back-and-forth arguments we find in the play. There would not be a presiding official like Athena, and if there were, he or she would have no vote. And the jury in the court of the Areopagus, which probably comprised only eleven or twelve members on stage, would have been much larger, perhaps 150 members. Despite differences, however, the trial has some familiar elements of a ritual performance. The two sides present their arguments orally, in a public space, before a large audience (the theater audience as well as the jury on stage). Each member of the jury probably came forward individually to cast his vote into one of the two urns that were on stage in such a way that the audience could probably see that the votes in the end would be equal. The first ten jurors' votes are accompanied by iambic trimeter couplets, spoken alternately by the Furies and Apollo (711–730); these are followed by three trimeters spoken by

21. See Gagarin 1975, where I argue that Athena's vote makes the jury's vote a tie and does not break a tie as many other scholars think.

the Furies and then a longer speech by Athena as she casts her deciding vote (731–743). The visual spectacle of this orderly procedure would help convey the message to the Athenian theater audience, and also to the non-Athenian spectators, that at Athens there was a divinely sanctioned, fully transparent judicial process that embodied fair and equal justice for all participants and reached just verdicts. Finally, after delivering the verdict, Athena then persuades the reluctant Furies to accept it.

The next trial scene comes in a comedy, Aristophanes' *Wasps*, produced in 422. The main character, Philocleon, is addicted to jury duty, so his son Bdelycleon decides to prevent him from leaving the house. To ease the pain of no longer judging cases, he allows Philocleon to set up a court at home. The first step is to assemble all the necessary paraphernalia, which takes some time (798–862).[22] After some prayers, the first case is called with an indictment that closely resembles the form of an actual indictment (894–97):[23] a dog who has eaten a cheese is charged with theft by another dog (with whom he did not share the cheese). The trial that follows (905–994) is a humorous parody but contains many elements of an actual trial, including many of its performance features. These are often exaggerated, as when the defendant's puppies are brought in to weep and beg on his behalf. And instead of the subtle interaction between litigants and the jury of an actual trial, the jury, represented by Philocleon alone, directly engages the litigants in dialogue. The trial is an obvious parody, and thus is not a direct window to reality, but it must bear some relation to reality to achieve its effect.

Aristophanes' play suggests that by this time the jurors who judged most forensic performances had changed significantly. The last half of the fifth century saw a significant expansion in the use of the courts, to the point that in other plays, Aristophanes could make jokes about the large number of trials held at Athens.[24] Earlier in the century (ca. 460) the traditionally aristocratic Areopagus council—the body that acted as jury for Orestes' trial and for many Athenian trials in the sixth and early fifth centuries—had seen its power considerably reduced and most of its duties given over to more demo-

---

22. As Blanshard observes (2004a:21–23; 2014:254–355), the laborious (and humorous) task of finding household items equivalent to actual court paraphernalia supports the view that Athenian courts were defined by the apparatus of litigation, not (as in later periods) by a special building.

23. The indictment in *Wasps* is quite similar to the later indictment of Socrates; see chapter 5.

24. For example, *Clouds* 206–208. In *Wasps* 799–805, Philocleon mentions a prophecy that someday trials would take place in a "little court" (*dikastēridion*) in people's homes. This may be an allusion to the increasing number of trials at this time.

cratic popular courts. The need for more jurors to staff this expanded court system led to the payment of a modest daily stipend for jury service of two obols, later increased to three obols.

In *Wasps*, Aristophanes portrays Philocleon as a typical Athenian juror—a poor, cantankerous old man with little to do in life but serve on juries. He enjoys being pandered to by litigants and takes delight in convicting as many of these litigants as he can. Although this picture is clearly a parody, it has impressed many readers, who assume that it is essentially true, even if a little exaggerated. Evidence shows, however, that the jurors were a more mixed group socioeconomically, and that the total audience, including jurors and bystanders, was a fairly diverse group.

One type of evidence that sheds some light on this question are jurors' *pinakia*, or small strips of bronze that were used to identify jurors and also to assign them (by lot) to a specific jury.[25] Beginning in about 378, each of the six thousand jurors selected for the jury pool in a given year was given a *pinakion*, which he had to present whenever he wished to be selected to serve on a jury. The *pinakion* was stamped with an official seal, the juror's name and (usually) patronymic, and at a later point his tribe. Because these *pinakia* made the allotment of jurors a much easier process, a few years later their use was expanded to the point that almost all citizens had a *pinakion* that could be used in the selection by lot of Council members and officials as well as jurors. To prevent anyone altering people's names, the letters on the *pinakia* were inscribed by punching tiny holes in the bronze.

The majority of names on the jurors' *pinakia* are persons unknown to us, and thus probably poor, but about 35–40 percent are known (or their families are known) from other sources; most of these individuals would thus have been in the middle or upper socioeconomic levels of the community. And Kroll identifies 8–10 percent of the total as belonging to "upper-class families."[26] This suggests that the jury pool may have been more mixed than they are in Aristophanes' portrayal, though the majority probably did come from the poorest stratum of the population. Moreover, the poorer citizens may have been more eager to earn the daily jury pay and may thus have appeared at the place of selection earlier than the others, so that they would dominate the juries that were selected that day; nonetheless, most ju-

---

25. The standard treatment of these is Kroll 1972.

26. Kroll 1972:261–267. His figures (p. 263) are that out of 50 jurors, 18–21 are known from other sources, of which 4–5 come from upper-class families, and 29–32 are not known from any other source. To be sure, 50 is not a large sample, but the results are still suggestive.

ries would probably have included more than a few of the more prosperous citizens.[27]

In addition to jurors, the audience before whom the litigants performed their pleadings in the popular courts also included a number—sometimes a very large number—of other observers or "bystanders."[28] Litigants had to address both groups, the jury, which was seated closest to them on benches, and the bystanders, who probably stood behind and around them, separated only by a railing.[29] Litigants regularly refer to these bystanders and sometimes address them directly, often asking them not to create an "uproar" (*thorybos*) if they are displeased with what the speaker is saying. One speaker even reports that in a previous case his opponent's pleading made such an impression on the jury that "they were unwilling to hear a single word of mine" (Dem. 45.6). If this report is accurate, the jurors' unwillingness to listen was presumably supported by similar feelings among the bystanders and manifested itself in an unusually loud *thorybos* that must have continued until the speaker sat down.

The speeches themselves provide some information about the composition of the bystanders at trials in the popular courts.[30] It is likely that at least a few of the would-be jurors who were not selected for jury duty that day remained to observe the trials. In addition, foreigners are mentioned as being in the audience in seven cases, and they may, of course, have been present in other trials. These foreigners must have been relatively well-off individuals; they may have been in town on business, but they evidently had the leisure to devote part of their visit to observing litigation. Lanni also notes references in various speeches to politicians being in the crowd, to students attending with their teachers, presumably as part of their education, and some speakers mention having attended other trials themselves. Thus, this part of the audience at trials would have included some "members of the rich elite"[31] with considerable knowledge of Athenian political affairs and law.

27. Jones (1957:36–37) discusses arguments in several speeches that in his view are crafted for a wealthier than average audience, but it is impossible to know whether such speakers truly thought the jury would be wealthier than average or were just addressing them as such, perhaps as a means of flattery. Hansen (1991:183–186) points out that because a court case could last all day, men from the country were almost certainly underrepresented; the elderly, on the other hand, were probably overrepresented.

28. The standard treatment is Lanni 1997.

29. See, for example, Demosthenes 18.196: "I intend this entire long discussion for your benefit, jurors, as well as for that of the surrounding audience."

30. See Lanni 1997: esp. 186–187.

31. Lanni 1997:187. She argues that this undermines the recent understanding of Athenian litigation as involving elite speakers addressing an audience of the masses (see

The bystanders and the *thorybos* they could create remind us of the crowd of observers who were "shouting out" at the trial on Achilles' shield (see above).[32] In analyzing the Homeric scene, I argued that this crowd of onlookers, representing the community, was an essential feature of the dispute-settlement process depicted there and played a major role in determining the outcome. The fifth- and fourth-century bystanders, together with the members of the jury, played a similarly important role in classical Athens, where the judicial process also consisted of performances by the litigants that must have been sensitive to and affected by the audience's response. Even if a litigant was delivering a speech that had been written for him before the trial, he would still have to be sensitive to the audience's response (just as a stage actor delivering fixed lines is) and would make adjustments in his speech accordingly. And logographers, too, must have tried to anticipate the audience's reaction, occasionally including in the speech a request that the audience not make a *thorybos* in response to what is about to be said.

Even today, when a trained judge is in charge of the proceedings, trials can take on aspects of a performance.[33] This is especially true for cases that are argued before a jury, but even arguing only before a judge, attorneys have to be sensitive to the way in which the judge is responding. And in jury trials today, when the vote of a single juror can determine the outcome of a case, litigants and their attorneys even employ professional jury consultants who can help them determine how each juror is responding to the arguments of each side and advise them on changing their line of argument accordingly.[34] Litigation in the United States may be becoming more performative, moreover, as trials are increasingly being broadcast on television. Although scholarly study of this development and its effects has largely been limited to citing the opinions of those involved, one effect that seems undeniable is that television broadcasts give litigants and attorneys greater ability to monitor the audience's response (the audience now being not just

---

Ober 1989). See also Carugati and Weingast (2018), who conclude (179) "the identity of litigants and jurors, as well as these actors' preferences, were meaningfully pluralistic and could not be reduced to a conflict between masses and elites."

32. Lanni (1997:189) makes this connection, disputing those who have connected the Homeric onlookers with the Athenian jury.

33. Shrager 1999 gives a very interesting account of the performative skill of good trial lawyers.

34. This can be seen in the TV series *Bull* (CBS 2016–), in which a trial consultant regularly monitors feedback from the jurors' expressions and body language, from the public (via Facebook, Twitter, and other social media), and from a representative group it has assembled. It then advises its clients to adjust their arguments accordingly.

the jury but a much larger public) and to adjust their arguments accordingly.[35] One scholar has even speculated that the televising of trials has made them more political and less observant of the rule of law.[36]

In Athens, where no judge was in charge of the proceedings, the performative aspect of litigation must have been considerably more important than it is today. Of course, we cannot today judge the full effect of an ancient forensic performance, since no visual recordings exist, but the texts of the surviving speeches can give us some idea of the performative aspects of these pleadings. There is disagreement, however, about how closely the written versions that we have resemble the speeches that were actually delivered, and in particular whether speeches were sometimes revised after the speech was given and before it was "published" (i.e., copied and distributed or sold to others).

The main argument for revision is that in the two cases where we have both speeches from the same trial (Demosthenes 18, 19; Aeschines 2, 3), one speaker occasionally refers to an argument of his opponent that does not, in fact, appear in the opponent's speech; this indicates (it is argued) that the opponent revised his speech after the trial to remove the argument. Other explanations, however, can account for these sorts of discrepancies. Each speech was probably composed only after hearing the opponent's arguments in the preliminary hearing, but litigants were not bound to incorporate every argument they made at the hearing into their final version, and nothing prevented them from adding other arguments that they had not used earlier. Whatever the truth of the matter, for practical purposes we have to rely on the texts as we have them and cannot base arguments on speculation about what a speaker might have said.[37]

---

35. One small example of this is cited by Smith (1997:259). In 1994, during the highly publicized trial of the Menendez brothers, which was being shown on television, the defendants first wore suits in court. When the defense team learned that their appearance was being criticized by the television audience, however, they changed the brothers' clothing to pants and sweaters.

36. "The comprehensive and instantaneous feedback loop between trial action and voyeuristic, public reaction . . . politicizes the judicial process in three ways. First, in the public's perception, the trial operates on a larger social theme than the legal reality. Second, the trial focuses less on the crucible of adversarial testing and more on the political context of the larger social issues. . . . Third, television publicity sacrifices justice for disfavored minorities to advance political causes. In short, politicizing of trials erodes the rule of law with mob rule" (Lassiter 1996:1000). Lassiter does not provide any hard evidence (like statistical analysis) to support these views, and in my mind they remain only speculative. But it is worth noting that since Lassiter wrote these words, the "feedback loop" has become almost literally instantaneous.

37. On revision of speeches, see Worthington 1991; Harris 1995:10–11; MacDowell 2000:21–27; Todd 2005a:108–109; Serafim 2017:32–33.

Regardless, the logographers who wrote these speeches must have been aware that the manner in which they were delivered was of great importance for their success, and after composing a speech, they may have coached their clients on how to deliver it. A well-known anecdote from Plutarch, perhaps apocryphal, indicates that Demosthenes, at least, recognized the importance of delivery (*hypokrisis*):[38] "When someone asked him what the most important thing in rhetoric is, he answered, 'delivery,' and the second is 'delivery,' and the third is 'delivery.'"[39] Aristotle, too, recognizes the importance of delivery, though somewhat reluctantly, since from a Platonic perspective delivery has nothing to do with truth: "When rightly understood, [delivery] appears vulgar; but since the whole business of rhetoric addresses opinion (*doxa*), we must pay attention to it, not because it is right but because it is necessary."[40]

This historical sketch shows that performance was fundamental to Greek litigation from the earliest times. Thus, although drama sometimes portrays litigation on stage, its influence on the actual performance of litigation was much less than Hall and others suggest. The many similarities between the courtroom and the theater with regard to performance were not the result of direct influence so much as the fact that from the beginning both genres were performances, and they therefore naturally shared certain performance features.

Several consequences follow from the fact that Athenian litigation was at heart a performance. First, and perhaps most important, as performers, litigants constantly had to be aware of the audience's response to their pleading and adjust their argument accordingly.[41] Second, the emphasis on performance increased the importance of rhetoric and of the skillful use of rhetorical techniques in litigation. The ability to tell a convincing story and to create an effective character (*ēthos*) for oneself and one's opponent (and sometimes for others, too) became essential to the success of the case.[42]

Third, the traditional communal context for litigation and the importance of the community in both assessing and shaping the performance

---

38. *Hypokrisis* essentially means "acting," and is most often used with regard to theatrical performances, but it then became the regular word for rhetorical performance, too.

39. Plutarch, *Lives of the Ten Orators* 845b.

40. *Rhetoric* 3.1, 1403b36–1404a3.

41. Even if a litigant was reciting a prewritten text, he would still have been able to make adjustments, such as cutting short an argument that was eliciting the audience's disapproval or adding some remarks to an argument that was meeting with approval. I will return to the subject of the audience's response in chapter 5, when I consider how the "rule of relevance," which required litigants to stick to the issue, was enforced.

42. Rhetoric and storytelling will be the subject of chapter 4.

caused litigants (and the logographers who assisted them) to ground their pleadings in the traditions and values of the community. Thus, the actions and characters in the stories told by Athenian litigants tended to conform to common societal patterns and stereotypes, which were generally those found in the traditional myths, so that in the litigants' pleadings men and women, old and young, rich and poor, slave and free generally behave in ways traditionally considered appropriate.[43] And this meant that jurors tended to deliver verdicts that conformed not only to the law but also to the norms and values of the community.[44] And especially in trials in which political considerations were important, litigants appealed to the Athenian past, to the great men and great deeds that had become almost mythical by the fourth century.

Finally, like all performances, Athenian litigation followed rules. To be sure, in Athens the rules governing litigation were not as strict as those we have today, and they were enforced by the audience (jurors and bystanders) rather than by an authoritative judge (see chapter 5). But there were rules, nonetheless, both the formal rules (substantive and procedural) prescribed by written legislation and unwritten rules established by custom and tradition. Litigants had to follow these rules, even if they were less strictly enforced than such rules are today.

In sum, Athenian forensic pleadings were competitive performances involving the interaction of litigants and their audience, the litigants seeking to win the votes of the jury, and the jury in turn, together with other observers, seeking to keep the litigants in line with the rules governing the performance. We will be examining more closely some of the consequences of this in the chapters that follow. First, however, I want to look at a separate feature of Athenian litigation, negotiation, which in Athens developed some rather strange and unfamiliar forms.

---

43. On the stock characters in Lysias 1, see Porter 1997; Gagarin 2003. Similarly, the plots and characters for most tragedies were taken from the traditional stories of Greek mythology.

44. Shrager 1999 repeatedly shows how successful trial lawyers today effectively appeal to the norms and values of their community.

CHAPTER 3

NEGOTIATION

The next feature of Athenian law I will examine, negotiation, is not marginal in the way performance is; indeed, negotiation is a well-established feature of our own law and in many forms quite closely resembles negotiations in Athens. But Athens developed three unusual types of negotiation that have no parallel in our law or (to my knowledge) in any other legal system—proposals to swear an oath, to interrogate a slave under torture (*basanos*), and to have a witness testify.[1] These appear similar to other familiar types of negotiation, but their intent was not to negotiate a settlement to the dispute but rather to prepare for a rhetorical argument in support of a litigant's case. Thus, they functioned in ways that we would consider marginal and need to be taken into account in assessing the Athenian legal system. This chapter will thus begin with a brief overview of the more ordinary forms of negotiation and then proceed to a more detailed examination of these three less familiar types of negotiation.

In all cultures, people commonly negotiate to find an acceptable resolution of their differences, whether or not they have taken, or are contemplating legal action. Normally one disputant proposes a certain course of action to the other, or a third party, often a friend or family member, or in our system a lawyer, may propose a course of action. Recipients of a proposal can either accept it and follow the proposed course of action or reject it, sometimes offering as a counterproposal either a modification of the original pro-

---

A version of this chapter was presented at the Symposion meeting in Tel Aviv in August 2017 (Gagarin 2018b). I am grateful for the feedback I received there from my respondent, Gerhard Thür (Thür 2018), and the other members of the audience. That paper contains an appendix listing all the examples of different types of negotiation mentioned in the orators.

1. These three types of proposals have traditionally been referred to as "challenges," a term I find inaccurate and misleading. My use of the term "proposal" is part of this chapter's attempt to situate these three types within the broader context of negotiation.

posal or something completely new. If at some point a proposal is acceptable to both sides, the dispute is resolved. If not, the dispute may end in litigation or in some other sort of hostile action, such as physical violence. For disputes that end in litigation, negotiation can still occur at any point up to the end of the trial and beyond.

In our legal system, negotiation occurs in most civil suits, either before the suit is officially filed or afterward. If the negotiation succeeds, the suit is settled out of court and no trial takes place. Even if a suit goes to trial, it can be settled by negotiation at any time before the verdict is delivered; and even after the verdict, the two parties can continue to negotiate if the losing side proceeds or threatens to appeal. Another possibility for civil disputes is binding arbitration, in which the two sides agree (or in some cases are effectively forced to agree) to accept a third party's decision. In suits between individuals, binding arbitration is less common, though the parties sometimes agree to it, but nonbinding mediation is often more desirable. The advantages of these sorts of negotiations are fairly straightforward: they allow both sides to avoid much of the time, expense, and emotional toll of a trial. Binding arbitration, which is becoming more common today, can have similar benefits, though it is apparent that in many cases companies are requiring their customers and employees to agree to binding arbitration from the start, when they first do business or accept employment, not so much because it saves time and money, but because on average it produces outcomes much more favorable to the company than litigation normally would.

In criminal cases today, negotiations between the accused and the public prosecutor (plea bargaining) are also common. The victim often plays no role in plea bargaining, but the victim and the accused may sometimes negotiate an agreement by which the victim will accept money in exchange for not pressing charges. Victims of crimes can also, and increasingly often do, bring a civil suit against the offender, and negotiations commonly occur in such suits, but these are usually handled separately from any criminal prosecution.

Negotiations in Athens were in many ways similar to those today. Negotiation was especially common in private cases brought by the *dikē* procedure, which was similar to the procedure in civil suits today. Negotiations could be handled privately by the two parties (often with the help of friends and family), or publicly in the nonbinding arbitration hearing that was required in most private cases before a trial took place. One purpose of this hearing was, if possible, to produce a resolution of the case. In homicide cases, the victim's relatives had a moral obligation to bring charges against the killer, depending on the circumstances, and people generally disapproved of the relatives if they accepted money from an intentional killer in exchange for agreeing not to bring suit. However, it does not appear that any law prohibited this. It would be difficult in any case to prove that a relative had accepted money (i.e., had been bribed) not to bring suit.[2] The *graphē* procedure did not accommodate negotiation so easily, because in many cases the prosecutor could be severely penalized if he dropped the case. But settling the case before, and perhaps also during, the preliminary hearing, which in a *graphē* was similar in many ways to the arbitration hearing in a *dikē*, seems to have been acceptable.[3]

Negotiation after a verdict was delivered was much less common in Athens. Today, the losing party will often appeal the decision, especially a large award in a civil case, and it may then be in the interest of both parties to agree on a smaller penalty than was awarded, thereby avoiding the uncertain outcome of an appeal. In Athens, where verdicts could not be appealed, such negotiations would have had little purpose. Possibly the losing side could propose paying a smaller amount in exchange for not bringing a suit for false witness, which would, in effect, reopen the case. Or if the penalty after a guilty verdict was assessable (and thus still needed to be determined), the two litigants might be able to quickly agree on a penalty before they each formally proposed a penalty to the jury. Or in a public case where the prosecutor had a weak case, but would be fined if he withdrew the case before trial, the two sides might agree that the accused would plead guilty but the accuser would only request a nominal penalty.[4] But we have no certain examples of any of these postverdict negotiations in Athens.

It is impossible to know exactly how common negotiations were in Athenian disputes, because litigants may have been more likely to mention cases in which negotiation failed than those that were settled by negotiation. Judging by the evidence of New Comedy, however, it appears that in situations where a young man had raped a young woman, the families of the two young people were very likely to negotiate a settlement, most often one that involved marriage between the assailant and his victim, after which the rape

2. In Antiphon 6 (according to the speaker), the victim's brother was first paid (by the speaker's enemies) to bring a homicide case (a *dikē phonou*) against him and then later was paid to drop the case. The brother's decisions about whether or not to bring charges are presented as being influenced strictly by money, not by moral or legal concerns.

3. See, for example, Dem. 59.53, 59.68–69. On dropping the charges in a *graphē*, see Harris 1999:133–138; Wallace 2006b; Harris 2006b.

4. It is possible that this happened in Demosthenes' case against Meidias (Dem. 21); if so, it would account for Aeschines' later claim (3.52) that Demosthenes "sold" the case for a mere thirty minas. See MacDowell 1990:23–28; Rubinstein 2000:209; Harris 2008:84–86.

would no longer be mentioned, as the two families resumed friendly relations.[5] If this was actually a common arrangement in Athens, and if other offenses were often treated in similar fashion, then many disputes could have been settled by negotiation before any litigation was initiated, and few of these would ever be mentioned in our sources.

Negotiation was a feature of Greek culture from the beginning. At the beginning of the *Iliad*, as the angry dispute between Achilles and Agamemnon is escalating, Nestor offers a very reasonable proposal to resolve the dispute (*Iliad* 1.254–284), but both leaders reject it. Later, Agamemnon sends several emissaries to Achilles with a proposal to resolve their dispute (9.115–161), but Achilles angrily rejects it. At the end of the poem, however, when Priam offers Achilles a wagonload of wealth for the return of Hector's body (24.553–558), Achilles accepts the offer in a moving scene, and the two enemies are reconciled.

A more complex scene in the *Iliad* with suggestions of litigation provides a good example of a proposal that is rejected by means of a counterproposal (23.566–611).[6] In the chariot race that was part of the funeral games of Patroclus, Antilochus finished second and Menelaus third, but when Antilochus is about to receive the prize for second place (a mare), Menelaus objects, claiming that Antilochus used unfair tactics. Menelaus first asks the assembly of Greek leaders to settle the dispute, but he then rather abruptly switches and says he will settle the dispute himself:

> But come, I myself will propose a settlement, and no one else, I tell you,
> among the Danaans will find fault with me, since it will be straight.[7]

He then proposes that Antilochus swear an oath:

> Come here, Antilochus, cherished by Zeus. As is right,
> stand in front of your horses and chariot, and take the pliant whip
> in your hands, the one with which you were driving earlier.
> Put your hands on the horses and by the earth-embracing earth-shaker
> swear you did not intentionally impede my chariot by trickery.[8]

---

5. See Scafuro 1997: esp. 238–259.

6. For further discussion of this scene, see Gagarin 2008:23–26.

7. 23.579–580. The verb Menelaus uses for "propose a settlement" is *dikazō*, whose performative sense I noted in chapter 2, note 12; the verb signals the quasi-juridical nature of the scene. The noun to be understood with *itheia* (straight) is *dikē*, "judgment, settlement"; cf. the trial depicted on Achilles' shield (chapter 2), where each elder tried to speak the straightest *dikē*.

8. 23.581–585. The "earth-embracing earth-shaker" is the god Poseidon.

Menelaus does not spell out the implications of his proposal, but he clearly implies that if Antilochus in fact denies that he intentionally used trickery and swears the proposed oath, Menelaus will accept the denial and drop his objection to Antilochus receiving the prize, although he probably will remain angry at the outcome and at Antilochus himself. Knowing this, he words the oath in such a way that Antilochus will be reluctant to swear it. Antilochus certainly did intentionally impede Menelaus's chariot; whether his maneuver was an unfair trick or a clever strategy is debatable.[9]

Antilochus understands the situation. He does not accept Menelaus's proposal and swear the oath, but neither does he explicitly reject the proposal; instead, he responds eloquently with a deferential counterproposal. He apologizes for his youthful impatience (nothing more) and then, while still claiming that he won the prize, he offers to give it to Menelaus as a gift and also to give him anything else he might want (587–595). His speech has its desired effect: Menelaus's anger is softened, and he responds with a counterproposal of his own that is equally eloquent and flattering: he will give Antilochus the prize, "even though it is mine" (23.610). This final proposal is acceptable: Antilochus takes the prize while tacitly acknowledging Menelaus's superiority but without admitting any unfair conduct.

This negotiation illustrates how the process can work if both parties truly wish to resolve their dispute, which, of course, is not always the case. The parties take turns offering proposals, each of which comes closer to being acceptable to the other until they finally agree. The same general process can be found today in such situations as determining the cost of an item in a flea market, or settling corporate lawsuits involving millions of dollars. The scene shows that from the earliest time, the Greeks recognized the important role of negotiation in the legal process.

All proposals follow certain unwritten rules. First, and most obviously, a person can respond by accepting the proposal and agreeing to do what is proposed or by rejecting it, sometimes offering a counterproposal along with the rejection. Acceptance and rejection can be explicit or can be conveyed only implicitly, as when the respondent simply does what is proposed or more often ignores the proposal and does something else or offers a counterproposal.

More importantly, when a party to the dispute offers a proposal, he implies his willingness to abide by the results if the proposal is accepted.[10] If

9. See Gagarin 1983, where I note that Antilochus is only following the advice of his father, Nestor, who recommends Antilochus's strategy as clever but not improper.

10. For example, if someone offers to pay a certain price for an item and the seller agrees to that price, under normal circumstances the person making the offer is obliged

he proposes an oath, for example, he implicitly commits himself to accepting the oath if it is sworn. Despite this expectation, however, it is not uncommon for an accepted proposal not to be successfully implemented, often because further disputes arise concerning various details of implementation. In the forensic speeches, for example, even if both sides have agreed to interrogate a slave under torture, they commonly cannot agree on the precise terms of the interrogation, and so no interrogation is ever conducted.[11] Most of the time, however, when a proposal is accepted, the agreement is carried out.

Even when an accepted proposal is fully implemented, however, a full resolution of the dispute does not necessarily follow. This depends on whether the proposal addresses the main issue in the dispute. If one party requests a document, for example, and the other side agrees to provide it and does provide it, this may resolve the entire dispute if the document in question is central to the dispute, but we have no actual example of such a resolution. More often a document will resolve only one specific point of the dispute, leaving other points unresolved, and thus the dispute as a whole will remain unresolved. For example, during his suit against Timotheus for the repayment of several loans, Apollodorus reports that when Timotheus proposed before the arbitrator that he, Apollodorus, produce the records (*grammata*) from the bank, he did indeed produce the records and let Timotheus examine them. He presents a witness to confirm this. Timotheus, however, disputed some of the details in the records and still has not paid his debt. Hence, the present trial.[12] Here, even though the document is produced, the dispute remains unresolved.[13] The determining factor is the proposal itself. If it addresses the central issue in the case, then its acceptance may resolve the entire dispute (though even then it may not). If, on the other hand, it is aimed at an issue that is not central to the dispute, then it will almost certainly not resolve the entire dispute even if the proposal is accepted and fully implemented.

In practice, these general rules are implemented differently in different types of proposals, so that each type must be examined separately. I have identified 173 proposals in the forensic speeches, but this number must be

---

to buy the item at the price he proposed and not then offer a lower price. Unforeseen factors may intervene and prevent the negotiation from succeeding, but the expectation is present nonetheless.

11. For example, Dem. 37.40–42; Isoc. 17.15–17.

12. Dem. 49.43–44.

13. For more on proposals to obtain a document, see Scafuro 2011:222–224; Harrison 1971:135–136.

treated with caution, as proposals are not always easy to identify. The vocabulary used to describe an act can help, though it is not decisive. The most important semantic marker of a proposal is the verb *prokaleō* (call forth, invite) or its cognate noun *proklēsis*. *Prokaleō* and *proklēsis* may be used for formal proposals that were offered in front of witnesses, often put down in writing, and sometimes submitted as evidence in a trial, but these terms may also be used to describe almost any kind of proposal. Moreover, the verb *prokaleō* can in some contexts simply mean "urge" or "encourage" when there is no question of a proposal.[14] In addition, a speaker can refer to a proposal without using *prokaleō* or *proklēsis* by saying that he or another person "offered" or "was ready" to do something, or that someone "requested" or "suggested" that something be done.[15] It can also be clear that a proposal has been offered by one side or the other (or by a third party) when a speaker describes disputing parties as achieving a reconciliation or as submitting to voluntary arbitration.[16]

Further difficulties arise because speakers are not always clear about the subject of the proposals they mention or allude to, making it impossible to know whether a proposal mentioned in one place is the same as one mentioned somewhere else. Also, when a speaker says that a person claims to have offered, it may be uncertain whether or not the proposal was actually offered. Finally, I have also counted hypothetical proposals because even if these were not actually offered, they are evidence of how proposals worked. Thus, precise numbers can only be tentative. With these caveats, I would identify 173 proposals in all, of which more than one-third (61) use *prokaleō* or *proklēsis*.

These proposals may be classified into seven types.[17] In order of frequency, they are (1) to resolve the entire case, or "whole-case resolution" (43 instances); (2) to interrogate a slave by *basanos* (36); (3) to submit to arbitration (28); (4) to swear an oath (23); (5) to resolve a specific issue in the case

14. Demosthenes argues (20.5), for example, that "the result of honoring more people than are deserving is that you (Athenians) will encourage (*prokaleisthai*) more people to do good."

15. See Thür 1977:59–67. Sometimes these terms are combined, for example in Dem. 45.48–49, where Apollodorus asks the jury to listen to the course of action "which I will now propose (*prokaloumai*). . . . For I request (*axiō*) . . ."

16. The flexibility of the vocabulary used to describe proposals makes it impossible, in my view, to identify a category of "formal" proposals by means of the vocabulary alone (cf. Thür 2018).

17. For a list of all passages that mention proposals, see the appendix to Gagarin 2018b.

(10); (6) to produce a document (8); and (7) to testify in court (4).[18] Four of these types are similar to proposals that are common today and operate in familiar ways: whole-case proposals, specific-issue proposals, arbitration proposals, and document proposals.

The most common was the whole-case proposal. For example, when Demosthenes sued Aphobus for ten talents, one-third of his overall claim against his three guardians for thirty talents, Aphobus "proposed (*proukaleito*) that he was willing to show me that the [total] estate was worth ten talents [i.e., one-third of what Demosthenes was claiming], and if it fell short of this, he said that he himself would make up the difference" (Dem. 27.50). Demosthenes reports that he asked Aphobus to demonstrate this value of the estate to the arbitrator, implying that he would accept the proposal if Aphobus did this, but Aphobus did not do so.

More often, however, whole-case proposals are more complex and often include matters separate from the actual dispute. Andocides reports, for example, that when he and Callias both claimed the same woman, Callias paid (bribed) Cephisius to bring charges against him concerning his involvement in the scandal of the Mysteries. Then Callias came to him and proposed that Cephisius would drop his charges if Andocides gave up his claim to the woman (And. 1.120–123). A proposal to resolve the entire dispute may also contain a choice of alternatives, as when Mnesicles proposes that Nicobulus and his partner either take back all the money they had paid (for a workshop) and leave (giving up the workshop) or keep the workshop and pay all the debts associated with it (Dem. 37.12). Nicobulus says he accepted the first alternative, but when the time came to return the money, Mnesicles (he claims) added further conditions and so no resolution was ever reached.

One more example illustrates the rhetorical possibilities for construing a wide range of actions as proposals. When Demosthenes was prosecuted for stealing public funds during the Harpalus affair, he passed a decree asking the Areopagus to investigate and report its findings. The Areopagus investigated and reported that Demosthenes did in fact take public funds. In his prosecution speech, Hyperides construes Demosthenes' decree as a proposal: Demosthenes "denied the charge and drew up a proposal (*proklēsis*) in the form of a decree, which he proposed to the Assembly"; Hyperides then concludes that "just as in private accusations, matters are often decided though proposals (*proklēseis*), so too has this matter been decided" (Hyp.

18. In addition to these specific types, speakers also occasionally refer to unspecified proposals (e.g., Hyp. 5, *Dem.* col. 3: "you offered proposals").

5, *Dem.* col. 2). By construing Demosthenes' decree as a proposal, Hyperides can argue that Demosthenes implicitly agreed to abide by the results if the proposal was accepted, and thus he must accept the Areopagus's report that he is guilty. Demosthenes, however, did not accept the report but questioned its lack of detail.

Specific-issue proposals may address an issue that would likely lead to an overall settlement if the proposal is accepted (e.g., in Dem. 56.40), but in other cases they address an issue that forms the background or only one part of a case, as when Euxitheus proposed that Euboulides, who was running a deme meeting, adjourn the meeting until the next day (Dem. 57.12–13). Euboulides "paid no attention to what I proposed," but even if he had adjourned the meeting, other issues would have remained in dispute.

Proposals for arbitration seem to have been the most successful type, especially if litigants were more likely to mention arbitration when it failed.[19] I am here speaking only of private arbitration.[20] Public arbitration was required in most private suits before they could go to trial; it was not a matter of negotiation. Within private arbitration we can distinguish between formal and informal arbitration.[21] Formal arbitration was a traditional procedure in which, as a rule, the two parties chose three arbitrators (though the number could vary), one selected by each party and the third by mutual agreement, and agreed to be bound by their decision. In informal arbitration, the two parties could mutually reach a compromise resolution, usually with the help of family members or friends.[22] In Athens, private arbitration

19. The only recent discussion of proposals for arbitration that I know of is by Johnstone (1999), who discusses it in his broader discussion of what he calls "dares" (73–92, 157–165). For recent discussions of arbitration in general, see Scafuro 1997:117–141, 383–399; Roebuck 2001; Harter-Uibopuu 2002:53–59; and Harris 2018b. For private arbitration, see Gagarin 2019:87–88.

20. At one point in his speech against Meidias (21.94), Demosthenes calls for "the law about arbitrators" to be read out, but the document preserved in our MSS purporting to be a law concerning private arbitration is clearly not genuine; see MacDowell 1990:317–318.

21. Scafuro, whose treatment of arbitration is the fullest, maintains the traditional distinction between arbitration (my "formal arbitration") and reconciliation (my "informal arbitration") on the basis of "whether a verdict has been given or a compromise has been proposed and accepted" (1997:122). See also Alwine (2015:31), for whom reconciliation "represented an agreement that the disputants affirmed," whereas arbitration "was a mechanism for reaching a resolution by handing over the decision to mediators who imposed a settlement." The Greek terminology, however, makes no consistent distinction between the two, and thus I treat them both as arbitration.

22. An informal arbitration, if unsuccessful, could lead to binding formal arbitration if both parties were willing.

often (but not always; e.g., Dem. 59.45–48) occurred before any litigation had begun, in an attempt to avoid litigation, which had several disadvantages, including restricting the possible outcomes and moving the dispute to a public stage.

We hear of many disputes in Athens being resolved in this way, and even if some of these were relatively minor disputes, the use of private arbitration must have helped reduce the burden of litigation on the courts. Arbitration proposals that were accepted generally succeeded, because both sides wanted them to succeed and were often willing to swear at the beginning that they would accept the result. Unsuccessful arbitration proposals are usually blamed on the other side's intransigence (e.g., Lys. 32.2), but in most cases both sides probably deserved a share of the blame. Even successful settlements may not have lasted. The settlement proposed by the arbitrators of the dispute over the property of Menecles, though accepted by all at the time, displeased the speaker greatly, and Isaeus 2 is essentially a continuation of the dispute that arbitration had supposedly settled.[23]

The fourth type of proposal in the forensic speeches that is relatively familiar is the proposal requesting to see a document, such as a will.[24] Such proposals were simple and straightforward, but most such requests that are mentioned in the speeches are denied. Even when successful, a request for a document did not necessarily resolve the main dispute, as we saw above in Dem. 49.43–44.

The four types of proposals discussed so far—whole-case, specific-issue, arbitration, and document request—appear often to have been offered seriously in the hope of resolving the dispute, or at least some aspect of the dispute, and it was not uncommon for these types to be accepted and for the two sides to reach an agreement. In that case, the agreement was binding according to "the law on agreements," which held that "whatever two persons agree on is binding (*kyrios*)."[25] To be sure, agreements sometimes fell apart as the two parties disagreed over the details of implementation, but binding agreements certainly kept many disputes from reaching the courts. And if one party tried to bring a suit concerning a matter that had been settled by agreement, the accused could then file a countersuit (*paragraphē*) claim-

23. See Isaeus 2.29–33. See also the dispute over Neaira between Phrynion and Stephanus, which is apparently settled to everyone's satisfaction (Dem. 59.45–58); one must wonder, however, how long the arrangement—that each of them would have Neaira on alternate days—could have lasted.

24. For example, Dem. 44.10–19, Dem. 45.8–9 and passim; in both these cases the request is refused.

25. For the law on agreements, see Phillips 2009; Thür 2013; Gagarin 2018c.

ing that his opponent's suit violated the settlement and was thus inadmissible and should be rejected.

The remaining three types of proposals include a practice that does not exist today, the *basanos* proposal that a slave be interrogated under torture, and two practices that were subject to special rules in Athenian law that do not exist today, to swear an oath, and to testify in court. All three, therefore, operate somewhat differently from the four familiar types that we have already discussed.

In a *basanos* proposal, one party to a dispute offers his own slave or slaves for interrogation under torture, or requests that one or more of his opponent's slaves be interrogated, or proposes the interrogation of a slave or slaves belonging to a third party, assuming the third party consents.[26] Usually the proposer specifies what question or questions will be put to the slave, and often he adds other conditions, such as that he will pay for any damage his opponent's slaves may suffer in the interrogation. Fairly strict (but probably unwritten) rules apparently applied to a *basanos*: the interrogation could be conducted by either party, but often an impartial public interrogator would be used; both parties had to be present; only simple questions that could be answered yes or no were allowed; and certain limits were placed on the severity of the torture.

The most obvious difficulty would have been to determine when a slave was telling the truth, since it was always possible that some additional torture would result in a different answer, making it impossible to know which was the real truth. The speaker's account in Antiphon 5 (31–41), confusing as it is, illustrates the sort of difficulty that might result, though this interrogation did not result from a proposal and only one party was present. The slave who was tortured gave one story first and then, the speaker says, changed his mind twice. The basic question, inherent in all such interrogations at all times, was: Did the torture force the slave to tell the truth, or did it only force him to say what the questioner wanted to hear in order to make the torture stop? Despite this difficulty, speakers almost unanimously express their complete confidence in the *basanos* procedure as the best way to elicit the truth.

Nonetheless, proposals to conduct a *basanos* are almost always rejected, so that the procedure does not actually take place. On the few occasions when a *basanos* proposal is initially accepted, some objection is always raised before the interrogation is actually carried out. One speaker, for example, describes how he and the banker Pasion reached an agreement to interrogate

26. See the magisterial study of Thür 1977; also Gagarin 1996; Mirhady 1996.

one of Pasion's slaves. But when they met to carry out the interrogation, having already chosen interrogators for the task, the speaker asked that the slave be whipped and put on the rack until they decided he was telling the truth. Pasion (not surprisingly) objected, saying that they had not chosen executioners and that he would only agree to an oral interrogation. The interrogators then said (according to the speaker) they would not interrogate the slave with torture but that Pasion should give him to the speaker, presumably to interrogate with torture (Isoc. 17.15–16).

This episode illustrates the kind of difficulty Athenian litigants faced because they could only interrogate a slave with torture if they reached complete agreement on the terms of the interrogation. It is possible that such interrogations occasionally did occur, but litigants, knowing that there was almost no chance that an actual *basanos* would be carried out, had little incentive to make a serious *basanos* proposal. Thus, most *basanos* proposals were made with no expectation that they would be accepted and carried out. Instead, as Thür has demonstrated, many of these proposals contained conditions that essentially ensured that they would be rejected.[27] The purpose of *basanos* proposals, then, was not to produce actual slave testimony that could be used in court. Rather, speakers sometimes describe *basanos* proposals in full detail, including the questions the proposer wished to ask at the interrogation. Sometimes the proposer even wrote these details down in an official document and introduced this document in court during his account of his *basanos* proposal.[28] This could have conveyed the impression that the *basanos* proposal was introducing material in court that was the result of an actual interrogation process, not just a proposed interrogation.

In other cases, a litigant might propose a *basanos* to provide rhetorical material that he could then use in his pleading. A common strategy was to use the opponent's refusal against him. Because litigants commonly claimed

27. See Thür 1977:233–261. As an example, in Antiphon 1, the speaker accuses his step-mother of poisoning his father. One argument he uses in support of his case is that on a previous occasion she had tried to poison him but she had been caught and had openly been accused by his father. The speaker proposed interrogating the household slaves to confirm this, but the defense refused (Ant. 1.6–7). The defense may have tried to refute this claim, arguing that even if their father had in fact accused his wife of trying to poison him long ago, this claim had no basis in reality and was worthless as evidence. Allowing the slaves to confirm the father's accusation under torture, which they might have done whether or not the accusation was true, would make the defense's task more difficult.

28. In our manuscripts, these documents are usually identified as a *basanos*, just as other such documents are identified as an oath (*horkos*) or a deposition (*martyria*). A *basanos* or a *horkos* could also be identified as simply a proposal (*proklēsis*).

that the *basanos* procedure was the best way to reveal the truth, a litigant could argue that an opponent who rejected a *basanos* proposal was rejecting the surest way to find the truth and thus was not interested in the truth. Antiphon was particularly fond of this argument and developed a special form of it, which we may call the hypothetical role reversal. After noting that the opponent had rejected his proposal, the speaker would argue to the effect that "if I had refused to reveal who was present when they made a proposal to me, or to hand over servants when they asked for them, or had rejected any other proposal of theirs, they would treat these refusals as very strong evidence that the charge against me was true. So when I offered them a proposal and they were the ones avoiding the test, surely it is only fair that this same refusal be evidence on my side, that the charge they are bringing against me is not true."[29]

In an oath proposal, a litigant either offers to swear an oath or offers to have someone else (usually a friend or family member) swear an oath, or he requests that his opponent swear an oath.[30] Oath proposals are often mentioned in the forensic speeches, but with one exception (see below), none of these was ever accepted. It appears, moreover, that the proposers of oaths almost always expected that their proposal would be rejected.[31] Most oath proposals are offers by a litigant to swear an oath himself or to have someone associated with him swear. These oath proposals are understandably never accepted. Such proposals essentially ask the opponent to allow the litigant to introduce as evidence an oath confirming a fact that the litigant is introducing as part of his case. Even if the opponent does not wish to dispute the fact, there is no reason why he should allow his opponent to present additional confirmation of the fact.[32] In some cases, the speaker says, "I am (or was) ready to swear" or "X is (or was) ready to swear," and it appears that the opponent is not even given a chance to accept.

Only on six occasions does a speaker report that someone else was asked

---

29. Ant. 6.27. The hypothetical role reversal is also used in Antiphon's two other court speeches (1.11–12, 5.38).

30. For oath proposals, see Mirhady 1991; Gagarin 2007b.

31. The oath in Dem. 59.60–63 may have been offered without expecting a particular outcome. As Apollodorus tells the story, the members of Phrastor's phratry proposed that he swear an oath concerning his son in order to have his son registered in his deme and phratry. They may have proposed it seriously, but Phrastor refused to swear and his son was not registered. Kapparis 1999:289–291 speculates that Apollodorus distorts the facts, omitting a significant clause in the oath offered to Phrastor and thus concealing the true reason why Phrastor declined to swear.

32. Moreover, since these proposals all occur in private disputes, the water clock would stop while the oath was read out.

to swear an oath, and all but one of these proposals were rejected. The one exception (reported in Dem. 39.3 and 40.10) occurred in unusual circumstances and resulted in two suits brought by a certain Mantitheus against his half-brother, whom he calls Boeotus. According to Mantitheus, his father, Mantias, refused to recognize Boeotus and a brother of his as his sons. To prove that they were not his, Mantias arranged with their mother, Plangon, that he would propose an oath for her to swear, stating that the boys were his; she would then, in exchange for thirty minas (3,000 drachmas), refuse to swear this oath, and her refusal would (implicitly) confirm that the boys were not his sons. When Mantias offered the oath, however, Plangon double-crossed him: she accepted the proposal and swore that the sons were his. Mantias then had no choice but to accept her oath (since he had offered it) and agree that the boys were his. Whatever the truth of the matter, it is clear that this oath proposal was expected to be rejected.

Two more aspects of oath proposals should be noted. First, some scholars[33] have suggested that if, as was very likely the case, women were not allowed to testify in Athenian courts, then when a speaker reported that a woman was willing to swear an oath and specified the content of this oath, this act could be seen as a way to introduce the woman's testimony in court.[34] This factor may account for some mentions of women's oaths, such as Dem. 29.33, where Demosthenes reports that several men testified but his mother said that she was ready to swear an oath. But the speaker in Is. 12.9–10 reports that both men and women were willing to swear oaths. A litigant could also report a woman's information without any mention of an oath, as, for example, Demosthenes does in 27.40 ("so my mother says"), and there appears to be no difference between this report and others in which a litigant reports that a woman was willing to swear an oath about something. In another case, Dem. 55, the speaker first reports what his mother told him she had learned from Callicles' mother about the damage done to the food in the house (55.23–24), and then later, in a discussion of the water on the road, he introduces a proposal he made that both mothers swear an oath apparently concerning rubbish on the road (55.27).

The second aspect is that offers to swear an oath are often treated as if they were actual oaths. In Isaeus 12.9–10, for example, the speaker reports that he himself and three relatives of Euphiletus (including one woman) were or are ready to swear oaths. He then adds, "you would rightly consider our oaths more credible than these men's words." Strictly speaking, "our

33. For example, see Harrison 1971:152.

34. Women's oaths make up less than one-fourth of all oaths that are reported (ca. six out of twenty-six).

oaths" refers not to oaths that were actually sworn but to oaths that were only offered, that is, proposals to swear oaths that were rejected. There was a long tradition in Greek literature, going back to Homer, of treating offers to swear an oath as if they were oaths.[35] Evidently, this tradition carried on into the forensic speeches, so that proposals to swear an oath may often have functioned as a means of introducing the oath in court while adhering to the traditional rule governing proposals, that the proposed oath was only actually sworn if the other party accepted the proposal.

Proposals to testify were also governed by the rule that a person who was asked to testify would only do so if he agreed; he could not be compelled to testify against his wishes. A litigant could not compel anyone to testify, but he could compel someone who refused to testify to swear an oath of exemption (*exōmosia*) that the testimony requested by the litigant was not true.[36] If a witness wished to swear an *exōmosia*, he would do so during the preliminary hearing before the trial. Then, during the trial, his *exōmosia* could be read out and he would simply confirm it. The *exōmosia* could include an account of the facts that the potential witness had refused to confirm.

In most cases, we do not hear anything about requests for testimony that were declined, though we may presume that there must have been a good number of these, since anyone who testified for a litigant in court risked being sued for false testimony if his side won the case. Requests that someone swear an *exōmosia*, however, seem to have been relatively rare, since few instances of this are mentioned in the surviving speeches. Occasionally, however, a litigant would request in court that someone testify even though he had already sworn an *exōmosia* at the preliminary hearing. The requested witness would then have to be present in court to confirm his *exōmosia*.[37]

We only have four examples of this, two of them in the same speech, but they all follow the same pattern.[38] The speaker in each case tells the jury

---

35. See Gagarin 2007b:43–46.

36. On the request for testimony and the *exōmosia*, see Carey 1995 and Thür 2005. Thür argues, against the consensus of other scholars, that "in the *exōmosia* the witness does not excuse himself by 'not knowing'; rather, he takes an oath that the statement devised by the litigant and formulated as the witness's knowledge is not true" (2005:147); but cf. Martin 2008.

37. The litigant could issue a summons to the requested witness to appear in court. If he did not appear, he could be fined one thousand drachmas. This may have happened in Aes. 1.45–50, where Aeschines appears to be uncertain whether Misgolas is present in court and will ("most shamefully") confirm the testimony Aeschines has prepared for him or whether he has ignored the summons, which indicates that he is willing to pay the one thousand drachma fine.

38. Aes. 1.45–50, 1.67–69; Dem. 45.58–61; Is. 9.18–19.

that he has prepared a deposition for a particular witness to affirm in court, and he gives a fairly detailed description of the deposition. He adds that he does not expect the person in question to accept the proposal and affirm the deposition, but that the speaker wants the court to know what sort of person the potential witness is.[39] Then the speaker may also ask the clerk to read out the deposition he has prepared, or he may have the *exōmosia* read out, after which the requested witness normally affirms his *exōmosia*.[40] It is clear that in these cases the litigant's motive in proposing that someone testify and then composing an actual deposition for the requested witness was not to produce the witness's actual testimony in court but to introduce into court a hypothetical deposition that the person had refused to confirm despite being asked. By this means, the speaker would give the impression that he was introducing a person's actual testimony, when in fact the person had refused to confirm the requested testimony.

The last three types of proposals we have considered—to conduct a *basanos*, to have someone swear an oath, and to have someone testify in court—were all subject to special rules unique to Athens. Nothing like them exists in our own law or (to my knowledge) in any other legal system.[41] Because these rules restricted litigants' ability to obtain the information they desired unless their opponent agreed, and because litigants could not compel their opponent to agree to a *basanos* or to an oath, nor could they compel a witness to testify, these proposals were virtually always rejected. Indeed, in most cases they were not intended to be accepted; rather, they were often formulated in such a way as to make their rejection almost certain. The proposer's intent was not to resolve the dispute but to introduce the information unofficially in his pleading and to lay the groundwork for various additional arguments he wished to make, such as accusing his opponent of

39. Aeschines 1.67 is the most explicit about this, although in the other three cases the speaker says essentially the same thing: "I am aware that he will refuse to affirm the testimony and will perjure himself [namely, by swearing that he has no knowledge]. Why then do I ask him to testify? So that I can show you what sort of men his way of life produces."

40. Some scholars have claimed that the proposed witness actually swears an oath of exemption in court, but Thür (2005:167–168) argues convincingly that the actual oath swearing took place before the trial.

41. We know very little about legal procedure in other ancient Greek cities, but Athens may have been unusual in this respect even among Greek poleis. The laws of the Cretan city of Gortyn do have rules for witnesses and oaths (but no mention of *basanos*). These specify cases in which a witness should testify or an oath should be sworn; they appear to leave little or no room for the sort of agreements required by Athenian law. See Gagarin and Perlman 2016:138–139.

resisting a sure means of obtaining the truth. In short, none of these three types of proposals could be considered a serious means of negotiation; they were offered so that once they had been rejected, they would provide rhetorical support for the proposer's case in court.[42]

We do not know how or why the rules governing the *basanos*, oath, and testimony proposals were created or developed into the forms we find in the classical period, but already in Homer, in the dispute between Menelaus and Antilochus after the chariot race in book 23 of the *Iliad*, an oath is proposed and implicitly rejected in a way that suggests that at that time unwritten rules existed similar to those governing oath proposals in classical Athens.[43] In the dispute between Orestes and the Furies in Aeschylus' *Eumenides*, moreover, when the Furies complain to Athena that Orestes is unwilling "to receive or give an oath,"[44] their language evokes the offering or requesting of oaths in Athenian law. These examples suggest that the Athenian rules governing oath proposals were a direct development of the community's traditional rules and customs about swearing oaths.

We have no information about the previous history of either *basanos* or testimony proposals before the classical age, but the requirement that both parties agree to a *basanos* proposal may have been influenced by the similar requirement for oath proposals.[45] Testimony proposals, on the other hand, probably developed separately from the other two, perhaps growing out of the general rule that no one could be compelled to testify in court, a rule that may have been instituted when the law against false testimony (*pseudomartyria*) was enacted.[46]

One other feature common to these three types of proposals was their

---

42. Johnstone argues (1999:72) that litigants sometimes used "dares" (his term for proposals) to exacerbate a dispute before litigation is initiated, and that when the dispute came to court, the dare (or the account of the dare) would function "as a way of establishing and securing the relationship between a litigant and the audience of jurors." I would agree with the first of these points but am not so sure about the second.

43. *Iliad* 23.581–585, discussed at the beginning of this chapter.

44. *Eumenides* 429: ἀλλ' ὅρκον οὐ δέξαιτ' ἄν, οὐ δοῦναι θέλει. The Furies are accusing Orestes of killing his mother and are complaining that he refuses to swear an oath that he did not kill her (because he did, in fact, kill her), or to offer some other oath instead. For "giving an oath," see Dem. 55.27: "I gave [i.e., proposed] an oath to his mother and I proposed that my (mother) swear the same oath" (ὅρκον ἐδίδουν ἐγὼ τῇ τούτων μητρί, καὶ τὴν ἐμαυτοῦ τὸν αὐτὸν ὀμόσαι προὐκαλούμην).

45. The *basanos* proposal in Antiphon's *First Tetralogy*, which was probably composed earlier than any of the other existing forensic speeches, indicates that this type of proposal was fully developed by the last third of the fifth century.

46. We do not know when this law was enacted.

place in the unique structure of Athenian forensic pleadings,[47] and this may also have led to their increasingly rhetorical use. As I noted in chapter 1, when a litigant wanted to introduce any sort of written evidence in court, he paused in his speech and had a clerk read out the text of a previously submitted document. This structure, in which the litigant's own speech is interrupted periodically for the reading of prearranged texts, is analyzed by Aristotle in his *Rhetoric* as a combination of what he calls *entechnoi pisteis*, or "artistic proofs"—that part of the speech that the litigant (or his logographer) wrote with "art" or "skill" (*technē*)[48]—and *atechnoi pisteis*, "nonartistic proofs"—the documents which, because they already existed, required no *technē* on the part of the litigant (or logographer) but could be inserted into the speech just as they were.

Aristotle lists five "nonartistic proofs": laws (*nomoi*), witnesses (*martyres*), contracts (*synthēkoi*), interrogations (*basanoi*), and oaths (*horkoi*).[49] In Aristotle's analysis, a litigant needs no rhetorical skill to produce these nonartistic proofs; he just takes an existing document and inserts it in his speech. This is partly true of laws and contracts, which existed independently of any litigation, though even with these it would require skill to select the right part of the law or contract to read out and to decide the best place to insert this into one's speech. The three types of proposals we are considering, however, are different. They were always created by the litigant himself (or by his logographer).[50] And they were generally created only during the course of litigation or when litigation was likely to occur. Thus, litigants and logographers not only used their skill to place these documents at points in the speech where they would be most effective, but they also crafted the texts of the documents to be as effective as possible in supporting the litigant's case.

The origins of this unusual structure of forensic discourse, in which the litigant's pleading was interspersed with the reading of documents, are obscure, but the structure itself is already clear in our earliest speeches, those

---

47. There is no hint of such a structure in the laws of Gortyn.

48. Aristotle's main categories of "artistic proofs" are *ēthos*, or "character" (of the speaker); *pathos*, or "emotion" (as a means of connecting with the audience); and *logos*, "reason, logic, argument."

49. *Rhetoric* 1.15.1; cf. *Rhetoric* 1.2.2, where only witnesses, *basanoi*, and *syngraphai* (also "contracts") are named. For problems that arise in applying Aristotle's analysis to the actual surviving speeches, see Carey 1994a.

50. This is obviously true of *basanos* and oath proposals. It is possible that some witnesses wrote their own depositions, but unless the testimony was completely straightforward, they would almost certainly have done so in consultation with the litigant; see Thür 2005:153.

written by Antiphon in the late fifth century,[51] where the *basanos* proposal in particular is subject to much rhetorical manipulation. And the same structure persists through the entire corpus of surviving speeches down to the late fourth century, ensuring that the three rhetorical types of proposals continued to be an important factor contributing to the rhetorical nature of Athenian forensic discourse.

Oath, *basanos*, and testimony proposals make up about 40 percent of all proposals. If we add to these a number of whole-case, specific-issue, and other proposals that are not intended to resolve the dispute but are primarily intended to make a rhetorical point, it seems that about half of all proposals were probably offered as part of or in preparation for a rhetorical argument and not with the expectation of resolving the case. In light of this, we may want to rethink the meaning of success as it applies to proposals. In several places above, I have discussed the success of a proposal as being a matter of whether or not it succeeds in resolving the dispute, or at least in resolving some issue that is part of the dispute. In these terms, we could conclude that the likelihood of a proposal's success depended in large part on whether or not the proposer offered his proposal seriously in the hope of reaching a settlement. By this criterion, the most successful proposals appear to have been those for arbitration, followed by whole-case and specific-issue proposals. However, the many proposals that were not offered in the hope of resolving the dispute should perhaps be evaluated by a different criterion. If a litigant's purpose in offering a proposal is to use it rhetorically in support of his case, then the success of his proposal would more fairly be judged according to how effectively it does in fact support his case. This criterion is more difficult for us to assess than whether the dispute is resolved, because even if we know the outcome of a case (and we rarely do), we have no way of knowing for certain how effective a particular argument was in persuading members of the jury.

Proposals, then, were a vital element in the negotiation process in Greece from the beginning. Those that were genuinely intended to resolve the dispute were sometimes, though certainly not always, effective. Even if the success rate was low, however, the benefits of ending the dispute would be great, whereas the cost of failure would leave one no worse off than before. Proposals that were offered for rhetorical reasons, on the other hand, are harder to assess. It is easy for a modern critic to see the weakness of many of

51. Specifically in Antiphon's three court speeches (1, 5, 6); the three Tetralogies lack any nonartistic proofs, though a *basanos* proposal is offered in 2.4.8.

the arguments based on such proposals, but Athenian juries may have found them more persuasive. A great many such proposals are offered in the surviving speeches, and their frequency seems to be fairly constant over time. This means that litigants and logographers must have concluded from experience that these rhetorical proposals would help their case. And as with proposals that were seriously intended, even if the success rate for rhetorical proposals was low, they probably did little harm to the litigant's case and may have done a great deal of good in some cases.

CHAPTER 4

RHETORIC

As I showed in chapter 2, comparisons of Athenian trials as performances to dramatic performances of tragedy and comedy can be instructive, but we must always bear in mind that there is an essential difference between the two. Poets strove to please their audience and win the prize for first place, but win or lose, they could return the following year for another attempt. A forensic speaker could also aim to entertain his audience, but no amount of entertainment value could compensate for the loss of his case. The trial scene on Achilles' shield, discussed in chapter 2, shows that from the time of Homer, forensic competitions consisted primarily of speeches by the two litigants. This made it vitally important for a litigant to deliver a persuasive speech. In addition, because there was no real forensic science in Athens, in most cases very little, if any, hard evidence was available, and the most common type of evidence presented in court, witness testimony, could be problematic. This made the effectiveness of the litigant's speech especially important, in most cases probably the single most important factor in determining the outcome of his case.[1]

In Roman law and in virtually all modern legal systems, rhetoric is generally thought to have little or no legitimate place. This is one of the main reasons why modern scholars have traditionally condemned Athenian law. Recall Bury's assessment (cited in the introduction) that as a matter of course Athenian jurors were "swayed by the eloquence of the pleaders working upon their emotions" and were "unduly influenced by the dexterity of an eloquent pleader." In practice, rhetoric plays a significant role in all legal systems, including our own, and this is not a bad thing. Indeed, it is hard to

1. There has been a surge of interest recently in the subject of rhetoric in the forensic speeches, one indication of which is the number of books and articles with the title "The rhetoric of X," including Hesk 1999; O'Connell 2017; Roisman 2003, 2005, 2006; Todd 1998; and Yunis 2005. Note also the Centre for Oratory and Rhetoric, established by the Classics Department at Royal Holloway, University of London, in 2010.

imagine a closing argument in any legal system that is not rhetorical. As a result, the same sort of criticism as Bury's is sometimes directed at our own legal system as, for example, after the verdict in the trial of O. J. Simpson a quarter century ago. Many members of the public felt that Simpson was guilty but was acquitted because the rhetorical arguments of his lead attorney, Johnnie Cochran, persuaded the jury to ignore the facts and concentrate instead on charges of racism in the Los Angeles police department, which (people felt) had no relevance to the case. Such a conclusion is far too simple. In Simpson's case, both sides made use of rhetoric, but Simpson's lawyers presented a stronger case than the prosecution did, in part by persuading the judge that the issue of racism was relevant. Rather than trying to eliminate rhetoric from legal argument, we would do better to recognize its role and try to understand it better.

The condemnation of rhetoric in the Athenian legal system originated in Athens itself, where philosophers and others criticized rhetoric in general and particularly rhetoric in the courts, giving some of the same reasons as critics do today. Even litigants in their pleadings would sometimes criticize their opponents for their skill in speaking or for using a clever logographer, and would warn their listeners not to be deceived, but they never extend this criticism to a condemnation of the entire legal system. Conversely, speakers often declare their inexperience or inability to speak well as a way to counter possible accusations of clever speaking.[2] These sorts of arguments, of course, are crafted with just as much rhetorical skill as the arguments they are criticizing.

Criticism of rhetoric in legal pleading began in the fifth century, when the role of the popular courts expanded rapidly, and the ability to speak well in court increased in importance. The increasing focus on rhetoric was also part of the fifth-century intellectual movement associated with a group of thinkers called the sophists, especially Protagoras, who said, "there are two arguments (*logoi*) on each subject opposed to one another," and whose teachings included how to "make the weaker *logos* stronger."[3] Critics were

2. Such criticism is common enough that it has been studied as "the rhetoric of anti-rhetoric" (Hesk 1999); see also Wallace 2015:59–61. Speakers like Demosthenes, who could hardly pretend to be inexperienced, had other means of defending themselves against such criticism (e.g., Dem. 18.276–277); see Wallace 2006a:425.

3. Two *logoi*: Diogenes Laertius 9.51 = DK B6a (δύο λόγους εἶναι περὶ παντὸς πράγματος ἀντικειμένους ἀλλήλοις). Weaker/stronger: Aristotle, *Rhetoric* 2.24.11, 1402a23 = DK B6b (τὸν ἥττω λόγον κρείττω ποιεῖν). For the meaning of these sayings as they apply to rhetoric, see Schiappa 2003: 89–116. Note in particular that the second saying only urges making the weaker *logos* stronger, not *the* stronger, as it is often misinterpreted.

quick to respond to these developments. Aristophanes satirizes both of Protagoras's teachings in his *Clouds*, where the Stronger Logos is a character on stage representing traditional views and a straightforward rhetorical style; he is defeated in a debate by the rhetorical trickery of his opponent, the Weaker Logos.[4] Suspicion was directed especially at the use of rhetoric in court. The earliest logographer, Antiphon, who began writing speeches for others around 430, was said to have come under suspicion because of his cleverness (*deinotēs*), a reputation clearly due to his rhetorical skill.[5]

In the fourth century, the best-known critic of rhetoric was Plato.[6] In the *Gorgias*, after being questioned by Socrates, Gorgias says that his particular knowledge is knowledge of the "rhetorical art/craft" (*rhētorikē technē*), and that he himself is a *rhētōr* and can make others *rhētores*.[7] Socrates then leads him painstakingly to assert that his *technē* is thus about speech and further that he "can persuade with words jurors in the courts, councilors in the Council, and assemblymen in the Assembly and in every other gathering" (452e), and further (453a) that rhetoric is the "craftsman of persuasion" (*peithous dēmiourgos*). Gorgias also says (454b) that rhetoric's persuasiveness is about just and unjust things (*dikaia te kai adika*), but later admits that the *rhētōr* both knows and doesn't know about just and unjust things. In a follow-up discussion with Polus, Socrates concludes (465a) that rhetoric is not a *technē* (because it cannot give an account of itself) but only a matter of experience (*empeiria*) and (465b–e) that it is a kind of flattery (*kolakeia*), akin to cooking, which (unlike medicine) seeks to make food good to the taste but not necessarily healthy. Rhetoric, in other words, seeks the appearance of truth, not actual truth.

In Plato's later work *Phaedrus*, Socrates and Phaedrus conclude that persuasion is most effective when the audience is ignorant and thus that a *rhētōr* who is ignorant of good and evil can persuade a city to do evil instead of good (260b–d). Later in the dialogue, Socrates advocates a kind of philosophical rhetoric whereby speakers will have knowledge of the matters they are discussing, but he returns to his criticism of rhetoric in the courts in his

---

4. The close link between Aristophanes' debate and a trial is indicated by the Greek word *agōn*, "contest, competition," which was used to designate either litigation in court or the debates found in many comedies and tragedies, including the one in the *Clouds*.

5. Thucydides 8.68. Cf. Philostratus, *Lives of the Sophists* 1.15: "Comedy attacked Antiphon for being clever (*deinos*) in legal matters and for composing speeches contrary to justice and selling them at a high price to those who were most in danger [of conviction]."

6. See Yunis 2017.

7. *Rhētōr* literally means "speaker" but is often used to designate a public speaker or politician; see chapter 1, note 12.

latest work, *Laws*, where he maintains that pleading in court ought to be a fine thing but it is "discredited, being an evil *technē* with a fine name [that is, rhetoric]. In the first place, it claims to be a device for conducting lawsuits and, when one is pleading a case or is a co-pleader for another, to have the power to win in every trial, whether justly or not" (*Laws* 937e). Therefore, if the judges, who in Plato's legal system are specialists and few in number, think anyone is trying to overturn justice, that person should be banished from the city (938b). This is essentially the same view as expressed in the *Gorgias*, that rhetoric has no concern with justice or knowledge but seeks only victory.

Plato's view of rhetoric won out over that of his fourth-century rival Isocrates, who attached much importance to the ability to speak well in advocating the best policy (though Isocrates never calls this ability rhetoric), and Plato has continued to influence views of rhetoric even today. In an examination of rhetoric and Athenian law, for example, Yunis remarks, "because from the point of view of rhetoric victory is the only objective, everything else—justice, law, statutes, communal welfare—is reduced to merely instrumental interest."[8] From this Platonic perspective, the large role that rhetoric played in Athenian litigation would certainly seem to support the criticisms of Athenian law voiced by Bury and others. This same perspective has led to the view that holds in most modern legal systems, which considers rhetoric incompatible with, or even antithetical to, law, and which has therefore devised rules to minimize the role of rhetoric and restrict its use so that it does not unfairly influence a judge or jury. Legal decisions, it is generally thought, should depend on the facts and the law, neither of which should be determined by the rhetoric of litigants, attorneys, or judges.

Legal theory, however, does not necessarily correspond to legal practice. H. L. Menken may have been exaggerating when he observed, "The best courtroom arguments that I have ever heard were not designed to unearth the truth; they were designed to conceal, maul and destroy the truth,"[9] but there is certainly an element of truth in his words. Litigants, attorneys, and judges today all make use of rhetoric, and not always in the service of unearthing the truth. Many studies emanating from the "law and literature" movement have shown that although rhetoric may be more pronounced and more obvious in trials before juries, it is present in trials before judges, too, and not just in the pleadings in court but in supposedly objective texts, such

8. Yunis 2005:192–193.

9. *The American Mercury*, January 1928 (cited from Menken 1995:88). A cynic might add that people are generally happy to have rhetoric deployed in support of their own case but condemn it when it is employed by their opponents.

as the legal briefs lawyers compose or the judicial opinions judges issue.[10] Judicial opinions may appear to present a dry, purely objective argument starting with the facts and the law and deriving a logical conclusion from them, but the many cases heard by panels of judges in which one or more dissenting opinion is issued make it abundantly clear that the judges' pure objectivity is only a façade. As one contemporary analysis of legal reasoning concludes, "in some legal systems, the form of judicial opinions, or, rather the 'motivation' of the judgment of the tribunal or court, is quasi-syllogistic. As everyone knows, however, the appearance of purely deductive or demonstrative argumentation, so far as it exists, is nearly always misleading."[11]

This reevaluation of the role of rhetoric in modern law leads to an understanding of law as not a strict science but a blending of rhetoric and science, in which the rule of law depends on both the observance of the law and the rhetoric needed to show what precisely constitutes observance of any particular law. Rhetoric is essential in forming the conflicting pleas of the two parties in a trial or in some cases the opinions of two or more judges on appeal. We should resist thinking of conflicting pleas or opinions as true or false, right or wrong. Rather, the same facts and the same law can legitimately be judged from different (but legitimate) perspectives or according to different (but legitimate) values, leading to different (but legitimate) results.[12] Thus, the role of rhetoric in law today is not essentially different from what it was in Athenian law, though it undoubtedly had a larger role in Athens than it does in our system or most other legal systems.[13] And al-

10. The bibliography for rhetoric in law, especially in the form of storytelling, is vast. See, for instance, Goodrich 1998; Amsterdam and Bruner 2000; MacCormick 2005; Laws 2013.

11. MacCormick 2005:237. See chapter 6, note 33, for an example of such pure deduction. See also MacCormick 2005:279: "It is in itself a discussable question, for any given topic of rational discourse, whether the topic is one which does admit of two or more 'discoursively possible', that is essentially reasonable, outcomes. Hence the claim that a certain matter was one on which there was nothing to be done but make an authoritative decision is one which it is always reasonable to problematize in a further discourse. The fact that legal finality imposes a closure for the law's practical purposes on such decision-making cannot insulate it from further inquiry at the bar of critical reason." Another way of putting this is that arguments made by lawyers and judges must be rationally persuasive, but they are not necessarily rationally demonstrative or conclusive.

12. See Scheppele (1989:2082) for the argument that stories may diverge not because one is true and one false but because of different perspectives. Moreover, the jury never has the real world facts to match the story against. "In law, both at trial and on appeal, all courts have is stories."

13. Even Roman law was not immune from the presence of rhetoric, although scholars usually see it as pure legal science. See Tellegen-Couperus and Tellegen 2013.

though Athenian litigants (as noted above) occasionally criticize their opponent's use of rhetoric, they generally accept the presence of rhetoric in law as legitimate.

Perhaps the aspect of forensic rhetoric that is most crucial for litigation is storytelling. As one scholar recently noted:

> Law is inescapably a storytelling as well as a rule-making enterprise. Clients tell their lawyers stories, so do witnesses; lawyers then edit and recast them to fit the models that match the stories to legal categories and are dramatically appealing to judges and juries; judges then produce their own narratives, both of the "facts" of the particular case and of the course of precedents that are called upon to supply the rule of decision; and majority and dissenting judges often tell the stories differently. The very simplest of disputes—like a dispute over which party's actions "caused" or "contributed" to a harm—cannot be resolved without listening to competing narratives."[14]

Storytelling, in other words, plays an essential role in litigation in all legal systems; the difference between its role in Athenian law and in our law today is just a matter of degree.[15]

To understand how rhetoric, and in particular storytelling, affected Athenian law, it is useful to begin by distinguishing its role in establishing the facts of the case from its role in establishing the applicable law. Facts and law are not entirely separable, but it is easiest to begin by examining each of these areas separately. For this I will use one of the best-known cases from classical Athens, Lysias 1, *On the Murder of Eratosthenes*.[16] Only the defense speech survives, but most readers have judged that this speech, written by Lysias, who was one of the most successful Athenian logographers, is one of the more convincing of the surviving speeches. It was probably composed for the defense of Lysias's client Euphiletus around 400.

Euphiletus has been accused of murdering Eratosthenes, but he maintains that the homicide was justified according to the law. In relating the facts of the case, he tells a lively story, admitting that he killed Eratosthe-

---

14. Gordon 2016:177. This explains why a contemporary handbook for trial lawyers advises, "One of your primary roles is that of storyteller. . . . When you prepare for trial, step back from the microscope and consider your overall story. Its clarity and credibility will probably play as great a role in the outcome as any single event or piece of crucial evidence" (Bergman 1989:10–12). A very interesting study of the use of stories in US trials is Schrager 1999 (see note 18 to this chapter).

15. For a slightly different perspective from the one presented here, see Asper 2019.

16. Todd's full commentary on this speech is excellent (Todd 2007:43–148). Much of the argument that follows is developed at greater length in Gagarin 2003 and 2014.

nes after finding him in bed with his wife. He begins by recounting how his marriage had been a happy one until the day Eratosthenes saw his wife at a funeral and decided to seduce her. The affair went on for some time, during which Euphiletus remained completely in the dark. But one day an old woman, the servant of another woman whom Eratosthenes had previously seduced, informed Euphiletus about the affair. He was stunned to learn of it, he says, for he always thought she was an exemplary wife and mother. His first step was to confront his wife's maid, who allegedly had acted as a go-between. Using harsh threats, he persuaded her to confess everything and to agree to help him catch Eratosthenes in the act. The next time Eratosthenes visited, the maid reported it to Euphiletus, who gathered a group of friends and then burst into the bedroom, finding the two lovers in bed together. The group seized Eratosthenes and bound his hands together, whereupon Euphiletus ran him through with a sword.

The story is carefully crafted to take the reader through the events exactly as they were experienced by Euphiletus himself, so that we feel the same betrayal and anger as he does. And although the structure of the story is highly sophisticated, the prose is clear and vivid with a few telling details that make the events memorable. Moreover, like almost all stories told in the forensic speeches, it makes use of a common literary story pattern with stereotypical characters. In this case, Lysias is drawing on what Porter calls "the comic adultery scenario":[17] the husband is a bit boorish, he is having poorly concealed sex with the maid on the side, his wife was first seduced at a funeral (one of the few public occasions where men and women mixed), and the maid acted as a go-between. And since traditional stories incorporated and promoted traditional norms of behavior, they appealed to the jurors' sense of justice, which was largely derived from these traditional norms.[18]

---

17. Porter 1997:422. Porter presents a detailed analysis of the similarities between this scenario and Euphiletus's account, which, he notes, contains very few details. He concludes, wrongly I think (Gagarin 2003), that Lysias 1 is a fictional speech cast in the form of a court speech.

18. The same is true in today's courtroom. Schrager gives a fascinating account of how a prosecutor in Philadelphia composed stories in a case involving drugs and murder that incorporated story patterns based on Christian ideas of sin and punishment in one trial and then of sin and forgiveness in a second trial. "Good lawyers compose their stories with careful attention to the evidence and the law. But they reach beyond these givens to tie the circumstances, which are always unique, to plotlines already deeply embedded in listeners' minds, to mythic narratives whose familiar moves reveal how the world is and how people, faced with fateful choices, act for good or for ill. This larger meaning is crucial to the story's effectiveness as a means of persuasion, a rhetorical de-

Lysias's rhetorical skill and use of traditional story patterns also help conceal the absence of any evidence supporting the story. Euphiletus offers no evidence for any of the events that took place before the actual night of the murder of Eratosthenes; his account is not confirmed by either his wife or the maid, the only others present. The murder itself is carefully planned and staged, and although Euphiletus presents the friends who accompanied him at the very end as witnesses,[19] they would have seen only what he wanted them to see. And if they testified falsely in support of his account, no one else had been present who could dispute their account. Thus, for all we know, most of this story could be complete fiction. It may of course have been true, or mostly true, but the story persuades listeners of its truth not because it is supported by evidence, but because of the rhetorical skill with which it is told.

In another case from about the same time, Antiphon 1, the speaker uses similar techniques to tell a fairly convincing story. He is accusing his stepmother of killing his father, and his narrative similarly draws on a traditional story pattern, this one from tragedy.[20] Alluding to the death of Agamemnon at the hands of his wife, Clytemnestra, he relates how the accused stepmother ("this Clytemnestra") planned the murder with the help of a maid whom she tricked into thinking she was only administering a love potion, which in fact was a poison. The speaker even relates a conversation between the accused and the maid in which the former deceived the latter. He offers no proof and probably had no information about what was said during the meeting (if in fact there even was such a meeting). Thus the account probably came entirely from his imagination. And in this case, too, adherence to a traditional story pattern undoubtedly helped make the speaker's story more persuasive.

To return to Lysias 1, the prosecution also gave a speech, of course, but because it has not survived, we cannot know exactly what they might have said. Certainly they must have told a different story. They might have denied that Eratosthenes ever seduced Euphiletus's wife, and they probably accused Euphiletus and his wife of deceitfully luring Eratosthenes into a compromising position in order to kill him. A similar scheme to lure men into precisely such a situation is portrayed in Demosthenes 59.64–69, where the

---

vice" (Schrager 1999:7). Much the same can be said of trials in the United Kingdom, as Griffith-Williams observes (2013:94, with note 16): "English barristers learn, in the course of their advocacy training, how to tell a convincing story on behalf of a client . . . [one that fits] with the audience's social attitudes and values."

19. Todd (2005b:70–71) notes that one aspect of Lysias's rhetorical skill is the careful placement of information about one of these friends, Sostratus.

20. Apostolakis 2007.

speaker describes how Stephanus and Neaira pretended that their daughter was a common prostitute. Then, when a man came to visit her, they would wait until the couple was actively engaged in sex, and would then burst in and seize the man and threaten to hold him until his family or friends paid a stiff ransom for seducing their daughter. It is not impossible that Eratosthenes' relatives alleged a similar scheme in this case, though the objective here would have been not ransom money but death, perhaps in retaliation for some earlier injury.[21]

The jury would then be presented with two different stories, one beginning with a peaceful, happy state before the trouble began and ending with the criminal trouble-maker caught and punished, the other beginning at a slightly later period, with Eratosthenes in a state of innocence, proceeding through his being seduced, entrapped, and murdered. This story is still unfinished, but it is clearly hoped that the story will soon end with Euphiletus being punished for his crime.[22] We can never know for certain what actually happened before the murder, and the jury could not have been certain either,[23] but after hearing the two speeches, they would have had to decide in favor of one side or the other without any further guidance beyond the two speeches they had just heard. As the (fictional) defendant in Antiphon's *Second Tetralogy* tells the jury: "Your task is to recognize that we litigants are likely to judge the matter by favoring our own side (*kat' eunoian*) and each of us is likely to assume his case is just (*dikaios*). But you must view the events with a righteous mind, for their truth (*hē alētheia autōn*) is only discernable from what is said (*ek tōn legomenōn*)."[24] Since Athens did not have a fixed standard of proof such as "beyond a reasonable doubt," the jurors could only judge by which story seemed to them most likely, or in other words, which speaker was the more persuasive. And this decision must have depended heavily on the rhetorical abilities of the two speakers (and their logographers).

The same is true of law today. In many (perhaps most) cases a judge or

---

21. Although Euphiletus strongly denies that he had any previous encounters with Eratosthenes (Lys. 1.4, 1.43–46), Todd notes (1998:165) that his wife and Eratosthenes' mother attend a festival together, which implies that the two families were on good terms and makes it unlikely that Euphiletus did not know Eratosthenes.

22. Today, too, it is not uncommon for the prosecution and defense to begin their stories at different times; see Scheppele 1989:2094–2097.

23. Scheppele (1989:2088–2094) presents a very interesting discussion of the difficulty (perhaps impossibility) of ever arriving at an objective truth. She shows how the attempt to strip away the point of view of participants in and observers of an event does not necessarily lead to an objective truth, which always relies on someone's assumptions.

24. Ant. 3.4.1–2. It is unlikely that a defendant in a real trial would be so honest about his own bias.

jury cannot know for certain where the truth lies, and the rhetorical skill with which each side has presented its case is certainly one of the factors that influences their decision. The high success rate of certain well-known trial lawyers is not due entirely to their superior ability to find hard evidence. Rhetorical skill, and in particular the ability to tell a good (convincing) story, is also an essential factor in their success in most cases.

Not only was the Athenian jury's understanding of the facts of a case thus significantly influenced by the rhetorical skill of the two litigants; the same was also true of their understanding of the law.[25] As noted earlier, at the beginning of each year, all members of the pool of six thousand jurors would swear an oath to "judge according to the laws and decrees of the Athenians." But judging according to the law was rarely a straightforward matter: the text of a law did not necessarily make clear the law's full meaning, nor did it tell jurors if, or in what sense, the law was applicable to the case at hand. In some cases, moreover, more than one statute may arguably have been applicable, so that differing statutes might have to be considered.

A related difficulty was that the laws a jury was given on which to base their decision were supplied by the litigants themselves and may not have been the most relevant or the only relevant laws. When a litigant wanted to make use of a law (or part of a law), he could introduce the text in court as a document, read by the clerk,[26] or he could simply speak about the law in his pleading, perhaps quoting a few words of it but without presenting the actual text. When a speaker introduced the law as a document in court, we can have some confidence that the text was quoted correctly because the penalty of death was apparently prescribed for anyone who cited a non-existent law.[27] And because each litigant was required to submit the texts of any laws that he wanted to introduce at trial during the arbitration proceedings (and probably also during other pretrial hearings), his opponent would have been able to check the quotation for accuracy and would then presumably bring a capital case if his opponent had cited a law that did not exist.

Litigants apparently did not object to minor changes in wording or par-

25. The following analysis is based in part on Gagarin 2014.

26. When a law is formally introduced in court (and read out by the clerk), our manuscripts usually provide only the notation *NOMOS* without preserving the text of the law. Occasionally a text is preserved in our manuscripts, but only rarely can we be (fairly) confident that this is the actual text of the law that was cited, and not a later creation.

27. The speaker in Dem. 26.24 reports that the legislator "defined the penalty, if one provides a non-existent law, as death." There is no other evidence for this law, but even if there was no such law, we can be fairly certain that a litigant who introduced a non-existent law in court would be exposed by his opponent.

tial quotation; indeed, the latter was probably the rule, since some Athenian statutes were rather lengthy and in most cases they would contain a number of provisions that were not relevant to the litigant's argument. Thus, in Dem. 58.14, the speaker asks the clerk explicitly to "read out this part of the law for me." In one case (Dem. 43.57), we can compare the introduced text with the original law, which was part of Draco's law on homicide, preserved in a fifth-century copy on stone. The speaker in this inheritance case is interested in degrees of family relationship not homicide, and so he not surprisingly omits many other provisions of the homicide law not relevant to this issue. The order of provisions in the text of the actual law and in the text of the law that he cites is also slightly different, and one clause of this part of the law has been omitted in his citation, but otherwise the citation is accurate.[28] This degree of modification was evidently acceptable.[29] Thus, when Demosthenes complains (18.121) that Aeschines removed parts of a law he cited, he is only accusing him of doing what many litigants do in quoting laws: they cite that part of a law that they consider relevant to their case, and as long as the quotation is accurate, this use of the law is generally considered proper. Of course, the opposing litigant may disagree about which part of a law is truly relevant, but he would be free to introduce the part that he considers relevant in his own speech. There is nothing improper, moreover, if a speaker quotes laws that support his case but says nothing about laws that may not support it, though of course, he may be well advised to deal with a law that poses obvious difficulties for his argument and try to counter its force (as Epicrates does in Hyp. 3, *Ath.* 13).

Litigants can also introduce laws that may seem to us not to be directly relevant to the case. At the beginning of Aeschines 1 (1.12, 1.16), for example, Aeschines has the clerk read out to the court the law on *hybris* and a law (or laws) regarding the conduct of school-age boys. These laws have nothing directly to do with the charge in the case but are introduced to contrast Timarchus's character with Solon's.[30] Finally, when litigants introduce a law by mentioning or describing it or even quoting part of it in their speeches without formally introducing the text as a document, there would be no control on the accuracy of their description or quotation, though there is little evidence to suggest that outright falsification was common in this practice.

28. For a comparison of the precise wording of the text as found on the inscription of the law and the text in our manuscripts, see Gagarin 2018a. See also Stroud 1968:49.

29. See Bonner (1905:59): "it was sufficient if the quotation was not materially different from the original law."

30. See De Brauw 2001–2002:170–174.

After they had heard the pleadings, the jurors would know the words of the law or laws that the litigants had provided, but it may not have been clear just how these words should be applied to the case they were confronted with, or, in some cases, which of the laws that were provided was the most relevant. Most jurors would have had a general knowledge of commonly cited laws from their experience serving on previous juries or otherwise attending trials, and some may have known quite a bit about the Athenian laws. But whatever their knowledge, for each case they would also have been provided with a limited number of laws that were either presented as documents in court and read to them by the clerk, or were described to them by the litigants in their own words. In the latter case, jurors surely might have suspected that the litigant's explanation of the law was not completely objective and almost certainly favored the litigant's case,[31] and this would have made it more difficult for them to know which verdict was truly in accordance with the laws.

One way to avoid the problem that jurors may not have known for certain just how the laws that were presented applied to the case they were deciding would be to adopt a view of Athenian litigation recently proposed by some scholars that downplays concerns about the precise meaning of statutes and argues instead that the main function of an Athenian trial was not to apply the law to the case at hand, but rather to resolve the dispute presented by the litigants. According to this view, "statute law in Athens does not supply the rules according to which the *dikastai* [jurors] must proceed, but rather the limits within which they must resolve the dispute."[32] This would mean that jurors had to take various laws into account in reaching their decision, but they did not have to decide about the precise meaning or applicability of any particular statute or choose between competing statutes, for these merely provided guidance. This view has some validity for some cases, but I think we must take much more seriously the repeated emphasis in the speeches that the jurors had a duty to decide according to the law. Unless the jurors completely disregarded their oath—and there is no evidence that they did—in most cases they would have had to confront dif-

31. See Yunis 2005:201–208, though he exaggerates when he says, "They [speakers] introduce the law not to make an argument about the legal or statutory basis of the case, but to create in the *dikastai* a feeling that will move them to decide in the speaker's favor for the sake of the community as a whole" (2005:208). Litigants introduced laws to support arguments they were making in the hope of persuading the jury, not simply to create a feeling that would move them.

32. Todd 1993:59; this issue is discussed further in the introduction, with notes 12–13.

ficult questions about the meaning and applicability of different statutes to the case they were judging. And in deciding these questions, they had no help from any source except for the pleadings of the two litigants.[33]

Litigants regularly discuss the meaning and relevance of the laws that they introduce in court and others that they mention in their pleadings. Often they tell jurors what these laws mean and how they are or are not relevant to the case at hand.[34] Litigants also often explain the legislator's purpose in enacting a statute and argue that this should influence the jury's understanding of the law.[35] But when two litigants disputed the meaning of a statute, or cited different statutes in support of their opposing positions, the jury had no other guidance to help them decide which of the litigants' pleadings was the correct, or the more correct, interpretation. Thus, the litigants' discussions of the law in their pleadings amounted in essence to an important source of law for Athenian jurors and others at the time, the most important source besides the statutes themselves.[36]

Of course, litigants' speeches did not have the formal authority of statutes, and the discussions and explanations of laws in the speeches were nothing more than the opinions of the speaker (and his logographer); in most cases, moreover, as Antiphon's fictional defendant admits (Ant. 3.4.1–2, cited above), each speaker undoubtedly presented the laws in a way that would favor his own case. Naturally, speakers would try to give jurors the impression that their opinions were authoritative, but in fact these opinions would carry weight only to the extent that the jurors, or a majority of them, were persuaded to accept them. Even then, it would take more than one case to establish any litigant's interpretation as the accepted meaning of a law. No single case had the kind of authority that, for example, a decision of the US Supreme Court has today. But in the absence of any similar judicial authority, litigants' speeches would have been the Athenians' only guide to the meaning of a law besides the texts of the statutes themselves.[37]

---

33. See Scafuro 1997:50–54.

34. See, for example, Lys. 3.41–42.

35. Lys. 3.42.

36. I am here using "source of law" in the modern, legal sense, not in the historical sense. The Athenians themselves did not have any concept of a source of law in the legal sense.

37. Harris (2013c:11–12) argues that the jury knew the laws independently of the litigants' speeches: they had enacted the laws, they heard the texts directly from the clerk, they heard lots of cases, and thus had a working knowledge of the law, and in most cases the dispute was about facts, not laws. However, a speaker might say that the jurors had enacted a particular law (e.g., Dem. 42.18), but this could only have been true for the few laws that had been enacted recently, and not all jurors would have been pres-

It is thus no surprise that in Lysias 1, Euphiletus explains to the jury the meaning of a number of laws, several of which he has the clerk read out to the court. His discussion of the law begins when he admits killing Eratosthenes but argues that the killing was justified because he was simply following the law (25–27):

> He admitted his guilt, and begged and entreated me not to kill him but to accept compensation. I replied, "It is not I who will kill you, but the law of the city. You have broken that law and have had less regard for it than for your own pleasure. You have preferred to commit this crime against my wife and my children rather than behaving responsibly and obeying the laws." So it was, gentlemen, that this man met the fate which the laws prescribe (*keleuousi*) for those who behave like that.

Euphiletus then (28) has the clerk read out "the law." He does not say which law this is, and no text survives in the manuscripts, but it was probably a law on adultery,[38] perhaps the *graphē moicheias* mentioned in *Ath. Pol.* 59.3, which may have prescribed death for adultery either as the sole penalty or as a possible penalty if the penalty was assessable.[39] Then, after again noting that Eratosthenes had offered to pay him ransom money, Euphiletus repeats his argument that he was merely obeying the law (29): "But I did not accept his offer. I reckoned that the law of the city should have greater authority; and I exacted from him the penalty that you yourselves, believing it to be just, have established for people who behave like that."[40]

---

ent when a law was enacted (see also below, note 40). Second, only some of the laws discussed by litigants were read out in court, and even then, their meaning and application to the case were not always clear. Third, if a juror learned the law from other cases, his knowledge would have come in large part from the speeches in those cases. Fourth, most cases involve both facts and laws. For example, Lysias 1 may concern a fact—did Euphiletus entrap Eratosthenes (Harris 2013c:385)—but it also depends on an understanding of the law. Did the law that Euphiletus cites allowing the killing of an adulterer allow him to use any means he wished to find Eratosthenes in bed with his wife? Or was there another law prohibiting entrapment (which the prosecution would surely have cited), and would Euphiletus's arrangement with the maid have fit that law's definition of entrapment?

38. The precise meaning of *moicheia* is disputed, and "adultery" is not an exact equivalent because the law applied to a man's daughter or sister as well as his wife (see Dem. 23.53, quoted below, and Todd 2007:44–49). The common alternative, "seduction," however, is also inexact, and "adultery" better fits the act in this particular case.

39. See Carey 1995:410–412. For cases in which the penalty was not fixed but was "assessed" only after a guilty verdict, see chapter 1 at note 52. If the penalty was assessable in adultery cases, death may have been assessed in some cases but not others.

40. Pretending that the jurors in a case were the same people who enacted this law was a common rhetorical practice. See Blanshard (2004b), who discusses the differ-

The problem with Euphiletus's argument at this point is that even if the law he has just cited prescribed death as the punishment for adultery—and it is perhaps more likely that the penalty was assessable—it certainly did not authorize a person to execute a violator without a trial. Euphiletus thus has another law read out, "the law from the stele on the Areopagus" (30). The text of this law is also missing in the manuscripts, but it was almost certainly the law that is preserved in Demosthenes 23.53: "If someone kills a person unintentionally in an athletic contest, or seizing him on the highway, or unknowingly in battle, or after finding him on top of his wife or mother or sister or daughter or concubine kept for producing free children, he shall not be exiled as a killer on account of this."

Euphiletus tells the jury that this law expressly says that "a man is not to be convicted of homicide if he captures an adulterer in bed with his wife and exacts this penalty from him." The paraphrase is accurate until the last clause, which speaks as if death were the penalty for adultery. This effectively changes a law that allows justified homicide into one that punishes adultery. This reinforces Euphiletus's earlier assertion that Eratosthenes "met the fate which the laws prescribe for those who behave like that" (27, cf. 29). This is a distortion, but because the law could be construed as declaring adultery a crime punishable by death, and because all Euphiletus needs for an acquittal is that the law allows him to kill Eratosthenes, the distortion serves the purpose of supporting Euphiletus's account of events, which sees Eratosthenes as the criminal and Euphiletus as the lawful punisher.

We can tell from some of the language used in the law that this is an old law, probably enacted by Draco more than two centuries earlier. In Lysias's time, it was still in effect,[41] but it seems to have been little used, since none of the many other cases of adultery mentioned in oratory or in comedy is handled in this way. Most commonly the adulterer is held for ransom, as Eratosthenes evidently expected to be in this case, or is subject to a variety of degrading punishments.[42] Thus, killing an adulterer on the spot may have seemed to many Athenians a cruel remnant of the distant past, and Euphiletus clearly understands that the jury may be reluctant to approve of his action,[43] especially since the prosecution almost certainly argued that his actions amounted to entrapment. Euphiletus's story seeks to give the im-

---

ences between the jury and the *dēmos* and the power of rhetoric to bridge the gap between them.

41. Some fifty years later (in 353) Demosthenes (23.53) treats the law as valid, though in doing so he may be influenced by his overall argument in that speech.

42. Phillips (2017:51–54) gives many examples of adulterers who had suffered various penalties other than homicide.

43. See Lanni 2016:39, with note 119.

pression that he killed Eratosthenes as a direct consequence of the rage he felt when he discovered the adultery, but even in his telling, the facts appear to show that the killing was planned beforehand and thus premeditated. Thus, it would certainly be questionable whether or not this law about justified homicide applied to Euphiletus's case.

If, as appears to be the case, no single statute governed adultery but rather a variety of statutes existed that might apply in different circumstances, jurors in such cases would have had to decide which law applied and in what sense it applied to this case, and in making this decision they would have had to rely primarily on information presented by the two litigants. And Euphiletus has told a persuasive story about the meaning of the law concerning adultery and its application to his case. Its persuasiveness is enhanced, moreover, by the vivid use of direct speech at crucial points, including when Euphiletus quotes himself (26): "It is not I who will kill you, but the law of the city. You have broken that law and have had less regard for it than for your own pleasure. You have preferred to commit this crime against my wife and my children rather than behaving responsibly and obeying the laws." This speech sounds like a judge explaining to a convicted man why he must be punished. We will never know whether Euphiletus actually said anything like this, but it hardly matters. The vividness of the scene and the formal, judicial quality of Euphiletus's pronouncement, followed quickly by the reading out of the law in its archaic language, would have encouraged the jurors to think that Euphiletus was presenting an authoritative explanation of the law.

To reinforce his argument about the law on adultery, Euphiletus has another law read out. The text of this law is also missing, but Euphiletus explains it to the jury as follows (32–33):

> You hear, gentlemen, how it provides that if anyone forcibly shames [i.e., rapes] a free man or boy, he is to pay double the damage; if (he forcibly shames) a woman—one of those for whom it is allowed to kill—he shall be liable to the same penalty. Thus, gentlemen, he thought that those who use force deserve a lesser penalty than those who persuade; for he condemned the latter to death but made the penalty double damages for the former, thinking that those who act with force are hated by their victims whereas those who use persuasion thereby corrupt their minds.

Scholars disagree about the accuracy of Euphiletus's conclusion, that the legislator prescribed a more severe penalty for adultery than for rape, but at the very least it oversimplifies matters.[44] In my view, the most accurate

44. Among recent discussions of this question, see Harris 1990; Carey 1995; Omitowoju 2002; Todd 2007:130–134.

conclusion would be Omitowoju's, that in Athens "there was no real legal distinction between seduction and rape."[45] Both were considered offenses against the woman's husband or other male protector, not the woman herself. As with some other offenses, moreover, rape and adultery were both subject to several different laws, which prescribed different procedures and penalties. The law just introduced by Euphiletus probably provided for a *dikē biaiōn* (lit. "suit against the use of force"), but the law on justified homicide that he introduced in 1.30 would have applied to a rapist caught in the act as well as an adulterer. Rape, and perhaps adultery, too, could also be prosecuted by the more serious procedure of *graphē hybreōs* ("insolent assault," see below), for which the penalty could be death. Thus, serious or less serious punishments were possible for both crimes.

Whatever the accuracy of his arguments, Euphiletus has given a clear and not implausible explanation for the severity of the law on adultery, and it is likely that at least some jurors found his case persuasive. The prosecution, however, almost certainly also discussed some laws, very likely including the law on homicide, which clearly prescribes a trial for those accused of homicide and death or exile for those convicted. They would probably have emphasized that the law required them, as Eratosthenes' relatives, to punish his killer. They also may have cited one or more laws on adultery, perhaps including a law about holding an adulterer for ransom and prohibiting entrapment. In any case, the jury would have been left to choose between competing arguments about the meaning and relevance of various laws relating to adultery and homicide. Each juror would have to determine for himself which litigant's story about the laws was more correct in this case, guided only by the bare texts of whatever laws had been read out in court together with the two litigants' explanations of the meaning and applicability of these and any other laws they may have discussed. As one speaker explains, "They [the jurors] have sworn to decide according to their most just understanding, but their decision based on this understanding relies on what they hear. Thus, when they cast their vote according to this understanding, they are behaving rightly."[46] The jurors, in other words, are dependent on the litigants' two speeches that they have just heard for their understanding of the law.

The rhetorical effectiveness of the litigants' speeches thus played a significant role in determining not only the facts of the case but also the meaning of the laws and their application to the case at hand. Moreover, because

45. Omitowoju 2002:131; see also her discussion of Lysias 1 on pp. 63–70.

46. Dem. 23.96. Cf. Cohen (2015:171), who notes that litigants themselves adduce the laws they wish; the jury is left with just those laws, the two speeches, and their own understanding of things.

Athenian juries voted simply for conviction or acquittal without giving any explanation of their vote, no litigant could know whether most jurors accepted his own or his opponent's account of the facts or the laws. A litigant could talk with jurors after the trial, but they could almost certainly not talk to each of the hundreds of jurors or even a majority. The views of the jurors undoubtedly differed, and many jurors may have had mixed views or would not be able to say exactly which law or laws were most important for them. Only where the vote was overwhelmingly one-sided and one could talk to a reasonably large number of jurors, all of whom gave the same reasons, could someone be confident that a particular argument about facts or laws had prevailed in the case, and this probably happened rarely, if ever.

If the jury voted for acquittal in Euphiletus's case by a large majority, this would certainly convey the message that a person might be allowed under certain circumstances to kill an adulterer found in bed with his wife. This would not necessarily have made Euphiletus's argument the authoritative interpretation of the law on adultery (or homicide), but if defendants in other similar cases used similar arguments successfully, then this interpretation could achieve a kind of de facto authority, and could be relied on with some confidence by others. But no previous interpretation could be relied on with absolute certainty, and in any new case, a litigant would still have to try to persuade a jury that the true meaning of the law favored his case.

Litigants in all legal systems, including our own,[47] may try to explain the meaning of laws to judges or juries, but absent authoritative decisions about the meaning or application of a law, Athenian litigants undoubtedly tried more often than others. Most Athenian laws were also written in more general language, at least with regard to their substantive content, than they are today, which made them easier for ordinary jurors and litigants to understand but also meant that there was more room for argument about a law's precise meaning or application.[48] One example often mentioned in this regard is the law on *hybris*, which we might translate as "insolent assault." As

47. Even if the US Supreme Court has determined the authoritative meaning of a law, it is still possible, especially if the justices were divided and if some time has passed, for someone to bring a new case to the court in the hope of getting the justices to alter or modify their previous decision.

48. Some technical language is used in Athenian laws, but it is largely confined to procedural matters; specialized procedures received technical names, and some ordinary words are used in technical ways. Prosecuting and defending, for example, were designated by the hunting metaphors "pursue" and "flee." But the meaning of terms such as these was usually unproblematic and did not affect the substantive language of laws, which for the most part remained general; cf. chapter 1, note 79, on the law against perjury.

cited in one case (Dem. 21.47), the law begins, "If anyone commits *hybris* against anyone, either a child or a woman or a man, whether slave or free, or does anything illegal (*paranomon*) to any of these."[49] That is the entire substance of the law; details about the procedures to be used in such cases follow. Nothing further is said that might guide the jurors in deciding what specific conduct amounted to *hybris*. They had to use their own judgment, guided only by their own understanding of the ordinary meaning of the term *hybris* and the arguments of the two litigants.[50]

The general vagueness of Athenian substantive laws may thus have caused some litigants to spend more time interpreting laws, and this, together with the absence of other means of providing an authoritative determination of a law's meaning, would undoubtedly have given litigants' interpretations more influence on the jurors' decisions about what various Athenian laws meant than is the case today, though even today "applying the law always means interpreting it."[51] At the same time, however, the precision of the specific accusation in a case may have rendered agreement on the general sense of the law less important (see further chapter 5).

Returning to Lysias 1, Euphiletus tells two stories, one about the facts of the case and one about the applicable law. The first story is legally a defense speech against a charge of homicide, but rhetorically Lysias has turned it into a prosecution speech accusing Eratosthenes of adultery and asking the jury to affirm the punishment that has already been inflicted on him for that crime.[52] And consistent with this emphasis on adultery in the story he tells about the facts, Euphiletus's story about the law is also a story about the law on adultery.[53] Thus, although we can analyze his stories about facts and law separately, they are inextricably connected.[54]

---

49. Dem. 21.47: ἐάν τις ὑβρίσῃ εἴς τινα, ἢ παῖδα ἢ γυναῖκα ἢ ἄνδρα, τῶν ἐλευθέρων ἢ τῶν δούλων ἢ παράνομόν τι ποιήσῃ εἰς τούτων τινά.

50. On the open texture of Athenian law, see Carey 1998:98–99. He notes (1998:99) that a law on marriage that speaks only of living together (*synoikein*) is subject to further definition by the speaker in Dem. 59.122, who gives his own definition of what *synoikein* means. Harris (2000:78) agrees that in the absence of substantive definitions, Athenian "litigants pay careful attention to substantive issues and questions about the interpretation of law."

51. MacCormick 2005:121.

52. See, for example, Todd 2005b:69–70; 2007:44.

53. To be sure, one of the three laws he cites (in 1.30) is a homicide law, but he presents this law to the court as if it were a law on adultery, like the other two laws he cites.

54. "Issues of law and issues of fact were inextricably mixed together for [the jury's] non-expert deliberation" (Scafuro 1997:52). Scheppele 1989 has an excellent discussion of stories in contemporary law; her analysis shows that interpretation of the law and interpretation of the facts are not separate processes.

Considerations of law and considerations of fact were especially closely connected in Athenian law. Unlike in US law, where in jury trials a judge decides questions of law and a jury decides questions of fact (at least in theory), in Athens the jury decided the whole case in one vote. Their judgment, therefore, was necessarily influenced by arguments about both the law and the facts, and in deciding on a verdict, the jurors would have had to combine their judgments about the facts and the law in such a way that even they themselves could probably not always say precisely how much they were influenced by each of these considerations. Litigants sometimes give a single explanation as to why the jury in an earlier case voted as it did (e.g., Dem. 21.75), but any such explanation has no basis in fact. Rather, litigants create explanations of previous jury behavior that will support their own case.

The necessity of arguing fact and law together stems from the basic structure of the Athenian legal system, which does not provide any means of deciding one without the other. This is clear from the special procedure of *paragraphē* (countersuit) created at the end of the fifth century, by which the accused could sue to stop the case against him on the ground that it was inadmissible because prosecution was prohibited by the amnesty, or the dispute had already been settled by binding arbitration, or some other reason. A *paragraphē* halts the original suit so that the *paragraphē* case can be tried first, with the accused now being the accuser.[55] In all the surviving speeches from *paragraphē* cases, except perhaps one that is uncertain (Lysias 23), the litigant discusses both fact and law.[56] Today, a defense claim that the case is inadmissible would be decided first, on its own merits, before any consideration of the facts of the case was allowed.

Finally, before concluding, I must note that forensic rhetoric often sought to evoke an emotional reaction in the jurors. Today, emotional appeals are generally considered irrelevant to judgments of guilt and innocence, and yet lawyers frequently find means of stirring up emotion by, for example, showing photos and other evidence of crimes or putting victims on the stand to testify. On the other hand, emotions, especially pity, are today generally considered legitimate factors in determining the punishment of a convicted person.[57] Some Athenian trials did have a separate punishment phase, but

55. There is nearly universal agreement among scholars that this reversal provided the original defendant the advantage of speaking first (e.g., Todd 1993:136–137), but I know of no evidence that speaking first was an advantage. Of Aeschines' three cases, for example, the defendant won two.

56. See Todd 1993:138–139.

57. See Lanni 2006:53–59; Konstan 2000:135.

the only surviving speech from this phase of a trial is Socrates', as represented in Plato's version of the speech (in his *Apology*), and this can hardly be considered typical. And since many Athenian cases had no separate punishment phase, emotional appeals could only be made in the body of the main speech. Thus, these do occur, though almost always as a supplementary argument to arguments about guilt or innocence.[58]

In particular, litigants commonly appeal to anger at one's opponent or pity for oneself or one's family.[59] However, speakers also criticize their opponent or other speakers for making such appeals just as often as they actually make such appeals to emotion themselves, and we must be careful not to take these criticisms at face value.[60] The particular type of appeal that is probably the most commonly criticized by litigants is one in which the opponent will bring his children up onto the speaker's platform (*bēma*) to join him in appealing for pity.[61] This practice, however, was probably far less common than its critics imply. It must have occurred occasionally, or there could hardly have been so much criticism (or satire) of it, but I know of no clear example of it in the surviving speeches.[62]

In sum, various factors contributed to increasing the importance of rhetoric in Athenian litigation. The absence of forensic science meant that litigants generally had little or no hard evidence, and the absence of authoritative judges who might rule on the meaning of a law or restrict the scope of an argument allowed litigants to plead in whatever ways they felt would be most persuasive. This meant that rhetoric played a much larger role in forensic pleadings than it has played in most other legal systems and gave greater incentive to litigants who could afford it to make use of logographers to help them present a stronger case. On the other hand, the Athenians were

58. See Griffith-Williams (2016), who shows that reason and emotion are generally both at work in forensic speeches both in classical Athens and today.

59. See Konstan 2000; Rubinstein 2003, 2014.

60. Cronin 1939 argues without justification that the large number of litigants who criticize others for appealing to the emotions is evidence for the frequency of such appeals to emotion. Konstan 2000 and Rubinstein 2004 and 2014 are more helpful, giving many examples of litigants who actually do stir up emotions.

61. For examples of speakers anticipating that their opponent will bring his children up to the *bēma*, see Dem. 19.310, 21.99, 21.186–188; Hyp. 2, *Phil.* 9 (col. 6); Hyp. 4, *Eux.* 41. Other speakers criticize the practice in general (e.g., Lys. 20.34; Plato, *Apology* 34c–d). The practice is satirized in Aristophanes, *Wasps* 976–979 (cf. 568–569). For a full list of references or possible references, see Whitehead 2000:64.

62. Aeschines (2.179) evidently has his children in court but not on the *bēma*. Andocides (1.148) appeals to the jury to act as his family (cf. Ant. 1.4), since his ancestors are dead and his children are as yet unborn.

also suspicious of rhetorical specialists, who might trick the jury into reaching the wrong verdict, so litigants generally concealed the fact that someone else had written their pleading for them. Whether a logographer was used or not, however, rhetoric retained its importance as the essential basis for establishing not just the facts of a case, but also the applicable laws. Disputes concerning the meaning of a law or the applicability of one or more laws to the case had to be decided by the jury, which had little that they could rely on besides the pleadings of the two parties. This did not mean, however, that rhetoric prevailed over all other considerations. In the next chapter, I will examine some of the ways the Athenians controlled litigants' rhetoric and reaffirmed the superior power of law. Despite the importance of rhetoric, it remained the servant, not the master of the law.

CHAPTER 5

RULES AND RELEVANCE

I now come to the question that lies at the heart of this study: if Athenian litigation was essentially a contest to determine the rhetorical effectiveness of the pleadings of the opposing litigants, what reason do we have to dispute Bury's conclusion that litigants "make a large use of arguments which are perfectly irrelevant to the case," and jurors were "swayed by the eloquence of the pleaders working upon their emotions"?[1] Must we accept the conclusion that litigants were constrained only by their sense of what would most effectively persuade the jurors?[2]

The Athenians themselves would certainly not have accepted this conclusion. Litigants repeatedly assert that Athens was a government of laws and that jurors decided cases according to the laws. As Aeschines puts it after noting that his audience will have heard these words many times before:

> There are three kinds of constitution in the whole world, sole rule (*tyrannis*), oligarchy and democracy. Sole rule and oligarchic cities are governed by the temperament of those in power, but democratic cities are governed by the established laws. . . . In a democracy the persons of citizens and the constitution are protected by the laws, whereas sole rulers and oligarchs are protected by suspicion and armed guards. . . . You whose constitution is based on equality and law must guard against those whose words or actions violate the laws, for your real strength is when you are ruled by law and are not subverted by men who break them. Whenever we pass laws our concern should be how to make laws that

1. Previously cited along with similar views of other scholars in the introduction at notes 5–10. See also Yunis 2005:192–193 (cited in chapter 4, note 8): "from the point of view of rhetoric, victory is the only objective. Everything else—justice, law, statutes, communal welfare—is reduced to merely instrumental interest."

2. "The only effective constraint was rhetorical; that is, litigants would constrain themselves from saying anything that might alienate their audience, the *dikastai*" (Yunis 2005:194–195).

> are fine and beneficial for our constitution (*politeia*), and once we have passed them, we should obey the laws in existence and punish those who disobey, if the city is to flourish.[3]

Many other litigants echo this insistence on the power of the laws and their role in protecting the citizens and the constitution, and we need to take it seriously. So I begin with a brief account of legislation in Athens.

Written law in Greece had roots in the prehistoric period, when the rules of conduct were orally preserved and transmitted. Before writing developed, they were sometimes expressed in verse and gathered together, as we find in sections of Hesiod's *Works and Days*, where rules concerning practical matters like agriculture (e.g., the best time for planting) are mixed together with rules about conduct toward others, such as:

> If someone grabs great wealth with his hands by force
> or plunders it by means of his tongue, as generally
> happens when profit deceives the minds
> of people and shamelessness drives away shame,
> then the gods easily make him obscure and diminish the household
> of this man, and his wealth only stays for a short time.[4]

Oral rules such as these contain the seeds of a substantive rule that could later be formulated as a written law against theft or fraud,[5] but in both Hesiod and Homer, the general rules, customs, and traditions that guide people's behavior and influence the settlement of disputes are called *themistes*, a word closely related to the earliest Athenian term for a (written) law, *thesmos*.

To illustrate the transition from oral rules to written laws, consider the *themistes* related to homicide.[6] In Homer, two different rules are cited concerning the treatment of homicide. The first is appealed to by Ajax in the *Iliad*, when he is pleading with Achilles to be reconciled with Agamemnon. Ajax argues that even someone whose close relative has been killed can put aside his anger.

---

3. Aes. 1.4–6. The first part of this passage is repeated in Aes. 3.6.

4. Hesiod, *Works and Days*, 321–326.

5. For clarity, I prefer to restrict use of the term "law" to rules that are authorized by some public process and written down. Scholars often speak of "oral laws," but unless they are written, rules almost always lack the precision and permanence achievable with writing; they also lack the clear authority of a public process. I will use the expression "oral law" to refer to a legal (or prelegal) system that does not use writing but relies on "oral rules," such as those portrayed by Homer and Hesiod.

6. This transition is examined in more detail in Gagarin 2007a and Gagarin 2008: 93–109.

A person accepts from the killer of his brother
or his dead son the blood-price,
and when he has paid a large compensation, the killer remains in the
community,
and the relative's heart and manly anger are curbed,
when he has received the blood-price.[7]

The second rule is cited by Odysseus near the end of the *Odyssey* as he considers the course of action that he and his son Telemachus should take after the two of them have killed all the suitors.

A man who kills just one man in his community
even one who leaves not many avengers behind
that man flees, leaving behind family and fatherland.[8]

These two rules are in direct conflict: a homicide victim's relatives can either accept compensation from the killer or pursue him into exile, but not both. They can coexist in the epic world because they are kept separate and are cited at different times and places. But if both rules are cited during the process of settling a dispute in the real world, with the killer offering compensation but the relatives demanding exile, or vice versa, there would have to be a compromise, taking into consideration the circumstances of the homicide, the situation of the two litigants, the history of their relationship, and other factors.[9]

Moreover, neither rule has much detail: nothing is said, for example, about the conditions of exile (where or how long), the amount of compensation, or what to do if some relatives want to accept compensation but others want exile. Being oral, moreover, the rules are not fixed, and as many studies have shown, oral poems are prone to change as they are repeated by bards over time. Oral rules were probably sufficient in the small communities of the eighth century, where families could negotiate these kinds of details, perhaps with the help of others in the community, and would only rarely need to use the trial procedure depicted in Homer.[10] And even if they did resort to a trial, the Homeric procedure appears to encourage the el

7. *Iliad* 9.632–636.

8. *Odyssey* 23.118–120.

9. It is possible that these two methods were proposed for resolving the dispute portrayed in the trial scene in the *Iliad* that we examined in chapter 2, with the killer proposing to pay compensation and the victim's relative insisting on the killer's exile. A possible compromise might involve some amount of compensation plus a short period of exile.

10. See chapter 2.

ders, together with the rest of the community, to find a compromise resolution. As Greek cities grew larger and more diverse, however, such negotiations would have become more difficult, and people would begin to need more precise and certain rules.

Alphabetic writing was introduced into Greece in the early eighth century, a little before the poems of Homer and Hesiod took their present form. It quickly spread through most of the Greek world, and for more than a century it appears to have been used exclusively for private purposes, such as dedicating an offering, or identifying the creator or owner of a pot. But between 650 and 600 we begin to find inscriptions with public texts, texts that speak for and are authorized by the community, and for the next century or so, the vast majority of these public texts are laws.[11] Those that have survived were mostly inscribed on stone, though a few are on bronze. We know that other laws were inscribed on more perishable materials, such as wood, but these have not survived to the present.

To illustrate the changes that occurred in moving from an oral rule to a written law, we can continue with the example of homicide, because one of the earliest surviving Greek laws is a substantial fragment from the Athenian homicide law written by Draco ca. 621 BCE. It survives only in a later republication, but its wording must be quite close to the original.[12] Here is a very literal translation:

> Even[13] if someone does not kill someone intentionally, he is to go into exile. The kings (*basileis*) are to judge (*dikazein*) guilty of homicide the killer or the planner, and the *ephetai* are to decide (*diagnōnai*).[14] Reconciliation, if there is a father or brother or sons, [is to be by] all of them; or the objector is to prevail. But if these are not (alive), up to the degree of first cousin once removed and first cousin, if all are willing to reconcile, [they are to be reconciled], but the objector prevails. But if not one

---

11. Accounts of lawgivers as early as the eighth century are found in Aristotle and other later authors, but these are generally recognized as largely legendary (Szegedy-Maszak 1978). Wallace (2009a:417–420), while recognizing the legendary nature of these reports, nonetheless takes them as evidence for some eighth-century written laws. In my view, however, the abundant material evidence shows conclusively that writing was not used to inscribe laws before the mid-seventh century.

12. See Stroud 1968:60–64.

13. The first word of the law (*kai*) is usually translated "and." I defend the translation "even" and argue that the text that follows applies to both intentional and unintentional homicide in Gagarin 1981, but this question does not affect the present argument.

14. The "kings" must be officials of some sort, probably the forerunners of the later Archon Basileus. The identity of the *ephetai* is uncertain; they are only mentioned in connection with early homicide litigation.

> of these is (alive), and he killed unintentionally, and the fifty-one, the *ephetai* decide he killed unintentionally, let ten phratry members admit him if they wish; and let the fifty-one choose these by rank. And let those who killed earlier be bound by this ordinance (*thesmos*).[15]

Leaving aside the many interesting and controversial details of this text, I will only note the most important point for our purposes, namely that the law first prescribes exile for homicide, and then adds rules for reconciling the victim's relatives with the killer, beginning with what are presumably the most common situations, when there are close living relatives.[16] If there are several relatives, then any decision about reconciliation must be unanimous. If we compare these laws with the oral rules concerning homicide in Homer, we can see that Draco found a way to incorporate both of Homer's conflicting rules into his new law, but gave the rule prescribing exile priority. This probably accorded with traditional practice in Homer's day, since in virtually all cases of homicide described in the Homeric poems, the killer goes into exile. But Draco kept reconciliation as a possibility, and in certain circumstances, such as accidental homicide, this may have been the common outcome.

Draco was followed in Athens by Solon, who in ca. 594 issued a large set of new laws, keeping only Draco's homicide law. Many laws dating to the seventh and sixth centuries are also preserved from other cities, indicating that a considerable amount of legislation was being written at this time. Some of this was the product of a single lawgiver like Solon writing a large number of laws for a city; other laws were single pieces of legislation, presumably enacted in response to specific concerns. Solon had some sort of mandate from the people, who were worried about growing enmity between the rich and the poor, and as far as we can tell, other lawgivers also had mandates to legislate. They wrote laws on a wide range of issues, but there is no evidence before the mid-fifth century of any systematic codification or the involvement of any professionals. The lawgivers we hear about were either the leaders of the community, who, among other things, enacted laws, or in some cases of civic strife were outsiders, who were called in to write laws for the city.

As far as we can tell, all these laws from the archaic and classical periods were displayed in a public place. Some were written on the walls of a temple or other public buildings; others were written on stone slabs or ste-

15. *IG* I^3 104 = *IG* I^2 115; Osborne and Rhodes 2017:504–511.

16. Even if the law only applies to unintentional homicide, as many scholars think, the combination of exile and compensation is notable.

lae erected in the agora or other public spaces. Some scholars think that only the elite could read these laws, and that their public display was not intended to allow ordinary people to read them, but rather to make a visual impact on nonelite, illiterate members of the community, thereby affirming the authority of the elite. I and others are convinced that these laws were meant to be read.[17] The Greek script, being fully alphabetic, was easier to read than scripts in Egypt and the Near East, where professional scribes did much of the writing, and although literacy in Greece was not high by modern Western standards, in my view, many members of the community could have read these texts or could have found someone to help them read them. The inscriptions themselves, moreover, use several techniques clearly designed to make the text easier to read, strongly suggesting that the purpose of public display was to allow a large number of people to read the texts if they wished.[18]

The public display of laws later became an important element in Athenian democratic ideology, which emphasized the availability of the laws for all to read. As we have noted, the language of the substantive portions of laws was generally simple and straightforward, with relatively little technical vocabulary. And the fourth-century legislative process lessened the possibility of conflicts between laws as much as possible, as Demosthenes notes in describing this process (20.93): "Next, opposing laws are repealed so that there is one law for each subject. This avoids confusion for private individuals, who would be at a disadvantage in comparison to people who are familiar with all the laws. The aim is to make the justice of law (*ta dikaia*) the same for all, simple and clear (*hapla kai saphē*) to read and to understand."[19]

The transition from oral rules to written laws had some important consequences. First, the texts were now fixed and durable. Second, the written laws were far more precise than the oral rules that preceded them were, or could ever have been, and included more details. Written laws would thus have limited a litigant's flexibility in pleading his case to a significantly greater degree than the old oral *themistes* did.

In addition to substantive rules, Athenian litigation was also subject to many procedural rules. Some of these were written, often together with substantive rules. For example, as noted in chapter 4, the procedural rules that

---

17. See the works cited in chapter 1, note 64.

18. For example, the earliest laws were written with marks that indicated where a new word began; see Gagarin and Perlman 2016:53–55. In later Greek inscriptions, as people began to read more easily, these marks are no longer used.

19. This text is part of a longer passage (20.93–94) that is cited in full in chapter 6 at note 17.

make up most of the text of the law on *hybris* ("insolent assault"), as preserved in Demosthenes 21.47, are preceded by a clause that designates the substance of the offense:[20] "If anyone commits *hybris* against anyone, either a child or a woman or a man, whether slave or free, or does anything illegal (*paranomon*) to any of these people. . . ." Everything that follows, however, is procedural:

> Let any Athenian who wishes to whom it is permitted bring a public action (*graphē*) before the Thesmothetai and let them bring the case to the court within thirty days from the time of the accusation unless some public business prevents it, but if not, at the earliest possible time. Whomever the court convicts, let it immediately assess whatever penalty it thinks he deserves to suffer or pay. As for everyone who brings his own personal indictment according to the law, if someone does not prosecute or does prosecute but does not gain one-fifth of the votes, let him pay one thousand drachmas to the public treasury. If someone is assessed a sum of money for his *hybris*, if the *hybris* was against a free man, let him be put in prison until he pays.

Other procedural rules may have been written as separate, purely procedural texts, though we have no certain example of one that was.[21] Many procedural rules, however, were probably unwritten. In my discussion of forensic performances in early poetry (chapter 2), I noted that these performances were shaped by traditional rules, and that a performance that did not accord with these rules would not achieve its desired effect. Later, some of these early rules, such as the plaintiff speaking first or equal time for each litigant, probably became so established that there would have been no need to write them down. Even if such rules remained unwritten, they would never have been questioned. And later rules, such as the use of two urns for the votes in the fourth century, which in effect provided a secret

---

20. On the mixture of substance and procedure in Athenian laws, see, in general, Carey 1998; Wallace 2018a.

21. The speaker in Antiphon 6.38 may perhaps be referring to a written procedural law when he describes how his opponents tried to bring a homicide case against him but the Basileus, the official who oversaw homicide cases, "read them the laws and showed them that there wasn't enough time to register the case and issue all the necessary summonses." The Basileus (he later explains) "had to hold three preliminary hearings in three months and then hold the trial in the fourth month . . . but he only had two months left in his term of office" (Ant. 6.42). We do not know which laws the Basileus read out, but they may have included a law requiring three preliminary hearings one month apart.

ballot,[22] may also have been established only in practice and never put into writing.

Athenian laws, whether substantive or procedural or both, were never organized systematically. The legislative process was intended to avoid direct conflict between laws, but even so, victims often had a choice of several procedures they could use to prosecute an offense.[23] And because both substantive and procedural rules were often included together in written statutes, in choosing which substantive offense to charge the accused with, a victim generally was also choosing which procedure to use.

This is evident in a passage in Demosthenes 54 that is regularly cited in this regard. At the beginning of the speech (54.1), Ariston explains that as the victim of physical attack, he is bringing an ordinary suit for assault (*dikē aikias*), although he could have used one of two other procedures if he wished, the summary arrest of cloak stealers (*apagōgē lōpodytōn*)[24] or an indictment for *hybris* (*graphē hybreōs*). His choice, he argues, is a sign of his modesty and respect. He does not mention that the procedure of summary arrest was historically intended to be used against common street criminals or "muggers," which the offender in this case clearly was not, or that by using the *graphē hybreōs*, he would have turned the case into a much more serious public prosecution, putting himself at risk of a substantial fine. A simple *dikē* procedure for the offense of assault (*aikia*) was thus probably used in the vast majority of assault cases, even if alternatives were available.

Defendants sometimes complain that the prosecution is using an illegitimate procedure, one that was not intended for use in prosecuting the offense charged in the current case. In Antiphon 5, for example, Euxitheus, who is accused of homicide, complains bitterly and repeatedly that his opponents maliciously used a procedure of summary arrest of "wrongdoers" (*apagōgē kakourgōn*) instead of the ordinary suit for homicide (*dikē phonou*). The prosecution evidently chose this procedure in order to prevent Euxitheus from leaving Athens and going into exile, as he could have done if he was accused by means of a *dikē phonou*, but in court they apparently concealed this motive and argued instead that the procedure of summary arrest of "wrongdoers" was intended to be used for "wrongdoings" (*kakourgēmata*)

22. Each juror was given two tokens, one for acquittal and one for conviction. At the front of the court were two urns, one for the tokens representing the jurors' votes, the other for the discarded tokens. Each juror in turn then cast one of his tokens into the urn that held the actual votes and the other token into the urn for discards. In this way no one watching could tell which token he had put into the urn whose votes would be counted.

23. See Osborne 1985.

24. A heavy cloak was usually the most valuable item a person walking in the street would have with him.

and that homicide was a big *kakourgēma* (Ant. 5.9–11). This argument is logically correct, though traditionally only a small number of offenses (such as mugging, but not homicide) fell into this category. The officials allowed the case to proceed, however, thereby leaving it up to the jury to decide if this argument was legitimate.[25] The officials may have felt it was better to allow litigation to proceed rather than possibly face the charge at their *euthynai* (accounting) that they had prevented someone from obtaining the justice he was due.[26]

The most important procedural rule for our purposes was the so-called rule of relevance, the rule that all litigants must speak "to the issue" (*eis to pragma*). In addition to the written laws, this rule provided the other main restraint on litigants' pleadings. It is uncertain whether the rule was a formally enacted statute or only an accepted customary rule, but it certainly existed in some form. The *Ath. Pol.* reports (67.1) that in private suits "the litigants swore oaths that they would speak to the issue," and although litigants before the popular courts do not mention any such oaths, they repeatedly mention the need to stick to the issue. That such assertions are frequent in public as well as private speeches of all sorts makes it very likely that there was such a rule for all cases.[27] Lanni has noted that litigants before the Areopagus speak of a *nomos* requiring them to stick to the issue (e.g., Ant. 6.9), whereas litigants in the popular courts speak of some other standard, such as appropriateness.[28] A possible, though not the only, explanation for this difference is that there was a written statute for the Areopagus but only an accepted custom in the popular courts. In any case, it is clear that the rule of relevance was treated more strictly in the court of the Areopagus. But whether the rule was a written statute or an unwritten but widely accepted customary rule, litigants in the popular courts are clearly aware of the rule and take it into account in constructing their arguments.

This obligation, however, leads to some obvious questions. First, how did

25. Expansion of a criminal charge to include offenses that were not originally targeted by the legislation is not confined to Athenian law. In the United States, the Racketeer Influenced and Corrupt Organizations (RICO) Act of 1970 provided special procedures intended to make it easier to prosecute the Mafia and other organized crime, but it has since been used to prosecute other quite different crimes, such as the cover-up of sexual abuse by Catholic priests.

26. Other examples of the questionable use of a procedure include Lysias 13 and Hyperides 4 (*Eux.*).

27. Whether the rule was written or unwritten is debated: doubts are expressed by Lanni (2006:100–101). Rhodes (1981:718–719; 2004:137) accepts the rule without deciding whether it was written, and suspects that it was not confined to private suits.

28. See Lanni 2006:100–101.

the litigants (and others) know exactly what the issue was? If the prosecutor brought a case of assault or cloak stealing or *hybris*, some of these general categories would present a very wide range of specific charges that could be included in the accusation.[29] However, litigants and jurors did not have to address these general categories, because in Athenian law, as Thür has shown, the formal charge in each case was determined quite precisely by the plaintiff when he initiated his case by filing an *enklēma* (complaint) in an ordinary private suit (*dikē*) or a *graphē* (indictment) when the procedure was a *graphē* or public case.[30] The *graphē*, as the name indicates, was always written down when it was filed, and the *enklēma* was written by the early fourth century if not earlier.[31] This written document was read out at the beginning of the trial, and it determined the issue or issues in the case, so that any argument directed at a point that was included in the charge was relevant.

The trial of Socrates is a good example of a case in which the general charge, impiety (*asebeia*), may have been vague, but the specific complaint was more precise.[32] The formal indictment in this case is preserved by Diogenes Laertius and reads as follows: "Meletus son of Meletus of Pitthos indicted and swore an oath as follows against Socrates son of Sophroniscus of Alopece. Socrates does wrong (*adikei*) by not recognizing the gods the city recognizes but introducing other new divinities; he also does wrong by corrupting the youth. The proposed penalty is death."[33] Note that the

---

29. For cloak stealing, however, the accusation presumably had to specify that the accused had stolen a cloak.

30. Thür 2008: esp. 66–72 (German version, Thür 2007: esp. 143–149); see also Gagarin 2012; Harris 2013b; and the useful overview by Lanni (2018) with a response by Wallace (2018b). In other public procedures, the accusation sometimes took the name of the procedure; for example, it was called an *eisangelia* in the impeachment procedure (*eisangelia*). Thür thinks that the defendant's response to the accusation, often called an *antigraphē*, also helped determine the issue, but as far as we can tell, this response was commonly just a simple denial of the accusation (see, e.g., Dem. 45.46) and thus can be ignored for our purpose.

31. Harris (2013b:154–156) argues that "plaints" were preserved in the archives, but although some evidence suggests that public indictments were preserved in the Metroon, no good evidence exists for the preservation of private complaints. The evidence Harris presents shows only that various people, all of them in some way related to the original case in which a plaint was first filed, were able to cite the plaint at a later time. Even if these individuals possessed a written copy of the accusation (and they may just have remembered something that they heard), this would not mean that they obtained it from an archive. See further Lanni 2018:198–199.

32. To be sure, greater precision does not eliminate a litigant's flexibility in constructing his case. A broad range of more specific conduct could be included in "corrupting the youth," but the charge is still significantly more precise than "impiety."

33. D. L. 2.40. The parody of a trial in Aristophanes' *Wasps* contains a very similar indictment: "Cyon [Dog] from Cydathenaeum indicts Labes [another dog] from

general charge of impiety is not mentioned in the indictment that Meletus wrote; rather, he charges Socrates in the most general terms with "wrongdoing" (*adikein*) and then lists the more specific acts that constitute the alleged wrongdoing. And it is this list of specific acts that controls the arguments in this case.

In other words, the issue that had to be decided in this case was not whether Socrates was guilty of impiety, and there is therefore no discussion of Socrates' impiety per se in his speech, at least not in the versions of his speech in Plato's *Apology* and Xenophon's *Apology*.[34] Instead, Socrates argues entirely against the specific points stated in the indictment, denying that he recognizes other new gods, not the city's gods, or that he corrupts the youth. Any argument addressed to these issues was relevant under Athenian law. Failure to recognize the difference between the general procedural category of offense (impiety) and the particulars of the complaint has led many modern readers astray. A common assessment of Socrates' trial is that whatever he did, he surely was not guilty of impiety. This argument misses the point that impiety in general is not the issue in the case; the issue is the formal complaint alleged by the plaintiff. This complaint, as Lanni shows after a thorough review of the evidence, generally offered "a specific but brief description of wrongdoing by the defendant that would fit at least loosely under the statutory procedure through which the case was brought, and typically did not include allegations of other legal wrongs committed by the defendant against the plaintiff or others."[35]

To be sure, the specific charges listed in the indictment had to be considered instances of the general charge of impiety. In this case, "not recognizing the gods the city recognizes but introducing other new divinities" would quite clearly be impious; "corrupting the youth," on the other hand, may be more questionable, but apparently it was seen as such a severe violation of standards of conduct regarding the defenseless youth that it was considered an act of impiety toward the gods. But whatever the reasoning, the Basileus accepted the charge and allowed the case to proceed.[36]

These considerations may help explain why the Athenians, at least in some of their laws, like the law on *hybris* (see above), used only a very gen-

---

Aexone for wrongdoing (*adikein*), in that by himself he ate up the Sicilian cheese. The proposed penalty is a fig-wood collar" (*Wasps* 894–897).

34. There is a brief allusion to impiety in Plato's *Apology* (35d). Xenophon mentions impiety twice in his *Apology* (22, 24), but only after he has finished giving his version of Socrates' speech.

35. Lanni 2018:194.

36. Today, judges invalidate laws that are too vague, so a law against corrupting the youth (for example) would probably not be allowed to stand.

eral term for the offense, without specifying precisely what conduct would or would not be included in the general category of offense.[37] It was only necessary for the law to designate a general category as illegal, because anyone who brought a complaint under this category would have to spell out the specific behavior that constituted the offense he was alleging in this case, and this list of specific acts would then be "the issue" that controlled the arguments and the jury's decision in the case. Today, we try to provide more detail within the substantive laws themselves, thereby specifying much more precisely the charges that can be brought under a given law.[38] The Athenians believed in writing more general laws, which allowed a wider range of charges to be brought, but their rule of relevance meant that once the charges were specified, the specific accusation limited the arguments that could be made in the case. Athenian litigants were thus constrained to stick to the issue, though they may have had a wider scope for determining what was relevant to this issue than we would allow today.

The main question concerning the Athenian rule of relevance is, how was it enforced? Why, in other words, did litigants obey the rule to the extent that they did if there was no judicial authority to enforce it? Critics of Athenian law argue that litigants commonly introduce irrelevant arguments, including arguments that appeal primarily to the emotions or that are so far removed from the issue as to be unquestionably irrelevant, such as the noble deeds of one's ancestors. Such arguments allow litigants to deceive the untrained and unsupervised jurors so that they render verdicts that have little or nothing to do with the law. Litigants themselves, moreover, sometimes criticize juries in the past for allowing defendants to win acquittal by talking about their and their ancestors' brave deeds and good service to the city without having presented any arguments to support their innocence on the charges.[39] Scholars sometimes cite such passages as if they were good evidence for this practice, rather than the rhetorical tropes that they clearly are, but in no case are allegedly irrelevant matters, such as the good deeds of one's ancestors, raised by a litigant who does not also argue strongly for his own innocence (or his opponent's guilt) on the basis of facts relevant to the issue. In fact, litigants did to a large extent speak to the issue, and ju-

37. And in the process, they left many modern scholars frustrated in their attempt to determine just what *hybris* or impiety was in Athenian law; see, for example, Gagarin 1979.

38. See, for example, the legal definition of perjury (US Code 18), quoted in chapter 1, note 79.

39. Lys. 12.38, 30.1; Dem. 25.76. See Wallace 2018b. These and other arguments concerning public service are discussed in chapter 7.

rors probably did decide most cases according to the terms of the complaint, though we have to broaden our idea of relevance to appreciate this.

One reason to think that jurors tried to follow the rules in reaching their verdict is that all six thousand members of the annual jury pool swore a judicial oath at the beginning of their year of service. The complete text of this oath is not preserved anywhere, but different parts of the oath are cited many times, so that we can reconstruct its most important elements with confidence. The important clauses for our purposes came at the beginning: "(1) I will cast my vote according to the laws and the decrees of the Athenian people, and (2) concerning matters about which there are no laws [I will cast my vote] according to my most just understanding (*gnōmēi tēi dikaiotatēi*). And (3) I will listen to both the prosecution and the defense impartially (*homoiōs*), and (4) I will cast my vote concerning the issue (concerning) which the prosecution concerns."[40] The oath was well known, and litigants often refer to it in their pleadings, emphasizing the jurors' obligation to adhere to the oath. Of course, the fact that all jurors swore this oath does not make it certain that all of them observed all of its provisions in every trial, but, Aristophanes' *Wasps* notwithstanding, we have no good reason to think that they routinely violated it.

Let us consider the four clauses of the oath separately. To cast a vote "according to the laws" is sometimes presented as a fairly straightforward process: one needs only to establish the facts of the case and then decide whether they amount to a violation of the law. This is (theoretically) the way it works in our system: the judge tells the jurors exactly what the applicable law is and all they have to do is decide what the facts are and if they meet the requirements of the law. Differences of opinion about the facts may be inevitable, but we generally think that once the facts are decided, the verdict follows directly. As I argued in chapter 4, however, this is a misleading analysis of our own legal system and is certainly not true of the Athenian legal system, since it was not always clear just which laws were applicable to the case or exactly what these laws meant. Thus, a juror wishing to cast his vote in accordance with the laws would still have to make decisions about the meaning and applicability of laws, and among the main sources on which they drew in making these decisions were the pleadings of the litigants.

The second clause reinforces this conclusion, as it even more clearly re-

---

40. The text is reconstructed from different passages in the speeches, none of which quotes all four clauses. The clause in provision 2, "concerning matters about which there are no laws," is not as well attested as are the other clauses, but it is generally accepted as part of the oath. For recent discussions with full citations, see Mirhady 2007; Harris 2013c:101–137.

quires the jurors to make difficult decisions about which laws apply to the case and what these laws require. Whether the qualification "concerning matters about which there are no laws" was part of the actual oath is a matter of dispute, but this hardly matters. Even where laws clearly apply to a case, the two litigants may propose different interpretations of these laws, and it is then up to jurors to interpret those laws and decide how they apply to the facts of the case and whether other laws may also apply, and this will involve using their own (most just) opinion to arrive at their own individual understanding of the law consistent with justice—far from a simple or straightforward matter. Justice, of course, is the ultimate goal of most legal systems, but in most modern legal systems it plays only a small role in any single case. It has a much larger role in Athenian law, however, in part because jurors explicitly swore that they would use their "most just understanding" in reaching their verdict (see further chapter 6).

The third clause, that jurors should listen to both sides impartially, may be the least problematic. Jurors can hardly help but hear both sides,[41] but "listen to" (*akroasthai*), as opposed to "hear" (*akouein*), implies "pay attention to." "Impartially" is more difficult. Some jurors were undoubtedly biased for or against a litigant whom they knew or had heard about, especially in trials where both litigants were public figures; but the victory of Demosthenes over Aeschines in the trial On the Crown, after he had lost his two previous contests with Aeschines, suggests that jurors must have considered the merits of the case, regardless of their feelings about the two litigants. And cases where both litigants were as well known as these two were the exception. Thus, Aristophanes' parody of an Athenian juror, in the person of Philocleon in the *Wasps*, as someone who is always eager to convict no matter what the case may be, seems unlikely to represent many actual jurors.

Finally, the fourth clause, to "vote concerning the issue (concerning) which the prosecution concerns" (lit. "concerning that [concerning] which the prosecution is"),[42] refers to the rule of relevance, requiring the litigants to speak to the issue as it was specified in the complaint. Because the jurors could only judge concerning the issue if the litigants had spoken to the issue, this clause in itself would have provided a strong motive for a litigant to speak about the issue in the case even if he also addressed other matters.

41. Apollodorus (in Dem. 45.6) reports that in an earlier trial in which he was the defendant, the jury was so persuaded by the plaintiff's arguments (which he claims were all lies) that the jury "was unwilling to hear a single word from me." If this means that they actually did not allow him to speak (as opposed to not listening or paying no attention to what he said), this would have been an exceptional violation of their oath.

42. περὶ αὐτοῦ οὗ ἂν ἡ δίωξις ᾖ.

Additionally, one other factor constrained the litigants and prevented them from speaking too far outside the issue, namely, their audience—not just the jury but also the bystanders.[43]

Because Athenian litigation retained traditional elements of a performance, the litigants (like all performers) had to be attuned to their audience and had to respond to feedback from this audience. The primary audience for Athenian litigants, of course, was the jury, but in addition, other spectators were present, sometimes in large numbers.[44] Litigants frequently refer to these spectators, sometimes even addressing them directly, and when they do, they often refer to the *thorybos*, or disturbance, that an audience can make, sometimes asking the audience not to make a *thorybos* because of what the speaker is about to say.[45]

In part because litigants had to be responsive to the reactions of their audience, they would sometimes try to explain beforehand the relevance of a certain line of argument. For example, in the trial On the Crown, Aeschines is seeking to invalidate a decree honoring Demosthenes for always acting in the best interests of the Athenian people.[46] As part of his prosecution case, Aeschines wants to discuss Demosthenes' character to show that he does not deserve a crown, but he is concerned that the jury may think, as many modern scholars do, that a discussion of character is not relevant.[47] Thus, Aeschines begins his discussion of character by faulting Demosthenes for not mourning his daughter's death because (Aeschines claims) he was more concerned about Philip's death, which had occurred about the same time. Aeschines concludes from this (3.78) that "a bad father who hates his children could never be a good public leader, and a man who does not love his nearest and dearest will never feel concern for outsiders like yourselves; nor could a man who is base in his private life be of use in public life." A man's character, in other words, as indicated by his conduct in his private life, will remain the same when he enters public life; Demosthenes' private life is there-

43. Lanni 1997 provides evidence for a relatively high degree of learning among the bystanders, who included logographers and foreigners who happened to be in Athens and sometimes attended. Both groups were probably better educated than average.

44. Lanni 1997.

45. For example, Dem. 57.50; Lyc. 1.52; see also Bers 1985. All the references we have to the audience's reaction during trials is to this *thorybos*, which would suggest a communal rather than an individual opinion. There is no evidence, to my knowledge, that any individual juror or bystander voiced his opinion alone.

46. For a more extensive discussion of relevance in the case, see Gagarin 2012.

47. Even Rhodes, who accepts that Aeschines' and Demosthenes' political careers are relevant, nonetheless concludes that in this case the "sections on the litigants' characters . . . are irrelevant to the formal charges" (2004:155).

fore evidence for the kind of person he is in public. This conclusion would likely have been accepted by the jury because it recurs in other discussions of character in forensic oratory.[48]

Later in his speech, as part of his attack on Demosthenes' public career, Aeschines explicitly connects character and public service when he questions whether Demosthenes is truly "a friend of the people" (*dēmotikos*, "public-minded"). Aeschines' indictment had accused Ctesiphon of, among other things, lying in his decree when he claimed that Demosthenes "always acted in the interest of the *dēmos*" (Aes. 3.50). To act in this way, Aeschines argues, Demosthenes would have to be *dēmotikos*, which he is not.

> Yes, he is *dēmotikos* if you look only at the nice sound of his words . . . but if (you look) at his character and the truth, you will not be deceived. . . . I will reckon up with you the character that a person should have if he is *dēmotikos* and decent (*sōphrōn*), and I will set against this the sort of character a person probably has if he is oligarchic (*oligarchikos*) and worthless (*phaulos*). Then you should compare these two and see which one his life, not his words, belongs to. (Aes. 3.168)

In this way Aeschines defends his discussion of Demosthenes' character as relevant to an assessment of his public career, which is the central issue in the case. One may disagree with Aeschines' argument and judge the question of character to be irrelevant, but the point is that Aeschines is concerned to show that it is relevant and, therefore, that he is not speaking outside the issue when he describes Demosthenes' character.

Demosthenes does not disagree that character is connected with a person's actions. Although he derides Aeschines' method of assessing character, he not only defends his own character but also attacks Aeschines'. And like Aeschines, Demosthenes is concerned that this character attack may be considered irrelevant. He therefore justifies it as a necessary response to Aeschines' attack on his own character: "Despite my reluctance to defame, the slanders he uttered compel me to respond to his many lies by stating the necessary facts about him, and to show you the identity and origin of this person who so casually initiates the abuse."[49] This justification may seem rather implausible, especially as Demosthenes' abuse is far harsher than Aeschines' criticism; however, Demosthenes' strategy throughout his speech has been to assess his public career by comparison with what Aeschines did

48. Lanni (2006:60–61) cites other passages from the orators that make a similar point; she also gives references to earlier scholarship. See also Aristotle's discussion of *ēthos* in the *Rhetoric* (especially book 2.12–17).

49. Dem. 18.126; see also Dem. 18.9.

or did not do at the time. Such a comparison is not unreasonable: Aeschines had been his main political rival during most of the period in question, and it would thus not be unreasonable to assess Demosthenes' political actions by comparison with the main alternative at the time, namely, Aeschines' conduct and policies.

In our legal system, with a (theoretically) disinterested public prosecutor, the prosecutor's character or public career is (or should be) of no concern in any case he brings, but in Athens, an opponent in court would not uncommonly also be a political opponent, so that an assessment of one litigant's public conduct could quite reasonably be connected to an assessment of his opponent's conduct. Thus, Demosthenes' career is not unreasonably assessed by comparison with Aeschines' conduct, which then leads to a discussion of Aeschines' character. We may judge Demosthenes' harsh attack on Aeschines' family and upbringing to be both extreme and outside the bounds of relevance, but because Aeschines has connected policy with character, his own character, as well as his policies, could arguably be considered part of the issue. Demosthenes' policies may have failed, but no one else at the time, least of all Aeschines, offered a better plan or showed a character as public minded.

Now, the fact that both litigants argue that discussions of character are relevant in this case does not mean that all such discussions are relevant or that no Athenian litigant ever violated the rule of relevance.[50] In Demosthenes 45, for example, Apollodorus brings suit against Stephanus for giving false testimony on behalf of Phormio during a case that Phormio had brought against Apollodorus and won. Although more than half of Apollodorus's speech is clearly relevant to the issue, much of the second half (Dem. 45.53–85) is devoted to blackening the characters of Stephanus (53–71) and Phormio (72–85). These parts of the speech do occasionally touch on matters related to the issue in either this case or in Phormio's original suit, but Apollodorus also says (57) that he is trying to make the jury see what a villain Stephanus is, and then admits that "by fully lamenting all that has happened, I will alleviate the burden of my grief."[51] Whether or not the jury accepted this justification is unknown.

Many other speakers also discuss their opponent's character, which indicates that litigants and jurors must have thought that it was a legitimate concern. In our legal system, litigants are not usually allowed to discuss an accused's character, except perhaps in the punishment phase of the trial; but

50. See Adamadis (2017), who concludes that most character arguments could be relevant.

51. Dem. 45.57.

in a system where forensic science was unknown, and arguments about likelihood thus played a larger role, and because the Greeks tended to believe that a person's character was relatively unchanging, it was not unreasonable to think that the accused's earlier conduct could increase or decrease the likelihood that an accusation was true. A person's past history, moreover, and even perhaps his ancestors' accomplishments could be taken to be an indicator of whether he was likely or not likely to have done something wrong. Thus, litigants were allowed to mention their or their opponent's past record of generosity, kindness, and civic benefaction, or lack thereof, not because these in themselves provided a reason for acquittal or conviction (see chapter 7), but because these could provide some indication that he was or was not the kind of person who would commit the sort of wrong he was accused of.[52]

I should also note one generally accepted use of character in Athenian law that is also accepted in our law, namely, the use of rhetoric to portray the speaker's character, Aristotle's *ēthos*. For example, Lysias quite intentionally crafts Euphiletus's speech so that the speaker appears to be a rather boorish, slow-witted country fellow, understandably infuriated at the deception Eratosthenes and his wife had been practicing. Defense lawyers today keep suits in their closets so that male defendants may appear in court looking more respectable than they ever looked in their ordinary lives, and have many other legitimate ways of conveying decency, devotion to family or to God, and other virtues to the court. But modern law largely rejects criticism of one's opponent's character as prejudicial to the case.

For the Athenians, however, the character and previous conduct of a litigant's opponent helped create a fuller context for the case, and it seems that this was thought to help the jury decide the likelihood of his guilt or innocence. Thus, arguments about character that were not directly relevant to the issue in the case were allowed, but were always presented in addition to arguments that addressed the issue directly. This meant that the jury always heard some arguments about the issue, on the basis of which they could decide the case in accordance with their oath.

Modern law in general rejects contextualization of a case. As many scholars, including legal realists and law and literature scholars, have shown, however, the fuller context of a case may make it look very different from versions that reduce the full story of the case to a small set of facts deemed to be legally relevant. A litigant tells a story to his attorney, the attorney tells

52. For further discussion of character, see Lanni 2006:59–64. I will have more to say about a litigant's past civic service in chapter 7.

a reduced version to the court, the judge issues a ruling citing only selected facts in support, appellate briefs cite only facts deemed relevant to the appeal (often those for which there are precedents), and appellate judges cite only a few of these in support of their decision. At each stage the story becomes reduced.[53] By contrast, in Athens, the litigants told their stories directly to the court. In making their decisions, jurors may have concentrated on relatively few of these details, but nonetheless, the litigants' stories include more of the context of the case than we deem appropriate, and this context must have influenced the jurors' overall understanding of the case.

In general, however, despite occasional violations, litigants mostly did stick to the issue as they saw it, and the jurors were able to vote according to the issue, as they promised in their oath. Some jurors undoubtedly were biased in one way or another, but we have no serious evidence for the sort of regular or systematic bias parodied in Aristophanes' *Wasps*. The detailed accusation provided the framework for pleadings in Athenian courts, and this framework allowed a rather broad range of arguments to be made, as long as they could be shown to be relevant. And the standards for determining what was relevant were certainly broader than those we would accept today.

The requirement that prosecutors provide a detailed written accusation, which then determined the issues in the case, has also been seen as a means of promoting procedural fairness, in that it gave both litigants a clear guide to the main arguments that their opponents would be allowed to make according to the rule of relevance.[54] On the other hand, it also gave the prosecutor a significant advantage, because he could not only decide whether to bring charges against the defendant in the first place, and if he did, what procedure to use in prosecuting him, but he could also select the specific acts of wrongdoing he wished to accuse him of. As long as the specific acts could plausibly be construed as falling into the general category of offense—a decision made by the official who accepted the initial accusation—the case could proceed with much less ambiguity or uncertainty than the general category alone would allow.

Prosecutors today have a similar ability to decide whether to bring charges and if so, which charges, although in some cases a grand jury can go against a prosecutor's wishes and refuse to indict, and judges can always reject one or more charges for various reasons before the trial. In Athens, it seems that the bias toward allowing everyone to have his day in court gen-

---

53. Gordon 2016:177 (cited in full in chapter 4 at note 14). See also Conley and O'Barr 1990. Gordon (2016:176) also cites Mertz 2007 on how law school education teaches students to ignore all the facts of a case except for those deemed legally relevant.

54. See Thür 2007 (= Thür 2008).

erally prevailed, making officials very reluctant to reject a charge that was brought to them. In fact, we know of no case in which the accusation was simply rejected. In three cases (Antiphon 5; Hyperides 1, *Lyc.* and 4, *Eux.*), the officials in charge allowed the case to proceed despite objections from the defense, and in two others (Lysias 13; Isaeus 10), the officials allowed the case to proceed after the plaintiff had made a relatively small change in the wording of his accusation that would make the charge acceptable to them. This meant that in practice, Athenian prosecutors had a large degree of freedom in composing their accusation.

Another possible advantage for the plaintiff was that he could include several specific charges in the same accusation. For example, the prosecutors of Socrates accused him of not believing in the gods of the city, introducing new gods, and corrupting the youth. This could provide an advantage if one or more of the alleged acts was easier to prove than others so that the plaintiff could concentrate his arguments on these charges in order to secure a conviction. In our system (but not in Athens), accusations with multiple charges would require proof of each charge separately. For example, Demosthenes tells us that in the specific accusation in his case against his guardian Aphobus he listed each kind of asset that had been included in his father's estate separately (Dem. 29.31), and in his first speech against Aphobus (Dem. 27), he examines each kind of asset separately. A jury today would have to vote on each category separately, but the Athenian jurors simply convicted Aphobus, setting the damages at those that were written in the accusation (Dem. 29.8). They had no means of deciding each charge separately, and so it was all or nothing.[55]

Socrates' accusers probably focused on the charge of corrupting the youth, undoubtedly to remind the jurors of the involvement of his former students in the tyranny of the Thirty. And at least in Plato's version of his speech, Socrates, too, devotes most of his defense to this issue. But he also addresses the other two charges—not recognizing the gods the city recognizes and introducing new gods—and his prosecutors almost certainly addressed these charges, too. This was necessary because Athenian juries decided all the issues together, so that the inclusion of several allegations could favor the defendant if the prosecution neglected some charges. The defendant might then develop convincing arguments on some of these neglected points and thus cast doubt on the entire accusation.[56]

---

55. Cases where the penalty was assessable, of course, required two separate decisions if the first found the defendant guilty.

56. Today, if prosecutors file more than one charge, the jury then decides each charge separately. Prosecutors can also file just one charge, but the jury may have the

As a partial counterbalance to any prosecutorial advantages, the Athenians enacted laws against frivolous prosecution, which could put plaintiffs at considerable risk. We saw one example of this in the law on *hybris* (above): "if someone does not prosecute [i.e., does not carry through with a prosecution he has begun], or does prosecute but does not gain one-fifth of the votes, let him pay one thousand drachmas to the public treasury." This same or a similar clause was added to many *graphai*, and there were other sorts of penalties in other cases.[57] Thus, although plaintiffs may have had considerable latitude in devising their accusations, they had to take care to make them plausible.

Finally, regardless of which party had the advantage in litigation, it appears that by giving plaintiffs such free rein to include whatever they wished in their accusation, Athenian law allowed litigants to turn virtually any matter into a legal issue. A very wide range of wrongful conduct could be construed as illegal within at least one of the broad categories of offenses in Athenian law. This is indicative of, among other things, the Athenians' tendency to equate law and justice: conduct that was wrong, they felt, should be punishable, even if no law explicitly designated that conduct as illegal.[58] This may help explain why defendants almost never object to the charges on the ground that the acts alleged by the plaintiff are not wrong. They always argue that they did not commit the alleged act. They may add that even if they had, they would have been justified after all the terrible things their opponent did to them, but they do not deny that the alleged act would have been wrong.

One example where a litigant apparently admits that he did the alleged act but claims it was not wrong is Lysias 10, in which according to the plaintiff, the defendant will argue that the law against slander does not prohibit him from using the words he used in calling his opponent a killer.[59] But the plaintiff condemns this attempt to take refuge in a narrowly literal interpretation of the law, and such arguments are very rare. Defendants do sometimes challenge an accusation on the ground that the case should not have

---

option of convicting on a lesser related charge, such as second-degree murder instead of first-degree murder.

57. For details, see Harris 1999; Harris 2006b; Wallace 2006c; Scafuro 2015.

58. As far as we know, for example, there was no law specifically addressing the matter of corrupting the youth, but because virtually all Athenians would probably have agreed that corrupting the youth was wrong, Socrates' prosecutors were able to include this charge in a *graphē asebeia*. For the intricate relationship between law and justice, see chapter 6.

59. Lys. 10.6. We cannot be certain, of course, that the defendant did in fact make this argument in his pleading.

been brought in the first place, arguing perhaps that the matter was too trivial for the courts or had already been settled, or that the plaintiff had been paid to bring the case, or that he was only bringing it because he wanted some personal benefit. They also, as noted above, sometimes object to the procedure used. But even in such cases, the defendants always include arguments aimed at showing that the plaintiff's allegations are false. And no one ever makes the argument, which seems to be increasingly common today, that what he did may have been wrong but it was not illegal.[60]

In sum, Athenian legal procedure allowed the plaintiff to include in his accusation a broad range of more specific charges under a limited number of broad procedural categories. At the same time, the rule of relevance constrained the litigants to confine their arguments for the most part to the specific matters mentioned in the accusation together with other points that were arguably relevant to these matters, and constrained the jurors to vote on the basis of these specific matters and other arguably relevant points. The result was that to a large degree verdicts in Athenian courts were rendered "according to the laws and decrees of the Athenian people" and the jurors' "most just understanding" of these laws, in accordance with the oath that all the jurors had sworn. The limits for what was considered relevant were broader and more flexible than we would consider appropriate today, but litigants did not in practice have unlimited freedom to say anything they wished. I will take up later (chapter 8) the question of whether or not these considerations produced a legal system that adhered to the principles of the rule of law; but first I will consider the roles of justice and public interest in litigation.

---

60. For an example of this, see chapter 6, note 4.

CHAPTER 6

JUSTICE

My discussion of relevance has concluded that the Athenian rule of relevance, although broader and more flexible than our own, did much to keep the litigants and jurors focused on the issue, as it was defined by the initial accusation. In Athenian courts, information that shed light on the background and broader context of the specific acts in question was considered relevant, as were, in many cases, the characters of the plaintiff and defendant and others who were involved in these acts. In this chapter, I want to consider another factor that we do not normally allow in legal arguments but which in classical Athens seems to have been not just acceptable but essential, namely, justice. Justice was important not because it was thought of as relevant to the issue in the case, but because it was considered an inherent feature of the legal system.

Law and justice are obviously related, and in some of its senses, justice can be roughly equivalent to law ("the administration of justice"). Achieving justice, moreover, is almost by definition a goal of any society's legal system. Although most would agree that a legal system ought to be just and ought to promote justice in the society, in modern Western legal systems, the role of justice in litigation is relatively limited, and arguments based on justice usually carry little or no weight in deciding the outcome of a case. By contrast, in classical Athens, law and justice were so closely connected that speakers sometimes seem to treat the two as if they were synonymous.

Over the centuries, legal theorists have advanced widely different views about the relationship between justice and law. Strict legal positivists maintain that law is completely separate from justice. Natural Law adherents, on the other hand, give justice a central role in law, arguing that (to oversimplify) a law is not a law unless it is just, though they tend to apply this principle only to seriously unjust laws.[1] Most Western legal systems steer a mid-

1. See Campbell 2008.

dle course in which, although the substance of most rules has little to do with justice, law must meet certain standards of procedural justice: judicial decisions must be made according to clear and rational procedures, with proper adherence to basic principles, such as equal treatment, and laws must be enacted by a clearly defined, nonarbitrary process.[2] Justice may be taken into consideration in exceptional circumstances, but otherwise the justice of a particular law or procedural outcome is not a question for the law.[3] In practical terms, this means that the law does not concern itself with moral wrongdoing,[4] and arguments about justice carry little or no weight in legal decision making.[5]

The absence of considerations of justice from litigation in the United States is evident in the oath that jurors swear today. In the United States, there is no single oath, since each state has its own oath, as does the federal government. But most juror's oaths are essentially similar and conform quite closely to the following definition: "Juror's oath is a statement under oath by a juror that he will do his duty as a juror, that he will well and truly try the issues joined, and a true verdict render according to the law and the evidence."[6] Maine's version is fairly typical: "Do you swear that in all causes committed to you, you will give a true verdict therein according to the law and the evidence given you, so help you God?" Florida's version is similar: "you will well and truly try the issues between the State of Florida and the defendant and render a true verdict according to the law and the evidence." The notion of a true verdict is nearly universal, and the injunction to adhere to the law and the evidence is widespread, reflecting the common view in the United States that a legal decision is based on the law and the facts of

---

2. See Ross 1958: esp. 280–285.

3. The US Supreme Court, for example, can declare a law invalid because it conflicts with a provision of the constitution but not (in most cases) simply because it is morally wrong or unjust.

4. Thus we have the common scenario of a public figure admitting to having done something wrong but nothing illegal. See, for example, an article in the *New York Times* for January 26, 2011 (p. A14) about John Edwards, former senator and presidential candidate; the article quotes his lawyer as saying "John Edwards has done wrong in his life . . . but he did not break the law."

5. As one idealistic public-defense lawyer told me when asked about justice, "I don't have the luxury of thinking about it."

6. https://definitions.uslegal.com/j/jurors-oath/. Cf. the Wikipedia entry for "juror's oath": In the United States, a federal juror's oath usually states something to the effect of "Do you and each of you solemnly swear that you will well and truly try and a true deliverance make between the United States and ______, the defendant at the bar, and a true verdict render according to the evidence, so help you God?"

the case. Justice, to my knowledge, is never mentioned in a juror's oath in the United States,[7] and questions such as whether a particular law is just are not supposed to be considered.[8]

There are good reasons why justice does not have a significant role in modern law. In contrast to the (relative) precision and certainty of law, justice is subjective and messy. Laws have a fixed text, and though their meaning may be disputed, the text provides a secure starting point in deciding what the law is. Thus, we can recognize the laws of our community as authoritative even if we do not agree with some of them. On the other hand, there is no accepted authoritative code of justice, no "rule of recognition" telling people how to know whether or not a certain rule is in fact an authorized rule of justice.[9] Judges, litigants, and others may all have a sense of justice, and some people may find in a particular religion a set of clear moral rules, but in modern pluralistic societies there is no single authoritative set of moral rules that define justice.[10] Thus, two parties in a dispute will often both claim to have justice on their side, and both may have valid arguments supporting their claim, but the law requires (theoretically) an objective decision on legal grounds, not a decision between claims of justice. For these reasons, justice plays little or no role in most Western legal systems.

In the preface, I mentioned the familiar scenario of children disputing. In many cases, whatever resolution one of them considers fair will be rejected by the other as "not fair" (colloquially equivalent to "not just"), but a modified proposal that satisfies that child will then likely be rejected as not

---

7. At the swearing-in for new justices of the Supreme Court (and probably for many other lower-court judges, too), the oath that is sworn includes "I will administer justice without respect to persons, and do equal right to the poor and to the rich, and that I will faithfully and impartially discharge and perform all the duties incumbent upon me." The expression "administer justice" here means essentially that the swearer will administer the law, not that the decisions that he renders will be based on justice. (I thank Chris Kremmydas for bringing this oath to my attention.)

8. This is not to say that justice is never taken into consideration. There are instances of "jury nullification" and also less extreme ways to consider justice in reaching a verdict. See, for example, Burnett's firsthand account of jurors trying to resolve what they see as a conflict between law and justice (2001: esp. 129–139).

9. A "rule of recognition" (in H. L. A. Hart's sense) is a rule by which we can recognize that a particular rule is a rule of law and not some other kind of rule; see Hart 1994: esp. 100–110.

10. Legal systems that are closely tied to a religion, like Islamic law, will often have a religious text that provides written moral rules. But even a single moral code or moral authority may have conflicting rules and conflicting understandings of justice, in which case a judge or other authoritative person has to decide.

fair by the other.[11] It takes considerable skill to find a resolution that both sides will (often grudgingly) accept. To find such a resolution, however, one must also know the full background and context of the dispute. Almost all disputes have a history, often a long history; in some cases, there may be extenuating circumstances, and often the past conduct of each party may provide insight into the likely outcome of various possible resolutions. All these factors must be considered in arriving at a resolution that might (again, grudgingly) be considered fair by both sides.

In recognition of the imprecision and subjectivity of moral judgments, modern legal systems generally do not aim to resolve cases in such a way that the outcome of every case is just; instead, they seek to construct a judicial system that will promote justice overall.[12] Thus, they generally focus on procedural rules designed to create a "level (i.e., fair) playing field." For common law, this is thought to be best accomplished by an adversary system in which each side makes the best possible case and an impartial judge or jury decides according to a fixed standard, such as beyond a reasonable doubt, and clear rules, such as a unanimous verdict in criminal trials. Civil law systems have a different method, sometimes termed inquisitorial, in which a specially trained judge oversees the investigation of the case and generally plays a larger role in determining its outcome. Which system achieves justice more often is ultimately unknowable.

For the Athenians, by contrast, law and justice were intrinsically connected, so that their legal system aimed for outcomes that in every case were both lawful and just. They acknowledged that because of human error not every verdict was the correct one, but they believed that if a verdict was correct, then it was both lawful and just. The Athenians also tried to ensure just outcomes by means of procedural justice, using an adversary system similar to that of common law today. To initiate the proceedings, a plaintiff had to file an accusation specifying the charge in some detail. Sufficient notice of the charge and the preliminary hearing had to be given to the accused. If he was unable to attend the hearing for some good reason, such as illness or absence from the city, the hearing would be postponed, but if he

---

11. The fairness of a law is similarly debatable in many cases. A fair system of taxation, for example, could require everyone to pay exactly the same amount in taxes; or could require everyone to pay exactly the same percentage of their income or property; or could require the rich, who can better afford to pay, to pay a higher percentage than the poor.

12. For some of the limitations on the ability of our legal system to achieve justice, see Benforado 2015.

failed to appear for no good reason, judgment could be given against him in absentia.

The preliminary hearing was particularly important for achieving the goals of fairness and openness. At an arbitration hearing, and probably also at other sorts of preliminary hearings, each litigant had the chance to hear his opponent's arguments and see the evidence he would be submitting at the trial. Each litigant could also question the other, and in an arbitration hearing, each could try to persuade the arbitrator to rule in his favor. A litigant might not reveal all of his arguments at this point, but in seeking to persuade the arbitrator he would have to reveal most of them. He was also required to present any document he planned to introduce in court, and these would often indicate a line of argument he was going to pursue at the trial. This meant that his opponent could study this material before the trial and prepare his pleading accordingly. At the trial itself, each litigant could present whatever arguments he wished, though he was under an obligation to speak to the point. For guidance, the precise accusation setting out the issues in the case was made known to all parties beforehand, was posted in writing at the entrance to the court, and was read out at the beginning of the trial. Both litigants were given equal time to plead their case.

As for the jurors, in the judicial oath that was administered to the six thousand Athenian jurors each year (see chapter 5), they swore to "listen impartially to the prosecution and the defense," and to "cast their vote concerning the issue (concerning) which the prosecution concerns." The jurors also swore, "I will vote according to the laws and the decrees of the Athenian people, and concerning matters about which there are no laws (I will vote) according to the most just understanding (*gnōmēi tēi dikaiotatēi*)." This makes clear to the jurors that their verdict must be guided by both law and justice—by the law when its meaning and application to the case are clear and by justice when the law does not provide sufficient guidance—and it implies that there is no conflict between the two. In the Athenians' way of thinking, their laws were necessarily just, and justice was the necessary consequence of acting according to the laws.

One way in which the Athenians explained their conviction that all their laws were just is illustrated in Aeschines' prosecution of Timarchus (Aes. 1.177–178):

> Why do you think, gentlemen, that your laws are fine (*kaloi*) but the city's decrees are inferior and the judgments reached in court sometimes arouse criticism? I shall explain the reasons for this. It is because in enacting your laws your entire goal is that they be just (*dikaioi*); you do not consider profit or favor or enmity, but only justice and the public good

> (*to dikaion kai to sympheron*). And because, in my view, you are naturally more skillful than other men, it is reasonable to conclude that you enact the finest (*kallistoi*) laws.

This passage suggests not only that Athenian laws reflect the principles of justice,[13] in contrast to decrees and court verdicts that sometimes do not, but also that the Athenians regarded all their laws as ipso facto just.[14] Aeschines' claim clearly alludes to the new procedure for enacting laws that was put in place at the end of the fifth century. This required that all laws had to be thoroughly vetted before being enacted, so that one could plausibly claim that only just laws were approved.[15] Aeschines then contrasts this with the procedures for enacting decrees, which required only a vote in the Assembly, and for determining verdicts, in both of which the citizens could be led astray by deceit and trickery.[16]

Demosthenes further explains this legislative procedure and the claim that it resulted in laws that were ipso facto just (Dem. 20.93–94):[17]

> You see, men of Athens, the excellent method that Solon provides for enacting laws.[18] First, it (the law) comes before you, men who have sworn

13. This and other passages, including Dem. 20.93–94 (cited below) and several of the other passages cited after that, make clear that for the Athenians, justice is separate from law, not something derived from existing laws; see further below, with note 30.

14. The fact that a procedure existed for repealing a law—the *graphē nomon mē epitēdeion theinai* or "indictment for proposing an inexpedient law"—would not invalidate this claim, since, as the two cases brought by this procedure (Dem. 20 and 24) reveal, the questions posed in this procedure concerned the expediency of the law and the way in which it had been enacted. The justice of the law in question was not the issue in these cases, though of course if a law could be shown to be unjust, it would certainly be considered inexpedient.

15. For more on the process of enacting laws in the fourth century, see chapter 1, with note 13.

16. Even before the reforms at the end of the fifth century, Euripides has Theseus (an early mythical king of Athens) explain that written laws in themselves promote justice. In the *Suppliants* (429–434), first staged ca. 421, Theseus, in endorsing democracy, asserts, "There is nothing more detrimental to a polis than a tyrant. First of all, when there are no public laws (*nomoi koinoi*), one man holds power by keeping the law all for himself, and there is no more equality. But when the laws are written, the weak man and the rich man have equal justice (*dikēn isēn*)." See Gagarin 1986:123–124; Wallace (2016) argues that the promotion of equality and justice were central to law from the beginning, but the evidence for this earlier than the fifth century is questionable.

17. Part of Dem. 20.93 was cited in chapter 5 at note 19.

18. The attribution to Solon of a law that was enacted long after his time is common in Athenian forensic rhetoric.

an oath and exercise supervision over this and other matters.[19] Next, laws that contradict it are repealed so that there is only one law for each subject. This avoids confusion for private individuals, who would be at a disadvantage in comparison to people who are familiar with all the laws. The aim is to make the justice (*ta dikaia*) [of the law] the same for all, simple and clear (*hapla kai saphē*) to read and to understand.[20] Even before this stage, Solon ordered that the laws be placed in front of the Eponymous Heroes[21] and handed over to the secretary and for him to read them at meetings of the Assembly. The aim was for each of you to hear the laws many times and have a chance to study them at leisure and then enact those that are both just and in the public interest (*kai dikaia kai sympheronta*, "beneficial").

These and other passages promoted the idea that all Athenian laws were just, and that justice thus had the support of all the laws. And this understanding of the essential equivalence of law and justice meant that justice and the laws were equally important considerations in forensic pleading. A litigant could decide to put greater weight on one or the other, depending on the needs of his case and the overall strategy of his plea. But in many cases, litigants argue that their case has the support of both law and justice. For example,[22]

1. Isaeus 11.35: "This is what is especially just (*megala dikaia*); the laws also command this (*tauta kai hoi nomoi keleuousin*)."
2. Demosthenes 43.52: "The law (*ho nomos*) states this, and this is also what is just (*to dikaion*)."

---

19. The group that oversaw the enactment of new laws in the fourth century was not the jury but the Nomothetai (see chapter 1). But because the Nomothetai were probably a group selected each year from members of the jury pool, Demosthenes easily identifies them with the members of his current jury, even though only some of them would actually be Nomothetai at the time.

20. 20.93: πᾶσιν ᾖ ταῦτ᾽ ἀναγνῶναι καὶ μαθεῖν ἁπλᾶ καὶ σαφῆ τὰ δίκαια. The translation of this clause is difficult, especially *ta dikaia*, which English translators generally render simply "law." It is easier to translate into languages like Italian (e.g., Canevaro 2016:143) or French (e.g., Navarre and Orsini 1957:88), where the same word (*diritto*, *droit*) can mean both "law" and "right" (or "just").

21. Each of the ten Attic tribes had an eponymous hero. Statues of these ten heroes were placed in the Agora, and their base served as an official state notice board.

22. Most of the passages I cite here are included among the eighteen passages cited in Harris 2006c:169–170 and, with one additional passage, also in Harris 2013c:112–113. His conclusion, however, that they illustrate the primacy of law, is quite different from mine; cf. below, note 26.

3. Antiphon 5.9: "They have made my acquittal most lawful and most just (*nomimōtatēn kai dikaiotatēn*) for you."

4. Demosthenes 43.34: "Whoever of these two seems to you to speak more justly (*dikaiotera*) and more in accordance with the laws (*kata tous nomous mallon*), it is clear that you jurors will take his side."

5. Lysias 14.42: "Have they not acted unjustly and illegally (*adikōs kai paranomōs*)?"

6. Demosthenes 43.84: "Come to the aid of the laws (*tois nomois*) and take care of the dead so that their house does not die out. By doing this you will cast a vote that is just (*ta dikaia*) and in conformity with your oath (*ta euorka*) and in your interests (*ta hymin autois sympheronta*)."[23]

7. Demosthenes 23.2: "If you want to understand these things correctly and judge this case justly according to the laws (*kata tous nomous dikaiōs*), you must all pay attention not only to the words in the decree but also to their consequences."

8. Demosthenes 39.41: "Therefore, in accordance with the most just opinion and the laws (*kai kata tēn dikaiotatēn gnōmēn kai kata tous nomous*) and the oaths and this man's admission, I make a reasonable (*metria*) request of you, men of Athens, in asking for justice (*dikaia*), whereas his request is neither reasonable (*metria*) nor in accord with custom (*eiōthota*)."

All these passages imply that the speaker's case has the support of both law and justice; they also imply that if the law demands a certain course of action, so, too, does justice, and vice versa.[24]

There are, to be sure, some passages where only law or only justice is mentioned. For law without justice, consider:

9. Antiphon 5.85: "For you [my acquittal] is lawful (*nomima*) and in accordance with your oath (*euorka*); for you swore to judge according to the laws (*kata tous nomous*)."[25]

---

23. Harris (see above, note 22) translates *euorka* "in conformity with the laws."

24. Cf. Sickinger 2007:290: "Law and justice went hand in hand in the rhetoric of the courts." See also Xenophon, *Memorabilia* 4.4.12–13, where Socrates and Hippias agree that someone who is lawful (*nomimos*) is just (*dikaios*), and he who is unlawful (*anomos*) is unjust (*adikos*).

25. A few sentences later, the speaker addresses the jury as "fair judges of justice (*ta dikaia*)." Harris includes this passage in his lists (see above, note 22), but he mistranslates *nomima* as "just" and misidentifies the passage as Antiphon 5.7.

On the other hand, for justice without law, consider:

10. Demosthenes 52.2: "Therefore, I ask you, if you have ever judged any other case on its own, without favoritism for either side—neither for the prosecutors nor for the defendants—but with a view to justice (*to dikaion skepsamenoi*), judge in that way now."

All these passages taken together point very clearly to the conclusion that the Athenians were not committed, as some have argued, either to the primacy of law or to the primacy of justice but to the equal importance of both.[26] Those who consider one of these more important than the other seem to assume that there was a distance between law and justice, an assumption that the Athenians would have rejected. Rather, they were committed to a legal system that, as they saw it, produced outcomes that were both just and lawful. The laws were just, and what was just was in accordance with law. The distinction that we make today between doing wrong and breaking the law[27] made no sense to the Athenians. For them, to violate the law was to act unjustly, and acting unjustly could in most cases be construed as a violation of the law. We shall see an example of this below, where Aeschines declares that telling lies in a public decree is a violation of all the laws.

Because all laws were just, illustrations of justice could be found in the laws, as we see in the case in Hyperides 3, *Against Athenogenes*.[28] Epicrates is bringing suit against Athenogenes because, as he tells it, Athenogenes has caused him to suffer significant financial damage. We do not know the precise words of Epicrates' accusation, but he is probably using a suit for damages (*dikē blabēs*), alleging that Athenogenes caused him significant loss. Epicrates claims that he signed an agreement to buy a slave family and their perfume workshop from Athenogenes, but that Athenogenes withheld in-

---

26. For the primacy of law, see, for instance, Harris (2006c:170 = 2013c:113–114): "What these litigants wanted the judges to bear in mind as they decided how to vote was that they had sworn an oath and that oath required them to vote in accordance with the laws, not just in a way that seemed right to them. The message of the judicial oath is clear: it bound the judges to vote in accordance with the laws." For the primacy of justice, see, for example, Christ (1998:95): "Jurors determined how and whether to enforce laws on the basis of a more fundamental standard—namely, their sense of "what is just" (*ta dikaia*). The primacy of this standard is evident when litigants speak of a particular law as just."

27. See above, note 4.

28. I discuss this case and the law on agreements in much more detail in Gagarin 2018c.

formation about the large amount of debt the slaves had incurred, debt that Epicrates was now obligated to pay according to the agreement.

Epicrates anticipates that Athenogenes will base his defense on a law that "whatever one person agrees with another is binding," but (Epicrates argues) this only applies to agreements that are just.[29] Epicrates then goes on to cite four other laws that explicitly prohibit unjust conduct in various transactions. None of these laws specifically addresses the kind of unjust conduct alleged by Epicrates, but together they help define more precisely what could be considered unjust conduct in business transactions and thus they strengthen Epicrates' argument that Athenogenes' conduct was unjust and is therefore not protected by the law on binding agreements. Epicrates concludes that even though he signed an agreement with Athenogenes, he should not be held to its terms because the agreement was unjust. Instead, in accordance with both law and justice, he should be awarded the damages that he has suffered on account of Athenogenes' unjust conduct.

Epicrates' ability to find illustrations of justice in several laws does not, however, mean that justice is somehow derivative of law, as some have argued.[30] Rather, law and justice were two independent sources of authority, inextricably bound to one another in Athenian legal ideology, so that jurors were always supposed to vote in accordance with both. But the authority of justice remained independent of any laws.

The need for the jurors to take into account both law and justice is evident even in *graphē paranomōn* cases ("indictments for illegal proposals"), which by their very nature raise questions about the law. In these cases, in order to show that the decree in question is illegal, the prosecutor had to specify which law or laws the decree allegedly violates. This alleged violation is always one of the charges listed in the indictment, but it appears that it was never the sole charge, since all such indictments also list other, broader complaints.[31]

A narrow view of *graphē paranomōn* cases would put the entire weight of the verdict on the issue of whether the decree in question violated the law.

---

29. Hyp. 3, *Ath.* 13.

30. See, for example, Canevaro (2019:76), who argues that the decision of the Areopagus in a case reported in Dem. 59.78–84 "was not based on extra-legal considerations, on a higher principle of justice independent from the laws. It was based on a higher principle of justice that was extracted from, and explicitly recognized, by the laws." The fact that justice can be found in the laws, however, does not make justice a derivative of law.

31. Note that passage no. 7 above, which stresses both justice and law, is from a *graphē paranomōn* case (Dem. 23).

Such a view is proposed by Aeschines in a famous simile in his prosecution of Ctesiphon in the case On the Crown:

> For justice (*to dikaion*) is not something undefined, but has been defined in your laws. As in carpentry, when we would like to know what is straight and what is not, we set a ruler (*kanōn*) next to it by which it can be judged, so too in indictments for illegal proposals we have at hand as a ruler of justice (*kanōn tou dikaiou*) that tablet (*sanidion*) there with the decree and the laws written down side-by-side (*to psēphisma kai hoi paragegrammenoi nomoi*).[32] [To Demosthenes] Show that these agree with one another and then step down. (Aes. 3.199–200)

A law written on the *sanidion* next to the decree thus had a more explicit role in the case than laws typically did in other types of cases, and Aeschines' argument is that in this case, the verdict, and thus justice, will depend entirely on whether the decree and the law agree according to "the ruler of justice."[33]

In his response, Demosthenes rejects Aeschines' simile of the ruler of justice as confused and unintelligible, and proposes instead that he will explain clearly the justice of the case (Dem. 18.111): "Since he thoroughly jumbled the arguments he made about the laws that are written side by side (*peri tōn paragegrammenōn nomōn*), by the gods, I don't think you understood most of them, nor was I able to make sense of them either. So in a simple fashion, I will discuss the correct understanding of the issue of justice (*peri tōn*

32. Aeschines here refers to the use of a whitened board or tablet (*sanidion*), which could be erased after the text written on it was no longer needed. In *graphē paranomōn* cases, the decree and the laws that it was accused of violating were written next to one another on such a tablet, and the tablet was then posted at the entrance to the court. Aeschines' use of a "deictic *iota*" (*touti*—"that tablet there") indicates that he is pointing to the tablet at the entrance to the court as he speaks.

33. The *graphē paranomōn* procedure is often compared to the process of judicial review in US law (Lanni 2010; Sundahl 2009). In 1936, Supreme Court Justice Owen Roberts, in an opinion that declared unconstitutional one of Franklin Roosevelt's New Deal proposals, formulated a geometric image very similar to Aeschines' ruler of justice, the "T-square rule": "When an act of Congress is appropriately challenged in the courts as not conforming to the constitutional mandate, the judicial branch of the government has only one duty—to lay the article of the Constitution which is invoked beside the statute which is challenged to decide whether the latter squares with the former. All the court does, or can do, is to announce its considered judgment upon the question" (*United States v. Butler*, 297 U.S. 1 [1936]:62). Ironically, one year later in *West Coast Hotel Co. v. Parrish* (300 U.S. 379 [1937]), Justice Roberts provided the swing vote in the first case in which the Court switched from opposing to supporting government measures to regulate the economy, which included a few months later the National Labor Relations Act and the Social Security Act.

dikaiōn) in the case." The question of justice, in other words, is a separate issue that cannot be decided by the simple method of side-by-side comparison. Aeschines himself, moreover, earlier in his speech, had made clear that as in almost all *graphē paranomōn* cases, other matters besides the strict application of the law are also at issue and are, in fact, more important than alleged violations of the law. This is evident from the fact that after a relatively brief discussion of the laws allegedly violated by the decree (3.9–48), he devotes most of the remainder of his speech (3.49–260)—more than 80 percent—to the issue of Demosthenes' career. As he explains (3.50):

> The rest of my case is absolutely straightforward and easy for you to judge when you hear it. As prosecutor, I must surely prove to you that the praise of Demosthenes is false, and that he neither began his career by speaking for the best nor does he now continue to act in the interests of the *dēmos* (*ta sympheronta tōi dēmōi*). And if I prove this, Ctesiphon will surely be convicted justly (*dikaiōs*) with respect to the indictment; for all the laws (*hapantes hoi nomoi*) prohibit anyone from writing false things (*pseudē*) in public decrees.

As many have noted, there was almost certainly no law that specifically prohibited someone from making false statements in decrees—and no law to this effect had been written side by side on the tablet—but it was undoubtedly agreed by virtually all Athenians that lying in a decree was wrong, and so Aeschines can conclude that all the laws must prohibit it. For the Athenians, a standard of justice could be treated as having the support of all the Athenian laws, and so any clear violation of justice, such as lying in a decree, must also in some way violate the law. For the jurors, moreover, because there was no law, they would have to judge according to their most just opinion, and this would surely have caused them to condemn Ctesiphon, if it could be shown that he had made false statements in his decree.

Demosthenes evidently shares Aeschines' view that his career was the main issue in the case because he, too, devotes most of his speech to this issue, arguing that Ctesiphon's praise is true, and that his own career has been entirely devoted to speaking and doing what is best for Athens. For the Athenians, it would have been inconceivable for Demosthenes to argue that because no law explicitly prohibited false statements in a decree, Ctesiphon should be acquitted even if the praise in his decree was false. Everyone knew it was wrong to make false statements in decrees, and so Demosthenes must argue that Ctesiphon's praise is true. Even in *graphē paranomōn* cases, then, the necessity of addressing the issue of law did not eliminate the importance of justice. Just as in all other cases, in these cases, too, law and justice went hand in hand, two standards of equal validity. Any correct verdict must satisfy the requirements of both, and conflict between the two was impossible.

This is not to say that the Athenians did not recognize any difference between law and justice. The judicial oath, among other things, spoke separately of deciding according to the laws and deciding by means of one's most just opinion, and most of the passages cited above that speak of law and justice in the same sentence imply that there is some distinction between the two. One important difference was that even though all laws were inherently just, only a finite number of laws had been enacted. As a result, one could act justly without the support of any law, and many violations of justice were not addressed by any law.[34] This was not an obstacle for a prosecutor, however, since in most cases he could easily include the violation in the detailed accusation that he provided when he initiated his suit.

Meletus proceeded in this way when he accused Socrates of, among other things, "corrupting the youth."[35] Meletus implies that corrupting the youth is an act of impiety (and is, therefore, against the law), even though it seems on the surface to have little to do with impiety. There was almost certainly no law explicitly prohibiting corruption of the youth, but Meletus (and his audience) evidently took for granted that corrupting the youth was wrong, and by connecting this charge loosely with the charges about the gods, he was able to include it in the general category of impiety. Socrates, moreover, does not dispute the assumption that corrupting the youth would be a violation of the law, but instead maintains that he did not corrupt any of the young men who associated with him.

It seems, then, that almost any conduct that was considered wrong by most Athenians could be included as part of the specific accusation brought under one of the general charges in an Athenian court. In addition to arguing that "all the laws" prohibited the wrongful conduct, another strategy a plaintiff could use was to acknowledge that no law existed that specifically addressed the act of wrongdoing that he was alleging. Lycurgus, for example, maintains (Lyc. 1.8) that Leocrates' "crime (*adikēma*) is so terrible (*deinon*) and so great (*tēlikouton . . . to megethos*) that it is impossible to find an appropriate charge, or to specify in the laws any punishment sufficient for his crime." And Demosthenes in his prosecution of Leptines for passing an inexpedient law similarly implies that the laws cannot provide the jury with sufficient guidance in assessing Leptines' law when he reminds the jurors (Dem. 20.118) that they have sworn to judge according to the laws of Athens and "where there are no laws to judge according to your most just opin-

34. This is why the speaker in Demosthenes 44.8 could say of his opponents, whose claim to an estate was based partly on an adoption that was of questionable legality, "but even if their arguments from the laws are inadequate but clearly are fair (*dikaia*) and humane (*philanthrōpa*), in that case we shall also yield to them."

35. See chapter 5, with note 33.

ion (*gnōmēi tēi dikaiotatēi*). Fine. You must, therefore, apply that opinion [i.e., the most just opinion] to this entire law [of Leptines]." Demosthenes then asks and answers two rhetorical questions (Dem. 20.119): "Is it just (*dikaion*) to honor those who do good? It is. Is it just (*dikaion*) to allow someone to keep what has been given to him? It is."[36] Demosthenes' argument here is clear: even if Leptines' law violates no specific law, it is unjust, and Leptines therefore deserves to be convicted of enacting an inexpedient law.

In sum, most litigants maintain that both law and justice favor their side and should govern the outcome of the litigation. Justice can prevail, however, where there are no laws. On the other hand, the reverse is not true, because justice and the moral rules that accompany it are always a consideration in assessing any kind of conduct that might come before the court. Thus, there never could be a case in which conduct that violated a law was not also considered unjust.

One factor that may complicate the conclusion that the laws are always just is the possibility that norms may change over time, causing an old law to conflict with more recent notions of justice. In Lysias 1, for example, many scholars have thought that Draco's seventh-century law, quoted by Euphiletus at 1.30 (see chapter 4), that allows a person to kill an adulterer in bed with his wife was considered too harsh by the end of the fifth century and had fallen out of use. If that was the case, it seems that the prosecution would have had to confront the argument that the jurors were obliged, according to this law, to vote to acquit Euphiletus even if they considered his killing of Eratosthenes unjust. Euphiletus does not make this argument explicitly, but he insists that in killing Eratosthenes he was following the law, and that the law was "most just" (1.29, cf. 1.31). He thus implies that the justice of his act is not in question. What could the prosecution have said to refute this?

We can only speculate, of course, but I would guess that if the prosecutor discussed this law, he may have argued that the lawgiver's intent was shaped by conditions at the time, but that conditions were now different. Thus, the self-help prescribed for the seventh century could take the form of killing

36. In the one other surviving case that is prosecuted by a *graphē nomon mē epitēdeion thēnai*, the speaker claims that Timocrates "in violation of all the laws has enacted a law that is neither expedient nor just (*out' epitēdeion oute dikaion*)" (Dem. 24.1). The speaker proceeds to make clear that the laws that were violated were those governing the procedure for enacting a new law. He then adds that Timocrates also did wrong "because he introduced [a law] that is opposed to all existing laws (*pasin . . . tois ousi nomois*) (Dem. 24.32). This last expression (like Aeschines' "all the laws") implies that no specific law has been directly violated by the substance of the new law.

the adulterer, but the same self-help in the fifth century would manifest itself as holding the adulterer for ransom or in one of the other currently approved ways. In other words, the law was still valid, but it needed to be understood in the context of current conditions. Whether such an argument (if in fact it was made) could prevail is uncertain, and it seems to me more likely that the prosecution based their case primarily on an accusation of entrapment, since Euphiletus admittedly had not simply found Eratosthenes in bed with his wife and killed him but had arranged beforehand to be notified by the maid when Eratosthenes was in the house.

Another factor that some scholars consider important in discussions of justice and Athenian law is equity (*epieikeia*), which (it is argued) can influence the jury's understanding of the law and its application in some of the forensic speeches.[37] The basis for such arguments is often seen in Aristotle's discussion of *epieikeia* in the *Rhetoric* (1.13, 1374a25–b23)[38] as "justice that goes beyond the written law" (*para ton gegrammenon nomon dikaion*).[39] Aristotle's identification of *epieikeia* as a kind of justice is not, however, found in the speeches of litigants. *Epieikeia* occurs only nine times in the forensic speeches, and in these occurrences it never means "equity." Rather, its meaning ranges from something like "sympathetic feeling" (e.g., Isoc. 18.34) to "good conduct" (e.g., Lys. 16.11).[40] Equity as a philosophical concept may be beginning to take shape in the mind of Aristotle, but it has not yet entered into the language of the forensic speeches.[41]

The more important point to note is that whether we call it equity or justice or fairness, no Athenian defendant ever argues that although the strict application of the law might lead to his conviction, he should be acquitted because of extenuating circumstances. Extenuating circumstances are sometimes advanced as an argument for acquittal, but they are always in addition to other reasons for acquittal. Prosecutors may predict that a

37. Scafuro (1997:54–56) sees *epieikeia* as especially important in deciding the penalty.

38. The discussion of *epieikeia* in *Nicomachaean Ethics* (5.10, 1137a30–38a2) is less relevant to its use in litigation.

39. Harris has recently maintained that "an argument from *epieikeia* was not an appeal to extra-legal considerations but to a general principle of justice implicit in the written laws" (2013c:276 = 2013a:26). As Aristotle makes clear, however, *epieikeia* is something "beyond the law," what Brunschwig (1996:139) identifies as the "moral intuitions of the judge and those of the society in which he works."

40. *Epieikeia* occurs in Isoc. 18.34; Lys. 16.11; Dem. 20.155, 21.90, 21.207, 26.16, 34.40, 36.59; Hyp. 1, *Lyc.* 13 (col. 11.21).

41. See O'Neil (2001), who cautions against reading a modern notion of equity into the forensic speeches.

defendant will cite extenuating circumstances despite his obvious guilt, or a speaker may attribute such arguments to defendants in other cases, but these examples cannot be taken as evidence for what defendants actually argued. Nor can we rely on a speaker who explains that a jury acquitted an obviously guilty litigant because of extenuating circumstances; no speaker would actually know why a jury decided as it did, and if he did know, we could not trust him to give an unbiased account of the jury's decision. Because all laws were assumed to be just, moreover, Athenian litigants never had any reason to introduce the notion of equity as a separate concern into their pleadings. Equity is a corrective force, used when the strict application of the law produces an admittedly unjust result. For the Athenians, however, the application of their laws necessarily led to a just result; justice was thus always a consideration and equity was unnecessary.

In my view, then, the so-called equity arguments that are found in Athenian forensic speeches are not correctives to the strict application of the laws; rather, they are appeals to justice made in addition to arguments based on the law. Thus, to the extent that Athenian courts took what we call equity into account in reaching their decisions, they looked to justice in addition to law. The arguments that some scholars treat as equity arguments are better understood as arguments for justice, and these were completely acceptable to the Athenians, for whom an argument or verdict in accord with justice was also in most cases an argument or verdict in accord with the law. This is not what most people understand by equity today, and was certainly not what the English understood by equity when they created courts of equity and equity law as an alternative to the common law and its courts,[42] but it is what the Athenians considered law.

For the Athenians, the close, almost inextricable connection of law and justice meant that the strict application of the law included the consideration of justice. The need to consider justice, and if possible to achieve a just result in every case, significantly affected the nature of Athenian law. As I will discuss in chapter 8, it did not lessen the Athenians' commitment to the rule of law, but it did mean that they could be, indeed had to be, more flexible in their application of the rule of law than many modern views of the rule of law would allow, because in applying the laws to the case at hand, they had to take into account justice, which depended in part on the background and full context of the case. Only then could they be certain that the outcome was consistent not only with the law but also with justice. Thus litigants could introduce and the jurors could consider issues involv-

42. See S. Worthington 2008.

ing justice that were more loosely relevant to the legal issues (strictly understood) than we would consider proper today.[43] And the need to address the broader context of the case increased the importance of the rhetorical skill of litigants (and their logographers), as litigants had to sort through a larger, more complex set of issues and present them clearly to the jury in a way that would convince the jurors that both law and justice supported a verdict in their favor.

Considerations of justice, then, were an important aspect of the rule of law as the Athenians understood it; they were not the only considerations, however, that affected their understanding of law and the rule of law and made it different from our own. They also believed that law should benefit the community not just in the general sense of providing rules of conduct for the well-being of the community and resolving disputes that might threaten that well-being, but also in the sense that the outcome of each case should be beneficial to the community. As the speaker in Demosthenes 43.84 urges the jury (passage no. 6 above): "Come to the aid of the laws and take care of the dead so that their house does not die out. By doing this you will cast a vote that is just and in conformity with your oath and in your own interests (*ta hymin autois sympheronta*)." I turn next, therefore, to an examination of the various ways in which public interest shaped the Athenians' understanding of law.

43. In this way, Athenian law to some extent resembles the litigation process found in some tribal societies and found today in some quasi-judicial dispute-settlement procedures such as mediation or small-claims courts. In these arenas, opposing sides present their claims together with the same sort of broad array of considerations we find in informal, everyday disputes. In these processes, other considerations besides the strict letter of the law may enter into the discussion.

CHAPTER 7

PUBLIC INTEREST

In the last chapter, I argued that justice, though not necessarily relevant to the specific issues detailed in the accusation, was a fundamental consideration in every legal case because the Athenians believed that all their laws were just and therefore that all verdicts reached in accordance with the laws also had to be just. The evidence I cited to support this conclusion, however, also suggests another fundamental consideration, namely public interest. Consider the following three statements (all taken from passages cited in chapter 6).

> Aes. 1.178: "It is because in enacting your laws your entire goal is that they be just (*dikaioi*); you do not consider profit or favor or enmity, but only justice and the public good (*to dikaion kai to sympheron*)."
>
> Dem. 20.94: "The aim was for each of you to hear the laws many times and have a chance to study them at leisure and then enact those that are both just and in the public interest (*kai dikaia kai sympheronta*)."
>
> Dem. 43.84: "By doing this you will cast a vote that is just (*ta dikaia*) and in conformity with your oath (*ta euorka*) and in your interests (*ta hymin autois sympheronta*)."

Two other passages, not yet cited, similarly connect the laws and justice with public interest:

> Dem. 25.26: "The laws want what is just (*to dikaion*) and fine (*to kalon*) and advantageous (*to sympheron*)."
>
> Lys. 19.64: "[By acquitting me,] you will cast a vote for justice (*ta dikaia*) and in your own interest (*ta hymin autois sympheronta*).

These passages indicate that, like justice, public interest, or what was advantageous (*sympheron*) to the *dēmos* (and to the jury, which forensic speakers commonly identified with the *dēmos*), was an expected outcome of all cases that were correctly decided according to the laws and justice. Like justice, therefore, public interest was not a factor like character or the context of a dispute that was necessarily relevant to the specific issue in the case (though it might be relevant to the specific issues in some cases). Rather, it was a feature of their law that was in itself consistent with the law and with a lawful judgment in every case.

The requirement that law serve the public interest, not only in the general sense that public welfare benefited from a well-functioning legal system, but also in the sense that every individual law and the outcome of every case ought to serve the public interest, was a direct consequence of the requirement that the law (like the government) be democratic. For the Athenians, a democratic legal system, like a democratic political system, directly benefited the *dēmos*. As one speaker puts it, "In my opinion, the task of both a good citizen and a just-minded juror is to understand the laws in a way that will be beneficial to the polis" (Lys. 14.4).[1] Litigants thus tried not only to interpret the applicable laws in a way that supported their own case but also to show that the result of this interpretation would be beneficial for the polis. In theory, such an interpretation should not be difficult because, as Demosthenes notes in a passage quoted above (20.94), the legislative process instituted at the end of the fifth century ensured that the city would enact laws "that are both just and in the public interest."

In addition to laws and verdicts that served the public interest, other aspects of the legal system were also structured in a way that aimed to benefit the *dēmos*: laws were enacted that were clear and simple so that ordinary citizens could understand them. These laws were made accessible by the display of copies in public spaces. And ordinary citizens had easy access to the courts, where they could have their grievances heard by a jury of their fellow citizens. Public interest, in other words, permeated the Athenian legal system.

Athenian litigation thus aimed to secure verdicts that met three objectives: to accord with the applicable laws, to achieve justice, and to benefit the *dēmos*; and litigants tried to shape their pleading so as to meet all three of these objectives. Euthycles, the speaker in Demosthenes 23, states this three-fold objective succinctly when he explains the charges that he has

1. See Wallace 2006a; his chapter is subtitled "Community Justice in Athenian Courts." He concludes (430), "In Athens' courtrooms, as elsewhere, the welfare of the community was paramount." See also Wallace 2018a:16–20, esp. 16–17: "The administration of justice at Athens, so far from 'primitive,' was deliberately and even systematically organized, shaped not by procedural or substantive law but in accordance with democratic principles and the welfare of the community."

brought against Aristocrates' proposed decree (23.18): "I have undertaken to demonstrate three things: first, that the decree has been composed in violation of the laws (*para tous nomous*); second, that it is not in the interest of the city (*asympheron tēi polei*); and third, that the person for whom the decree has been written is unworthy (*anaxion*) of these privileges." In other words, the decree violates the law, is not in the public interest, and is unjust because Charidemus, the proposed beneficiary of the decree, does not deserve the privileges it would give him.[2]

Demosthenes also links the law closely to the public interest in another famous passage from the end of his speech against Meidias, where he addresses the jury (Dem. 21.224):[3]

> What is the strength of the laws? Is it that if one of you is wronged and cries out, they will come running up and be there to help? No, for they are only letters that have been written and would not have the power to do that. What, then, is their power? You are, if you strengthen them and make them always available for whoever needs them. Thus, the laws are strong because of you, and you are strong because of the laws.[4]

This passage makes clear that for the laws to benefit those members of the *dēmos* who may need them, they must have the support of the entire *dēmos*. The laws thus benefit both the community as a whole and the individual members of the community.

Scholars have often remarked that in contrast to modern Americans, the Greeks valued the community over the individual;[5] in fact, as this passage suggests, the relationship between the two is more complex. Whereas we often assume an opposition between the interests of the individual and the interests of the community such that the rights of one can often be thought

---

2. Demosthenes elaborates these three points in 23.19–21. The three charges were very likely spelled out in the indictment.

3. Every instance of "you" in this passage translates the Greek second person plural pronoun (*hymeis*). As often, the addressee here is both the jury and the audience as a whole (jurors and bystanders), and by extension the *dēmos* as a whole, whom the jury is commonly assumed to represent.

4. President Barack Obama included a variation of this same theme in his farewell address, January 10, 2017: "Our Constitution is a remarkable, beautiful gift. But it's really just a piece of parchment. It has no power on its own. We, the people, give it power. We, the people, give it meaning. With our participation, and with the choices that we make, and the alliances that we forge. Whether or not we stand up for our freedoms. Whether or not we respect and enforce the rule of law. That's up to us" (https://obamawhitehouse.archives.gov/the-press-office/2017/01/10/remarks-president-farewell-address).

5. See especially Wallace 2006a.

to conflict with the rights of the other, the Athenians tended to see the individual as embedded in and protected by the community. In their view, the well-being of the community ensures the well-being of the individual and vice versa; without a healthy, law-abiding community, no individual can prosper. Thus, the two are not in conflict but rather are mutually sustaining.[6] The imperative that the legal system should serve the interest of the *dēmos*, the community, thus meant that at the same time it should serve the interest of each citizen in the community.

As noted above, the view that the legal system should benefit the city is rooted in the Athenians' commitment to a legal system that is democratic in the full sense of being controlled by the *dēmos*. Two aspects of this community control have already been discussed: first, the institution of pay for jury service in the middle of the fifth century, with an increase in the amount later in the century from two obols to three.[7] The amount was small, but it provided a minimum level of sustenance for anyone who wished to serve, and thus ensured that juries would be broadly representative of the community as a whole, although men who lived far from the city were probably underrepresented and the elderly were probably overrepresented.[8]

Second, the Athenians also tried to ensure that all citizens had easy access to the legal system.[9] Litigation was inexpensive, involving only small court fees, and procedures for bringing suit were relatively straightforward. Using the *dikē* procedure required only that a person file a complaint with the clerk and then notify the accused, and the *graphē* procedure was only slightly more complex (though it could involve greater risk). The language of the laws regarding procedure, moreover, was relatively clear and simple. For a case of *hybris*, for example, the law prescribed, "Let any Athenian to whom it is permitted bring a public action (*graphē*) before the Thesmothetai and let them bring the case to the court within thirty days from the time of the accusation unless some public business prevents it, but if not, at the earliest possible time" (Dem. 21.47). These procedural rules would not have been hard to follow. The Thesmothetai were a group of six officials who met in the agora or central marketplace and were easily found. Thirty days is a reasonable limit, with more time granted if there is good reason. And the law goes on to spell out clearly the penalty in case one fails to secure one-fifth of

6. This interdependence of individual and community can be found in texts as diverse as Pericles' funeral oration (Thucydides 2.35–46) and Plato's *Republic*.

7. See chapter 1, note 26.

8. For the composition of the jury, see the discussion in chapter 2 (text at notes 25–27).

9. Further discussion of litigation procedures in Athens is in chapter 1.

the votes. If a person did not feel confident, however, and was afraid to risk such a penalty, he could always bring a less risky case of assault by means of a *dikē* (as Ariston does in Demosthenes 54). In all these ways, a poor Athenian with little education had far easier and more direct access to the legal system than such a person would have today.

In addition to providing a fairly easy means for citizens to obtain a hearing in court, the democratic legal system (like all legal systems) was intended to benefit the community by providing an effective means of keeping order and by punishing wrongdoing and compensating individuals for damage they had suffered. Speakers sometimes stress this aspect of public benefit by warning the jury about the precedent they would set.[10] Toward the end of Lysias 1, for example, Euphiletus asserts that he is acquitted by the laws and asks the jurors to reach the same decision as the laws (Lys. 1.36): "Otherwise, you will provide such immunity for adulterers that you will encourage even thieves to claim that they are adulterers, because they know full well that if they claim that this was their reason for entering someone else's house, then no one can lay a hand on them." With similar exaggeration, Apollodorus gives the same warning of general public harm at the end of his prosecution of Neaira, when he calls on the jury to convict her and then adds (Dem. 59.112): "It would be far more beneficial if this trial had never taken place than that once it has taken place, you vote for acquittal. For in that case prostitutes will be allowed to live with whomever they want and to claim anyone as the father of their children; and the laws will no longer be valid but the prostitutes will be able to do whatever they want." And a third speaker, Ariston, has a similar warning (Dem. 54.44): "Is it advantageous (*sympherei*) to each of you that people are allowed to beat up and insult others? Well, if you acquit him (Conon), there will be many (who do this); if you convict him, fewer." In all these passages, after asserting that their opponent is most certainly guilty,[11] the speaker warns that if the jury finds for his opponent, crime or unrestrained sexual license will overwhelm the social order. To have a proper deterrent effect, therefore, the jury must vote for conviction.

More commonly, discussions of public benefit involve personal public service, especially the liturgies, special levies (*eisphora*), and other services provided by a litigant or his family or by his opponent or his opponent's

---

10. Precedent in an Athenian context was necessarily more flexible than it is for us today. See chapter 8.

11. In Lysias 1, Euphiletus is actually the defendant, but he presents the case as if Eratosthenes were the defendant on trial for adultery (see chapter 4).

family.[12] Most such discussions involve public service that occurred in the past, but in inheritance cases it is not uncommon for a speaker to speak about the benefits of the future public service that he or his relatives will undertake if their claim to the estate is upheld by the court.

At the end of Isaeus 4 (4.27–28), for example, the speaker asks the jury to consider what sort of people the claimants are (*hoioi eisi*). He extols the public service of the two young brothers for whom he is speaking and their father, Thrasippus. They have never left the city except in its service, they have paid special levies (*eisphora*) when asked, and they have generally conducted themselves properly (*kosmious*). The speaker then contrasts these with the crimes and worthless life of Chariades, the opposing claimant to Nicostratus's estate, who spent most of his life away from Athens and has never served the city as a soldier or paid any special levy (4.28–29). The speaker concludes (4.30–31) that the brothers' public service, their good lives, and their close kinship with the deceased make them clearly more deserving of the estate.

Similarly, in Isaeus 6, a more complex case, the speaker (a family friend of the claimant, Chaerestratus) seeks to refute what he portrays as a main argument of the other claimants, that they are poor whereas Chaerestratus and his relatives are rich. He argues that although his friends have more money, they have spent it on the city, not on themselves (6.60–61):

> Phanostratus has already been trierarch seven times; he has performed all the other liturgies, and has been victorious most of the time. Chaerestratus, young as he is, has been trierarch, *chorēgos* for a tragedy, and gymnasiarch for a torch-race. Both have paid special levies. And there is a younger son who has also been *chorēgos* and paid a special levy. . . . If then the jury awards Philoctemon's estate to his friend, he will spend it [in] service to the city performing liturgies just as he has always done and even more. The other claimants, however, will just squander it and then plot against others.

One's first reaction to the introduction of public service in these cases may be that such arguments are, or ought to be, irrelevant to the issue of inheritance. But before accepting this conclusion, it should be noted that in inheritance cases a claimant always argued that he (or those on whose behalf he was speaking) deserved the estate because of his kinship with the de-

12. For the liturgy system and the special levies (*eisphora*), see chapter 1 at notes 35–36.

ceased or some other legitimizing factor such as a will. This point often required a complex discussion, because the cases that reached court usually involved claimants with complex connections to the deceased. Without the kind of record keeping that we are accustomed to, it was often questionable whether the claimant or someone in the chain of connections linking him to the deceased was or was not a legitimate child or spouse. The Athenians relied on witnesses to events such as marriages and births, and if these events occurred decades ago, there might no longer be any witnesses still living. Wills are introduced in some cases, but questions often arise about the genuineness of these or, if the will was made shortly before the death of the deceased, whether some malign influence was exerted against the deceased's true wishes.

These factors regularly created situations in which more than one party could present a reasonable claim to the estate. In addition to arguments that we might consider legal in a strict sense, therefore, claimants often argued that they deserved the estate because of the deceased's friendship with them or their family, or their devotion to the deceased, including tending to his burial and to his grave thereafter. In this context, public service is always presented as an additional consideration in the speaker's favor (or against his opponents). Moreover, all such discussions of public service in Isaeus's inheritance pleadings come at or very near the end of the speech and are presented as lending support to the speaker's legitimate claim, not as the main reason for his claim.[13]

In other types of cases, discussion of public service is often relevant to an issue in the case; when it is not, then discussion of public service is usually an ancillary argument, just as it is in inheritance cases. Some speakers, however, would have us think otherwise; these speakers warn against the practice of some litigants who (they allege) base their entire case on their public service because they have no argument for their acquittal on the basis of the facts of the case. Many scholars have taken these speakers' warnings at face value, but we must, as always, be suspicious about any claims that a speaker makes about a past case or about his opponent's arguments in the present case. These claims can take several different forms. For example, the prosecutor of Aristogeiton tells the jury (Dem. 25.76): "I have before now seen some defendants who were convicted on the facts of the case and had no way to show that they had done no wrong take refuge in the moderation and self-control of their lives or in the achievements and liturgies of their

13. Similar arguments based on public service occur in Isaeus 7.35–42, 10.25, and 11.49–50.

ancestors, or in other similar pleas, by means of which they moved the jurors to pity and goodwill." The speaker goes on to argue, however, that none of these refuges is available to Aristogeiton, who has led a wicked life, nor has he or his ancestors done any public service.

Another speaker accuses a certain Nicomachus of abusing his position as *anagrapheus*, or "inscriber of laws" (Lys. 30.1): "Some men on trial have seemed to be guilty but by demonstrating their ancestors' virtues and their own good deeds, they have obtained your pardon. Since, therefore, you accept pleas of defendants who show that they have done something good for the city, you should also listen to accusers who demonstrate that defendants have long been wicked men." The speaker then mentions that Nicomachus's father was a slave and insinuates that Nicomachus himself had a disreputable life as a youth, but then immediately proceeds to discuss the abuses Nicomachus committed while holding the office in question (30.2).

Another variation of this argument comes in Lys. 12.38: "He cannot even do what has become the custom in this city and say nothing to defend himself against the charges but tell you other things about themselves, and sometimes deceive you, showing you that they are good soldiers, or have captured many of the enemy's ships when they were in command, or have made once hostile cities friendly to us."

And a final example: Lycurgus predicts that the defendant's co-pleaders will cite their own public service in his favor (Lyc. 1.139). Lycurgus rejects this argument not because citing public service is wrong but because the particular service they will cite (sponsoring a choral production, etc.) is not distinguished enough; to earn gratitude they would need more significant service.

The message these speakers convey is that a defendant who has no valid argument for his innocence can still win an acquittal by citing his and his family's public service, but such statements must be understood for what they are—rhetorical moves to support the speaker's own case.[14] We have no reason to expect a speaker to give an accurate account of whatever earlier cases he has in mind (if any), or to be accurate in predicting what his opponent or his opponent's co-pleaders will say. Proclaiming the defendant's obvious guilt is a rhetorical move with no objective basis in fact, and (as I

14. Wallace at times seems to echo these speakers concerning the overriding importance of public interest (2006a; see above, note 1). See also Cartledge 2016:170: "In major political trials—in a sense all trials were political, of course—the overriding consideration for a juror was not necessarily the guilt or innocence of the defendant as charged, but rather what verdict and (where relevant) punishment would most likely further Athens' best interests as a democratic *polis*."

have noted before) any explanation of the jury's reasons for conviction can only be a guess.

The same holds true for the opposite argument, that the jury convicted the defendant despite his extensive record of public service. Aeschines reports, for example, that in Archinus's *graphē paranomōn* case against Thrasybulus, "he convicted him, even though his public benefactions were recent, but the jurors did not take these into account" (Aes. 3.195). Here the speaker does not even tell us that the defendant raised the issue of his public service. It was well known that men with strong records of public service could be condemned to severe punishment, even death for later misdeeds,[15] but because we do not know what arguments were actually made by the litigants in these cases and what reasons the jurors had for voting for conviction, such cases shed no light on the role of arguments concerning public service in forensic pleadings.

Rather than drawing conclusions about litigants' discussion of public service from other litigants' allegations about pleadings or verdicts in other cases, we need to look at how and why litigants actually introduce public service into their own cases. How important are such arguments? Do defendants in fact argue that they should be acquitted solely because of their public service?

I begin with thirteen cases.[16] In the first five of these, public service is clearly relevant either to the main issue in the case or to another significant issue raised by the prosecution.

Lys. 25.12–13: This is a *dokimasia* case in which the speaker's fitness for an office for which he has been selected is questioned. He was clearly involved with the recent government of the Thirty and he cites his public service to counteract the charges that he is hostile to the democracy.[17]

Dem. 18.267: The main issues in the trial On the Crown is Ctesiphon's assertion that Demosthenes has always spoken and acted for the benefit

15. The speaker in Dem. 24.133–36 recalls a number of such cases. See also Din. 1.14; Dem. 21.143–47; Hyp. 4, *Eux.* 35–36; Dem. 19.273, 19.277.

16. Johnstone (1999:166n4) lists thirteen defendants who cite their past services, but his list includes only mentions of liturgies and special levies; he does not include cases in which the speaker reports other sorts of public service, such as military service. Two of his examples are from speeches for inheritance cases (Is. 2.42, 11.50), which I have already discussed. On the other hand, I include two cases that are not on his list: Andocides 1.141–149 and Isoc. 18.58–65. In the latter, although the speaker is technically the prosecutor, it is a *paragraphē* case, so he is better treated as a defendant (see below, note 20).

17. See also Lysias, frag. 106 Carey, which was probably also part of a *dokimasia* speech.

of the *dēmos*.[18] Thus the list of liturgies that Demosthenes has performed, which is apparently read out in this passage, is clearly relevant to the charge.

Lys. 20.23: In this speech, Polystratus's sons are defending him against a charge that has something to do with his complicity in the oligarchy or the Four Hundred. He evidently was a member of this regime, so rather than deny it, the son defends him by citing the whole family's many services on behalf of the democracy. Among these are all of Polystratus's public services, with the implication that these can compensate for his membership in the Four Hundred. They also support the speaker's argument that there is little left in the estate and the city should therefore let them keep what's left. Public service in this case is also directly relevant to the main issue.

Lys. 19.56–63: The Aristophanes whose property is in question in this case is not the famous comic poet but a minor military commander. He was earlier convicted, probably of some military negligence, put to death, and his property was confiscated. Now someone is accusing him of having concealed some of his property to prevent it being confiscated. His son is defending him, and one of his arguments is that because of Aristophanes' generous public service, his estate was not as large as people had expected it to be. To support this argument he recounts at length not only his father's usual public services but also such services of his as ransoming prisoners of war and paying for the funerals of others when the relatives could not pay. This account is clearly relevant to the main issue in the case. The son also notes (19.62) that he himself is currently funding a trierarchy and pledges that he will continue to perform liturgies whenever he has enough money; thus the city will do better to let him keep what little he has rather than confiscating it, because a substantial portion of what would be confiscated would have to be given to the prosecutors, who would do nothing for the city.[19] This last point is not relevant to the main issue but is presented at the end of the speech as an additional point.

Ant. 5.75–77: Toward the end of this speech, which was delivered not long after the revolt of Mytilene in 427, the speaker Euxitheus reluctantly includes a defense of his father, a Mytilenean who (he claims) has been accused by the prosecution, probably of anti-Athenian conduct of some sort in connection with the revolt. Euxitheus claims that he is too young to know much about his father's activities in 427, but "I will tell you as much as I know in order not to let my father be unjustly maligned before you" (5.75).

---

18. See Gagarin 2012 and also above, chapter 5.

19. Thus the speaker's final plea (which was cited at the beginning of this chapter): by supporting my case "you will be voting for what is just (*ta dikaia*) and advantageous to yourselves (*hymin ta sympheronta*)" (19.64).

He then briefly tells (5.76–77) how his father did not support the revolt but could not prevent it, and after it was suppressed, he has been loyal to Athens, and has funded choruses and paid taxes. As in the preceding passage, this account is not relevant to the main charge of murder, but does address one of the lesser claims (of disloyalty to Athens) that the prosecution apparently included and that was probably an important factor underlying the case.

In the next case, discussion of the defendant's public service is not directly relevant to the accusation in the case but is presented in connection with an additional point that is loosely connected to the main issue.

Dem. 52.26: Apollodorus is defending his elderly banker father, Pasion, against the charge that he wrongly paid out some money. After specifically refuting the charge, he mentions other arguments that the prosecution may make, including allegations of a specific motive. In response to one of these potential motives, Apollodorus says, "perhaps he (the accuser) will say that my father made a private profit from the money. . . . Was he in this case a shameful seeker of profit (*aischrokerdēs*) when he was not with respect to special levies and liturgies and gifts to the city?" (52.26).

The remaining seven discussions of public service by a defendant all come toward the end of the speech, after the main issue has been addressed, and are presented as an additional consideration in the defendant's favor.

Lys. 7.31–32: The speaker first responds to the charge of removing a sacred olive stump, and then adds several additional considerations. He first asks that the jury disregard the indictment and not consider the prosecution's words more credible than the facts (7.30). Instead, "remember what I have said, and the rest of my conduct as a citizen (*tēs allēs politeias*)." He then reports (7.31–32) that he has performed all the duties assigned to him with greater zeal than required, mentioning trierarchies, choruses, special levies, and other liturgies, and he suggests that if he had been more modest in his public service, he would have attracted less attention and would thus not now be a subject of this (frivolous) suit.

Isoc. 18.58–65: The speaker was accused by Callimachus of depriving him of property during the reign of the Ten, who briefly succeeded the Thirty before the democracy was restored.[20] Underlying the specific charge is undoubtedly the broader charge of complicity with the Ten and very probably also with the Thirty. Thus, near the end of the speech, he reminds the jury of his one most notable service to the city, that at the disastrous (for Ath-

20. Technically, the speech is brought by the new procedure of *paragraphē* (counterplea), in which the speaker argues that the original suit is inadmissible. Thus the original defendant in the case is now the plaintiff; for the purpose of this chapter, however, I will treat him as a defendant.

ens) battle of Aegospotami he so surpassed the other trierarchs that he not only saved his ship but, after returning to Athens, together with his brother he continued to fight the enemy. Furthermore, when Sparta then took control of Athens, he and his brother brought grain into the city. In recognition of these services, the city voted them crowns and proclaimed them heroes. The speaker goes on to make common arguments about how he could not have harmed the city after doing all these things, but in this case, the mention of his services would also help counter any accusations of complicity with the oligarchs.

And. 1.141–149: Andocides was exiled in 415 for his involvement in two major religious scandals. He returned after the fall of the Thirty in 403, but in 399 was again accused of attending religious ceremonies from which he was barred by decree. It is questionable whether the decree in question applied to his situation, and the whole case can be seen as essentially a political attack on Andocides, who must show that he is a good citizen and does not deserve to be exiled again.[21] Andocides spends the first part of his speech defending the actions that led to his exile in 415 and arguing for his innocence in the current case. He then attacks the motives of the prosecution, and finally at the very end, he mentions the distinguished service (mostly military service) of his ancestors, which he is trying to emulate and will continue to do so if acquitted. No liturgies or special levies are mentioned in this account, but Andocides pledges to benefit the city in other ways.

Lys. 3.47: The defendant in this case relates at length his dealings with Simon, refuting Simon's accusation of wounding with intent (to kill). At the very end (3.47), he adds an appeal for pity, which he links to his public service: "Remember these things (Simon's crimes) and vote for justice (*ta dikaia*), and do not allow me to be unjustly (*adikōs*) exiled from my fatherland, on behalf of which I have risked many dangers and performed many liturgies. I have never done it any harm, nor has any of my ancestors, but I have done it much good."

In addition to these four cases, in which the defendant mentions public service at the end of the speech after addressing the issues in the case, there are three other cases in which the defendant also mentions public service at the end of the speech, but because we are missing the beginning of the speech, we cannot be certain whether the main issue in the case has been addressed earlier in the part that is missing. In two of the cases, however, the speaker tells us that the issue has been addressed earlier.

Lys. 21.1–10 (and also 21.19–22): This is not a complete speech but only

21. I should note that in a prosecution speech delivered in this case, the speaker denies at some length that Andocides has done anything good for the city (Lys. 6.46–49).

the final part, containing an account of the defendant's services and a peroration. Whether the charge was taking a bribe (as the title says) or something else, it very likely had a political dimension relating to the reign of the Thirty. The speaker begins (21.2), "Concerning the accusations, things have been made clear to you, men of the jury. But I ask you also to listen to me concerning other things, so that you may know what sort of person I am about whom you will be voting." He then relates in great detail all the liturgies and other services he has performed beginning when he came of age, including the amount of money spent on each (which was far more than required) as well as other details such as victories he won and how he ensured that his ships were always the best equipped. The opening sentences imply that these services are not directly relevant to the accusation, but if (as seems likely) the prosecution was trying to link him to the Thirty and thereby question his loyalty to the democracy, then this long account of services would serve as partial refutation of this underlying charge.

Toward the end of the excerpt, the speaker again mentions his public service, tying it directly back to the charge of taking bribes. First, he asks the jury not only to remember his liturgies but also to consider his private life, for "the most difficult liturgy is to conduct oneself moderately and with self-restraint" and so on (21.19). And shortly after this he argues, "I would be crazy if, after I spent my patrimony on you, I should accept bribes from others to do harm to the city."

Isoc. 16.35: In the surviving fragment, the younger Alcibiades begins (16.1–2) by asserting that he has clearly refuted the specific accusation in the case (that his father, Alcibiades, did not own a certain team of horses) and accusing the prosecution of spending most of its time slandering his father instead of discussing the actual charges in the case. Alcibiades thus argues that he must defend his father against their slanders, and proceeds to praise his father's life and accomplishments. In 16.35, he mentions his father's liturgies but says that although greater than those of most men, they were insignificant in comparison to his father's many other great deeds. If the prosecution really did spend much of its time maligning his father, then this defense of his life, including the brief mention of his liturgies, would certainly be considered relevant to the case. Even if they did not malign his father, however, this mention of his liturgies at the end of the speech would be a reasonable ancillary point after the main issues had been addressed.

Lys. 18.7, 21: In this case, the sons of Nicias's brother Eucrates are defending themselves against some sort of attempt to take away part or all of their inheritance. We do not know the precise charge, but the arguments addressing it were presumably made in the first part of the speech, which is missing, though we cannot be absolutely certain of this. In the fragment of the speech that remains, the speaker begins (18.1),

> Therefore, men of the jury, you must consider what sort of citizens (*hoioi politai*) we are and from what sort of family, as we ask you to pity us and to give us justice (*ta dikaia*) for the injustices we have suffered. For we are contending not only for our property (*ousia*) but also for our civic status (*politeia*), whether we will have a place in the city under the democracy. First, therefore, you should recall our uncle Nicias.

Nicias's family was aristocratic and highly distinguished. Nicias himself was the commander of the expedition to Sicily in 415–413 and died during it, but many members of his family probably supported or worked with the Thirty in 404–403, and it is very likely that the charge of complicity with the Thirty was implicitly or explicitly part of the accusation in this case. The defendants thus emphasize the services that they and their whole family provided to the city when it was a democracy in order to refute, or at least diminish, the charge of complicity with the Thirty. In this connection, the speaker mentions the liturgies and special levies contributed by their family (18.7) and later (18.21) mentions that he and his brother and their cousin are all currently serving as trierarchs and have been contributing to special levies (*eisphorai*). As in the preceding example (Isoc. 16.35), the discussions of public service in this speech are very likely relevant to the main issues in the case, even if they are only raised at the end of the speech after other arguments have also addressed the issues.

To sum up, these thirteen examples of defendants citing their public service include five cases where public service is certainly relevant to the main issue in the case, one case in which it is relevant to a related issue, and seven cases in which public service is only discussed at the end of the speech. In most of the latter cases, we are certain that the main issue was addressed earlier with other arguments, and when we are not certain about earlier arguments (because the beginning of the speech is lost), it seems very likely that the main issues were addressed earlier. And many of these ancillary discussions of public service are in fact relevant to either the stated issues or to the underlying issues in the case. None of these examples provides support for the claim made in some of the passages cited above (Dem. 25.76 or Lys. 30.1), that some litigants who are clearly guilty might be acquitted simply because of their public service.

Prosecutors also speak about their public service, though not so often as defendants do. I will discuss ten additional examples.[22] In the first three,

22. Johnstone (1999:166n4) lists eleven examples of prosecutors citing their public service, but I am excluding one from an inheritance case (Is. 6.60–61), which I have already discussed. There are many more prosecution speeches than defense speeches in our corpus, and Johnstone calculates that only 15 percent of the former mention pub-

performance of a specific liturgy is a central issue in the case, and in two of these the prosecutor's own performance of liturgies is introduced as a contrast to the defendant's misconduct, making it somewhat relevant to the main issue.

Dem. 50 passim: Apollodorus, who had funded a trierarchy for the past year, is suing Polycles, who has been designated trierarch for the current year but has not yet relieved Apollodorus during the first four months of the year, forcing Apollodorus to continue paying the costs of the trierarchy. Thus throughout the speech he describes all the expenses he incurred in this period and other difficulties he faced because of Polycles' dereliction of duty. Discussion of the liturgy in this case seems unavoidable.

Dem. 47.23, 54: As trierarch for the coming year, the plaintiff in this case was supposed to receive the ship's equipment from the previous trierarch, who had not delivered it. The speaker says very little about any other liturgies he has performed, but in the course of suing to recover the ship's equipment, he mentions (47.23) that he has often served as trierarch in the past. Later he recalls how the defendants allegedly came to his house and seized a little furniture. He says (47.54) that they expected to find much more, but because of the liturgies and special levies he had paid for, most of his furniture has been sold or pawned. All in all there is less mention of his service than we might have expected.

Dem. 21.151–174: The case concerns Meidias's conduct during a choral production funded by Demosthenes, but most of the speech concerns Meidias's other wrongs, which are primarily connected to this or another liturgy. Thus, these other wrongs of Meidias are as relevant as any arguments in the speech, and the same can be said for Demosthenes' own liturgies, which he introduces as a contrast to Meidias's liturgies.[23]

In four other cases, the prosecutor's or his family's public service is alluded to briefly in connection with a point that is arguably relevant to the case.

Dem. 19.230: In the course of contrasting his own conduct on the embassy that is the subject of the speech with that of the defendant Aeschi-

---

lic service vs. 52 percent of the latter. Excluding inheritance speeches would alter these percentages a little, but the general conclusion would still hold. Johnstone also notes (without listing them) that twelve prosecutors mention the defendant's public service, whereas only one defendant mentions the prosecutor's public service.

23. If the complaint in Dem. 21 only mentioned Meidias's alleged assault, then almost everything in the speech is irrelevant, since the assault itself is almost nowhere directly discussed. But the complaint probably also mentioned something about mistreating Demosthenes' *chorēgia* or Demosthenes himself in his role as *chorēgos*.

nes, Demosthenes claims that one man (i.e., himself), "although he was still paying for a chorus and a trierarchy, thought that he ought also to spend money voluntarily to ransom captives so that no citizen should suffer because he lacked resources."

Dem. 23.5: In the preamble, the prosecutor explains that he is unaccustomed to speaking in court, but although he does not normally speak out, he thought it would be dishonorable to be silent when he saw people doing a public disservice (*pragm' alysiteles tēi polei*), "and I earlier spoke out and accused people who were doing you wrong (*adikein hymas*) when I was sailing to the Hellespont as trierarch."[24]

Dem. 45.78, 85: Apollodorus, the plaintiff, anticipating that his opponent will criticize him because he is poor (having wasted his inheritance), defends the modest amount he has spent on public service (45.78). Later (45.85) he asks the jury not to penalize him because of his poverty and adds that his father gave the city a thousand shields and funded five trierarchies.

Lys. 12.20: After recounting how in addition to killing his brother, the Thirty had confiscated all of his and his family's considerable property, Lysias adds (12.20), "We did not deserve such treatment by the city, in view of all the choral productions we had funded, all the special levies we had contributed, and we had lived moderately and done everything asked of us."

In the three remaining prosecution speeches, public service has no direct relevance to the case but is mentioned briefly at the very end of the speech.

Dem. 54.44: At the end of his speech, Ariston says (54.44), "I would have much to say about how I and my father while he was alive have served you, funding trierarchies, serving in the army, and doing what was asked of us, and how the defendant had done none of these things. But there is not enough water [i.e., time] and the present discussion (*logos*) doesn't concern these things."

Dem. 58.66–68: At the end of a speech accusing Theocrines of being in debt to the city for several different matters, the speaker contrasts Theocrines' wickedness with the great deeds of his own grandfather and especially his grandfather's uncle. "For his sake, even if I happened to be like Theocrines, it would be reasonable for you to save me, as you certainly should do since I am better than he is and my pleading has been just" (58.68).

Isoc. 17.57–58: At the end of the speech, the speaker mentions that his father and Satyrus, king of Bosporus (where the speaker lives), always let Athenians buy grain even during severe shortages and always treated Athe-

24. Men who funded a trierarchy often sailed with the ship whose expenses they were paying.

nians fairly. "I ask you, therefore, on my behalf and on theirs, to vote in accordance with justice (*ta dikaia*) and not consider Pasion's false words more trustworthy than my (true) words" (17.58).

These passages reveal that except in cases where public service is directly relevant to the case, prosecutors, like defendants, mention their own public service only briefly, if at all. In some cases, they connect their public service to some point that is relevant to the case; in others, they mention it only briefly at the very end of the speech. Even when it is directly relevant to the accusation in the case, public service in itself is never mentioned by either the prosecution or the defense as the primary reason for conviction or acquittal.

All these (usually brief) references to the speaker's or his family's (or his opponent's) liturgies in cases in which it is not clearly relevant to the case suggest that these litigants wanted the court to know that they were good people, and thus that they would not have done whatever wrongs they were alleged to have done. Litigants today similarly try to present themselves as good people, but Athenian litigants had more freedom to mention specific evidence for their good character, whereas litigants today often have to do so indirectly.[25] In Athens, litigants could introduce evidence directly to show that they were good family men, or helped their friends, or served the city. And they could then argue explicitly that having done so many good things, they are not likely to have done the wrong they are accused of doing, as in the following two cases. As in the case of liturgies, however, these other good deeds are never presented as in themselves a sufficient reason for acquittal.

Dem. 34.38–40: In connection with a maritime loan, the plaintiff alleges that he and his partner are being robbed. "We, who have continually brought grain to your market" (34.38). He adds that they gave the city a talent, imported much grain at a below-market price, and gave another talent (34.39). "Based on this evidence, it is not likely that when we have given so much money in order to have a good reputation, we should bring a malicious prosecution against Phormio and throw away the reputation we acquired (34.40). He then repeats the facts of the case as he has presented them earlier.

Hyp. 1, *Lyc.* 14–18: After making his defense against a charge of adultery, at the end of his speech, Lycophron argues that the righteous conduct and public service of his entire life are the best evidence that the charge against

25. There are many ways today in which a veteran, for example, can make it known that he or she served in some combat zone, even if such service has no direct relevance to the charges in the case.

him is false.[26] He has never been involved in a lawsuit, he was a cavalry commander, he was crowned for bravery, and so on. "All this should be evidence for you that the charges against me in this trial are false" (1.18).

Two other passages openly acknowledge that a good life that includes public service can help a person who is later involved in litigation.

Lys. 25.13: "It was for this reason that I spent more than the city required of me, in order that you might have a higher opinion of me and that if some misfortune befell me, I might better defend myself in any future litigation."

Lys., frag. 106 Carey: "This is why I risked my life so often on your behalf and willingly spent so much of my family property for you, so as to do my part in helping the city prosper and if I ever was unjustly accused and stood trial, I could confidently give an account of what I had done."

These two passages allude vaguely to future cases, but the speakers probably have in mind cases in which public service is the main issue in the case, such as *dokimasia* cases and others. Overtly political cases would also include cases concerning the performance of a liturgy, *eisangelia* cases in which a person is accused of subverting the democracy, and *graphai paranomōn* cases concerning honorary decrees in which a person's public service is at issue, such as the case On the Crown (cf. the first five passages discussed above).

From this overview of discussions of public service in the forensic speeches,[27] we may conclude that except in cases that are overtly political, in which public service is relevant to the main issue, public service is generally mentioned only briefly, sometimes in connection with a subordinate argument that is relevant to the case, but most often at the end of the speech as evidence for the litigant's good character.[28] In such cases, information about public service would become part of the background and context of the case, just like character was. Litigants also occasionally presented their arguments about public service as arguments about justice, arguing that it was only just that a person's public service be rewarded by some consideration in court. Overall, therefore, public service is mentioned often enough that it must have been a significant consideration, but there is no indication that any litigant thought that mentioning his own public service would be

26. Because we have only a fragment from the end of Lycophron's speech, we do not know all that he said about the charge itself. The fragment ends with section 20, in which he calls on a co-pleader to speak on his behalf.

27. I believe I have included all substantial discussions of public service, but I may have overlooked some briefer mentions of it.

28. See Lanni 2006:63, where discussions of a litigant's service to the city are included in the section on extra-legal arguments "concerning the character of the litigants" (59–64).

the most significant consideration in his case, nor does any defendant do what some of the speakers claim, namely, emphasize his public service as the sole argument for his acquittal.

Another explanation some scholars have given for the presence of arguments about public service in the forensic speeches is that public service was only taken into account during the punishment phase of a trial, where it properly belongs and where it can legitimately be introduced in our own legal system.[29] The evidence does not support this claim. A punishment phase occurred mostly in public cases after a guilty verdict had been rendered, at which point the two sides each proposed a penalty and the jury had to choose between them. Since no actual speech survives from the penalty phase of a trial, we cannot know what role public service normally played.[30] But even if public service was introduced in many or all of the speeches that were delivered during the punishment phase of a trial, we still need to account for the many discussions of public service during the main pleadings, which are never presented as a reason for a lighter or heavier sentence. Moreover, in many trials, there was no separate punishment phase, so a litigant's entire pleading, including his public service, would be directed at winning a favorable verdict. And in inheritance cases, of course, there would be no question of punishment, so the only possible reason to introduce public service would be to influence the award of the estate.

In the Athenian democratic legal system, then, considerations of public service could be raised in any case, whether or not that service was relevant to the specific charge in the case. Litigants seem to have felt, however, that if their public service was not relevant to the issues in the case, then it should be mentioned only briefly, and preferably near or at the end of the speech.

Considerations of civic benefit play a far smaller role in litigation today. Although a well-functioning legal system is generally thought to benefit society, and a prosecutor may argue for a conviction in part because its deterrent effect will benefit society as a whole, litigants today would never argue (though they might suggest) that it is only fair that the court should rule in their favor because of their previous public service or that a verdict in their favor would benefit the city, state, or country more than would a verdict against them.[31] Modern legal systems, especially in the United States,

---

29. For example, Harris 2013c:131–136.

30. Plato's *Apology* contains Socrates' speech from the penalty phase of his trial (35e–38b), part of which is devoted to Socrates' idiosyncratic assessment of his service to the city (36b–37a), but we do not know how closely this resembles Socrates' actual speech or how typical Socrates' speech was of assessment speeches in general.

31. Even if nothing is said explicitly about public service, public servants like police officers may be more likely to receive the benefit of the doubt in court today.

place a high value on the protection of rights—both of individuals and of others—and this concern will generally override any other considerations, especially considerations of public benefit. To cite just one well-known example, in 2010 in the "Citizens United" case, the US Supreme Court struck down laws that prevented corporations, unions, and political action committees (PACs) from making independent expenditures and election communications on the grounds that such restrictions violated these entities' right of free speech. The court did not consider whether or not the community at large benefited from this ruling (and most people feel it did not).[32]

Whether or not the Greeks had any notion of individual rights is debated,[33] but it is clear that they more commonly thought in terms of a person's duties and obligations, rather than his rights. From earliest times, the Greeks took for granted certain basic rules concerning the treatment of people in general or of certain groups of people: the dead required burial, guests and suppliants were to be treated in certain ways, and so forth. But such rules were not generally expressed in terms of these people's rights but in terms of the obligations others have to treat these people in certain ways. Thus, the Greeks would view the proper treatment of guests by hosts a matter of the host's obligation not the guest's rights. And the same is true in legal matters: for example, the law on mistreatment of parents required children to care for their elderly parents; it did not say that parents have the right to be cared for by their children.

In perhaps the most famous example from Greek literature, Antigone insists on burying her brother, not because "the unwritten and unerring ordinances of the gods"[34] give her the right to bury him (or give Polyneices the right to be buried), but because these unwritten laws oblige her to do so. Athenian litigants speak similarly of obligations. In Lysias 1, for example, although Euphiletus cites a law that, in our view, would give him the right to kill a man in bed with his wife, he does not argue that this is his right but rather that it is his duty to do what the law commands. Or take the opening of Demosthenes' speech On the Crown (Dem. 18.1–2), where he appeals to the jurors to give him a fair hearing, and more specifically to allow

---

32. See Wallace 2006a:419–420 for the contrast between the "paramount importance of protecting individual liberties against public interference" in the United States today (which can be explained, at least in part, by the country's origin in a struggle against monarchic power) and the Athenian view of "the prior importance of the community over any individual," which can be traced to the emergence of law "as a means to protect the community against powerful or dangerous individuals."

33. See Miller 2009, who notes that the Greeks had no single word corresponding to "right" (in the sense of an individual's "right"). Cf. Wallace (2009a:171): "The Greeks called these not rights but 'powers,' *exousiai*."

34. Sophocles, *Antigone* 454–455: ἄγραπτα κἀσφαλῆ θεῶν νόμιμα.

him (as they would allow any litigant) to present his case in whatever way he thinks best, and not as his opponent wishes him to present it. A litigant today would be likely to speak of his right to a fair hearing or his right to present his case in whatever way he wishes. Demosthenes, however, appeals to the jurors' oath, in which they swear to listen to both sides equally, and he explains this as meaning that they have an obligation not to prejudge the case and to allow him to arrange his defense as he chooses. Thus he does not speak of his situation as involving his right to speak as he chooses; instead, it is the jurors' duty to let him speak as he wishes.

One can argue, of course, that the difference is insignificant because a duty implies a correlative right (e.g., my duty to pay you implies your right to be paid and vice versa),[35] but the Greeks generally, and Athenian litigants specifically, almost always speak of duties rather than rights, and even if duties and rights are two sides of the same coin, it makes a difference which side one looks at. The Athenians' focus on people's obligations directed their attention to the needs of the community and to asking how its members could help satisfy those needs. By contrast, the modern focus on people's rights directs our attention to the claims of individuals and to asking how the community can avoid restricting those claims. For us today, individual rights generally outweigh the community's interest; for the Athenians, it was the other way around. Thus, whereas we would rather see many guilty defendants acquitted rather than one innocent person wrongly convicted, the Athenians took a more nuanced view, taking into account the benefit to the city but not treating it as a sufficient reason to acquit a guilty defendant or convict an innocent one.

Because the Athenians expressly wished to have a democratic legal system, it may not be surprising that they created a system that had public benefit as one of its goals. Not only did the *dēmos* create the system, but the *dēmos* managed it and constantly worked to ensure that it was effective. The famous words of Demosthenes from the end of his speech against Meidias[36] make the point that the laws and the *dēmos* are inextricably linked in a common mission: to ensure the rule of law in the city. The natural conclusion deriving from this joint endeavor was that the *dēmos* would be the beneficiary if the system worked properly.

In sum, public benefit, like justice, was a fundamental objective of the Athenian legal system as a whole as well as of the individual laws enacted by the *dēmos* and the verdicts delivered by juries representative of the *dēmos*.

---

35. The classic analysis of legal rights and their correlative legal duties is Hohfeld 1919; see esp. 36–38.

36. Dem. 21.224, cited above at note 4.

Justice and public benefit were seen as fully compatible with one another, and both were compatible with the rule of law, which I will examine in chapter 8. On the other hand, public benefit did not have the same status in Athenian law as justice did. Justice was mentioned in the jurors' oath as a specific obligation (to "vote according to the most just opinion"), and a litigant could base his case on justice, as Epicrates, for example, does in Hyperides 3 *Against Athenogenes*.[37] Public benefit, by contrast, unless directly relevant to the main issue in the case, was always a supplemental argument and in most cases was only mentioned briefly, often at the end of the litigant's speech. Nonetheless, public benefit was unquestionably valued, and no juror would have wanted to render a verdict that would clearly result in harm to the polis.

---

37. See chapter 6 at note 28.

CHAPTER 8

THE RULE OF LAW

In an influential study of fifth-century Athenian democracy, Martin Ostwald (1986) argued that the reforms enacted at the end of that century resulted in a transition "from popular sovereignty to the sovereignty of law." Not everyone has accepted this conclusion, and scholars disagree about whether sovereignty lay with the laws or the *dēmos*. The difficulty in determining the relative authority of these two forces arises in the first place from the fact that the *dēmos* enacts the laws, but it has also prescribed the juror's oath, requiring that the *dēmos*, in its incarnation as a jury, be ruled by those laws. The premise of this book is that the Athenians created a democratic legal system, that is, one in which the *dēmos* is sovereign, but in this chapter I hope to show that the laws were also sovereign, and that Athens observed "the rule of law," though not in exactly the same way we do.[1]

If we ask, did the Athenians believe in the rule of law, the simple answer is clearly yes. Beginning early in their history they enacted a large number of written laws; they displayed these laws prominently in public where they were available for all to see; they created courts to enforce these laws; they subjected everyone in the city to these laws, including the highest officials and leading public figures; and they required all jurors to swear an oath that they would judge according to these laws. Moreover, litigants in court and others repeatedly praise the laws, urge adherence and obedience to the laws, urge the jury to vote in accordance with the laws, and explain the importance of the laws for Athenian democracy and the Athenian way of life in statements that go well beyond the general praise of the laws that one might expect in any legal system from litigants addressing a court. Thus, recent

1. Wohl (2010:32–34) also argues for the rule of law and of the *dēmos*, though by rather different means than I do. "Juridical discourse thus finds its mandate, I suggest, not in 'popular sovereignty' nor in the 'rule of law' alone, but in its own ability to unite the two. . . . Only through this [forensic] process is the abstract 'rule of law' actualized in the form of a verdict and 'popular sovereignty' converted into *eunomia*" (2010:34).

scholars have generally agreed that the Athenians were committed to, and generally adhered to, the rule of law, although they have understood this commitment in different ways.[2]

The real questions we need to ask, then, are what did the rule of law mean to the Athenians, how did they observe the rule of law in practice, and how did their understanding and observance of the rule of law fit with their insistence on popular control of the legal process? To answer these questions we must first make clear what we mean when we say that a community adheres to the rule of law, which is a complex concept that has been subject to many different analyses. I will begin with a rather simple definition of my own and will then supplement this with the clear and straightforward account in Bingham 2010.[3]

Before I begin, however, it should be noted that the Athenians' commitment to the rule of law was closely connected to their commitment to democracy and their democratic city.[4] Aeschines expresses this connection clearly in a passage I quoted more fully at the beginning of chapter 5 (Aes. 1.4–6):

> There are three kinds of constitution in the whole world, dictatorship (*tyrannis*), oligarchy and democracy; dictatorships and oligarchies are governed by the temperament of those in power, but democratic cities are governed by the established laws. . . . In a democracy the persons of citizens and the constitution are protected by the laws. . . . Your real strength is when you are ruled by law and are not subverted by men who break them. . . . We should obey the laws in existence and punish those who disobey, if the city is to flourish.

Any definition of the rule of law that will be applicable to Athenian law must recognize this democratic context in which it was observed.

---

2. See, for example, Cohen 2005a; Harris 2013c; Gowder 2014; Kapparis 2018:49–54. Lanni (2006:4), however, argues that the Athenian legal system "favored equity and discretion over the strict application of generalized rules, but managed to do so in a way that did not destroy predictability and legal certainty in the parts of the system where it was most needed," that is, in the homicide and maritime courts; and Wallace (2006:430) argues that "in Athens' courtrooms as elsewhere, the welfare of the community was paramount."

3. Some different perspectives on the rule of law are provided by Simpson (1995:227–258), who discusses the history of the rule of law in the nineteenth century, and MacCormick (2005), who analyzes the interaction of rhetoric and the rule of law.

4. Gowder (2014) has an interesting analysis, in which he connects the rule of law in Athens with democracy by arguing that the rule of law implies and depends on equity, and that the rule of law is thus consistent with the democratic power of the masses.

Some years ago, I proposed that the rule of law consisted of three main principles: (1) "the orderly and peaceful regulation of society according to a set of authoritative rules as opposed to disorder and violence"—that is, law and order (*eu-nomia*) as opposed to lawlessness (*a-nomia*); (2) "the principle that no man is above the law"—more specifically, that the wealthy and those in power are subject to the law just like everyone else; and (3) "strict adherence to the requirements of the law and the exclusion of extraneous 'non-legal' considerations, especially political considerations," from legal decision-making.[5] I concluded, rather optimistically in view of the insufficiency of the evidence, that all three principles seem to have been present in the Cretan city of Gortyn, which was the object of my study at the time.

I did not at the time discuss the rule of law in Athens, but the principle that most certainly applies to Athenian law is the second. Not only was every Athenian subject to the law, but officials and prominent citizens were regularly subject to prosecution and often suffered severe penalties, including exile and even death, not only for public crimes, such as treason or embezzlement of public funds, but also for failure to carry out their public duties satisfactorily, which could include such failures as suffering defeat in battle. There can be no doubt that in Athens everyone was subject to the law.

The Athenians also largely fulfilled the first principle, the orderly and peaceful regulation of society according to a set of authoritative rules. To be sure, they did not eliminate violence and crime entirely, but in general, Athenian society was peaceful, people could apparently walk the streets in safety almost never carrying weapons, and people generally resolved their disagreements through peaceful means, including using the courts.[6] And the Athenians enacted a set of authoritative laws to which they regularly expressed their adherence, not only in repeated statements in the orators and elsewhere[7] but also in the oath that every potential Athenian juror swore at the beginning of each year.

The most problematic of my three principles for Athenian law is the third, and in particular the exclusion of political considerations from legal decision making.[8] As the discussion in chapter 7 showed, political consider-

5. Gagarin 2004:173.

6. Not all scholars would accept this characterization of daily life in Athens, but in my view, Herman (1994 and more fully in 2006) makes a stronger case for it than do Cohen (1995) and others who believe that Athens was a continually feuding society.

7. For a sample of such statements, see, for example, Cohen 1995:52–55.

8. The requirement that political considerations should be excluded from legal decisions is not one of Bingham's eight principles of the rule of law (for which, see below). Bingham only refers to political factors in his principle of equality before the law (3), which implies that political figures should be subject to the same laws as everyone else, and the exercise of power (4), which implies that public figures should generally stay

ations in the form of a person's public service were not necessarily excluded from legal decision making. Some cases concerned political issues directly, and even in cases that were not overtly political, juries may sometimes have considered the political consequences of a verdict. But no litigant in a non-political case ever argues that his public service alone is sufficient to decide a case, and there is no good evidence that political considerations were ever the decisive factor in nonpolitical cases. I would conclude that political considerations may have influenced the outcome of some cases, though I would also note that political considerations can be an underlying factor in some cases in any legal system.[9] I would tentatively conclude, then, that although public interest was more acceptable as a consideration in litigation than it is today, the Athenians generally observed the rule of law in regard to the three principles set forth above.

My three principles are not exhaustive, however, and so I turn now to Bingham's account, beginning with his definition of the rule of law.[10] "The core of the existing principle is, I suggest, that all persons and authorities within the state, whether public or private, should be bound by and entitled to the benefit of laws publicly made, taking effect (generally) in the future and publicly administered in the courts."[11] For Bingham, then, the rule of law requires a public system of laws and adjudication procedures to which everyone, including all authorities, is subject. As I previously noted, when

---

away from legal decision making. Bingham also raises political considerations in his discussion of a fair trial (2010:93–96) but only as they affect judges, noting that judges in the United Kingdom are largely independent of politics, whereas those in the United States in particular are often political figures.

9. Political considerations may have been an important underlying factor is cases such as the trial of Socrates or Antiphon 5, but it is difficult to assess the degree to which political considerations may have influenced the verdict in these cases.

10. Lists of principles that make up the rule of law are also proposed by Harris (2013c:5–10) and Cohen (1995:56–57). Harris's list is explicitly drawn from Bingham's; Cohen's list, on the other hand, reflects principles that he claims are affirmed by the Athenian forensic orators. The only items in these lists that are not in Bingham are two of those on Cohen's list: no citizen should be tried twice for the same offense, and statutes should not contradict other provisions. Both of these were affirmed in Athenian law and need no discussion. Cohen cautions, however, that in practice the Athenian observance of the rule of law may not have been identical to our own, and he goes on to argue (1995:192) that the Athenians' view of their democratic legal system meant that the interests of the *dēmos* were a legitimate feature of the rule of law in Athens ("the radical democratic notion of the rule of law meant that in principle no individuals, whether magistrates or ordinary citizens, were above the law. It also meant, however, that the rule of law was inextricably connected to the court's perception of the interests of the *demos*").

11. Bingham 2010:8.

so defined, it becomes impossible to deny that the Athenians adhered to the rule of law.

Bingham proceeds to expand his definition by breaking down the rule of law into eight specific principles. Slightly abbreviated, these are as follows:[12]

1. Accessibility. "The law must be accessible and so far as possible intelligible, clear and predictable."

2. Law not Discretion. "Questions of legal right and liability should ordinarily be resolved by application of the law and not the exercise of discretion."

3. Equality Before the Law. "The laws of the land should apply equally to all, save to the extent that objective differences justify differentiation."

4. The Exercise of Power. "Ministers and public officers at all levels must exercise the powers conferred on them in good faith, fairly, for the purpose for which the powers were conferred, without exceeding the limits of such powers and not unreasonably."

5. Human Rights. "The law must afford adequate protection of fundamental human rights." Bingham enumerates these rights according to the Articles of the European Convention on Human Rights and the UK's Human Rights Act of 1998: (Article 2) "The right to life"; (Article 3) "The prohibition of torture"; (Article 4) "Prohibition of slavery and forced labor"; (Article 5) "Right to liberty and security"; (Article 6) "Right to a fair trial"; (Article 7) "No punishment without law"; (Article 8) "Right to respect for private and family life"; (Article 9) "Freedom of thought, conscience and religion"; (Article 10) "Freedom of expression"; (Article 11) "Freedom of assembly and association"; (Article 12) "Right to marry"; (Article 14) These rights shall be secured without discrimination on any grounds (sex, race, religion, etc.).

6. Dispute Resolution. "Means must be provided for resolving, without prohibitive cost or inordinate delay, bona fide civil disputes which the parties themselves are unable to resolve."

7. A Fair Trial. "Adjudicative procedures provided by the state should be fair."

8. The Rule of Law in the International Legal Order. "The rule of law requires compliance by the state with its obligations in international law as in national law."

---

12. Ibid.:37–129.

My own brief assessment of Athenian law in terms of these eight principles would come to the following conclusions:

1. Valid with regard to being accessible, intelligible, and clear, but some question its predictability (see below).

2. Valid, though the separation of law and discretion in legal judgments is not as simple as Bingham seems to imply and may not be possible at all.

3. Valid, if, for example, being a slave or a woman is an objective difference, as it was for the Athenians.

4. Valid. Since Athenian officials had very little individual power, they would be far less tempted to exercise it unreasonably than officials today.

5. Partly valid. Because, as noted at the end of chapter 7, the Athenians were generally focused on obligations and had very little concept of "rights," they would not have expressed a commitment to honor human rights in these terms; in practice, however, many of the specific points enumerated as rights were protected in the Athenian legal system, though they would have been viewed rather differently than they are today. These include (5.2) right to life; (5.3) prohibition of torture for citizens; (5.5) right to liberty and security, though the Athenians were more concerned with community liberty than individual liberty; (5.6) right to a fair trial; (5.7) no punishment without law; (5.8) right to respect for private and family life; (5.9) freedom of thought, conscience and religion, as long as these did not threaten to harm the community;[13] (5.10) freedom of expression, also as long as these did not threaten to harm the community; (5.11) freedom of assembly and association.

6. Valid, with far less cost and delay than today.

7. Valid, though fairness is very difficult to assess (see further below).

8. Probably not applicable, as there were no clear rules of international law, though some matters, such as conduct in war, were subject to a few customary rules or principles.

Bingham's eight principles seem clear and straightforward, but qualifications like "so far as possible" (1) indicate that, in some cases at least, adherence is a matter of degree, or that there can be exceptions to the rule; and "ordinarily" (2) implies that in some cases, questions of law should be resolved by the exercise of discretion not the application of law. Moreover, phrases like "objective differences" (3) have been understood differently in

13. See Wallace 1994.

different times and places.[14] Such considerations indicate, and most scholars would agree, that the rule of law is an ideal that is never fully achievable in practice. Thus, we must judge the Athenians in terms of their degree of adherence to the rule of law, not whether they observed it perfectly. And since Bingham's principles are clearly tailored to the practices of contemporary legal systems, we will undoubtedly have to make adjustments to apply them to classical Athens.

Bingham's principles include some additional concerns that need to be discussed to complete the picture drawn from my three simple principles. The first of these is predictability (Bingham's principle 1). The principle that the law should be predictable implies that legal decisions should also be consistent. In a recent article, Lanni argues that "Athens did not have a 'rule of law' in the sense that the courts did not enforce the law in a predictable or consistent manner."[15] She adds, "Athenian jurors did not feel constrained to apply strictly the statute under which the case was brought," citing in support "Aristotle's characterization of laws as a form of evidence, similar to contracts and witness testimony, rather than a decisive guide to a verdict."[16] Lanni continues to make her case for the unpredictability and inconsistency of the Athenian enforcement of the law in her 2016 book, where she argues, "The vagueness of Athenian statutes, absence of binding precedents, and broad notion of relevance meant that while Athenian courts enforced general norms of fairness and good citizenship, they did not reliably and predictably enforce the legal norms expressed in statutes."[17]

In response, I should note that Aristotle's characterization of laws as evidence, which is often cited in discussions of the role of laws in Athenian litigation,[18] concerns only the manner in which litigants can introduce the texts of laws in court; it has no bearing on the importance of the laws in litigation or on the obligations of the jurors, who had sworn an oath to judge "according to the laws and decrees of the Athenian *dēmos*." These certainly included the statute under which the case was brought, together with any

14. Race, for example, was judged by some in the United States to be an objective difference well into the twentieth century.

15. Lanni 2013:164. She continues, "The Athenian courts nevertheless played a vital role in maintaining social and political order." Predictability and consistency are also among Forsdyke's elements of the rule of law: "The principle that laws should be clear in meaning, accessible, and their application consistent and predictable" (2018:187). See also Harris (2013c:246–273 [an earlier version of which is Harris 2007a]), who is mostly concerned with precedent (see below).

16. Lanni 2013:166; For Aristotle on laws, see *Rhetoric* 1.15, 1375a24–b26.

17. Lanni 2016:48.

18. See, for example, Yunis 2005:200.

other relevant laws. The manner in which Athenian litigants introduced laws in court may have been unusual, but the jurors would have known that these documents were statutes (and not, for example, witness depositions), and would have been obliged, in keeping with the oath they had sworn, to vote in accordance with those statutes.

Predictability essentially means that the verdict in all cases with the same set of facts will be the same. In any system, however, whenever a case goes to trial, the outcome cannot be entirely predictable, because if it were, then there would be no need to go to trial. No two cases are absolutely identical, and the outcome of any trial is uncertain until the verdict is rendered. Thus, predictability is always a matter of degree, and certain differences between the Athenian system and our own make the predictability of the two systems difficult to compare.

Features of our own legal system that help promote consistency and predictability are the existence of fixed laws with precisely defined offenses; laws specifying fixed, minimum, or maximum sentences; and well-trained and knowledgeable attorneys for the prosecution and defense. This makes the outcome for some common offenses like driving under the influence (DUI) of alcohol or drugs fairly predictable, at least for cases with the same relevant facts, such as a first offender with a certain level of alcohol in the blood. Even in cases in which all these conditions are met, however, a judge may exercise discretion if some small difference is thought to be relevant. Juries, moreover, are probably even less predictable than judges.[19] Prosecutors, too, exercise discretion in deciding which cases to bring to trial and which specific charges to include, and this can affect the consistency and certainty of law enforcement. Some other sorts of offenses, moreover, are much less predictable in our system, even when the facts are essentially the same. Sexual assault cases, for example, often depend on intangible factors, such as the physical appearance of accuser and accused. In some places, such cases are predictable only because they are almost never prosecuted.[20] In other words, there is never absolute certainly, and when two experienced attorneys take a case to trial, this in itself indicates that the two have different expectations about the outcome.

19. The greater unpredictability of juries than of judges is an intuitive feeling shared by many, though I know of no evidence to support it. As Simpson (1995:228) notes in writing about the rule of law in the nineteenth century, the jury has always been a problematic factor for rule of law theories.

20. There is currently (2019) a lawsuit in Austin, Texas (and similar suits in other cities), brought by women seeking to force the local prosecutor's office to prosecute more rape cases.

The difficulty with comparing the Athenian system to our own results in part from the leeway given to plaintiffs in formulating a specific accusation under the broad, relatively unspecific categories of offenses, together with the leeway they have in many situations in choosing which general category to bring suit under. This makes it less likely that any two cases will present the same set of facts. The outcome of Athenian trials may also have been less consistent and predictable than in a system like our own, because all cases were decided by large juries, none by a professional judge, and because the jurors' oath explicitly recognized that there would be cases where jurors had to exercise discretion (their "most just understanding") and not simply rule according to the law. Thus, although a juror might hear many cases brought by the same general procedure, he would be unlikely to hear two cases in which the detailed and often quite extensive accusations were the same or even fairly similar.

Another factor that may have rendered Athenian verdicts less predictable than those today was the absence of a strict sense of precedent. Strictly speaking, precedent today applies to interpretation of the law and is primarily important in appeals, in which a written explanation of the ruling (the *ratio decidendi*) is given, but precedents are also cited in the initial trial stage. Precedent in a strict sense did not exist in Athens, in part because the large number of jurors would have made it impossible to record a *ratio decidendi*, but a looser sense of precedent is evident in a number of cases. These arguments for precedent take two forms, past and future.

Past precedents summarize the issue in a previous case, state the verdict, sometimes explain the reasons for the verdict, and then urge the jurors to vote in a way consistent with this earlier case. Often a prosecutor will use an *a fortiori* argument, claiming that the defendant in the present case has committed a far worse crime than a defendant in a previous case who was convicted and punished, and that the jury is therefore obliged to punish the current defendant. But even if some of the cases that are cited as precedents are fairly recent, this does not necessarily make the speaker's account reliable. Speakers often present the facts as if they were well known, but they construe these facts in such a way as to be most supportive of their own case. And when they add explanations of the jurors' reasoning or of their feelings in the past case, these are simply fabricated.

Consider the precedent of Euaion and Boiotus, cited by Demosthenes in his prosecution of Meidias (Dem. 21.71–77). "Many people know," Demosthenes begins, employing a common rhetorical strategy to make those in the audience who do not know the case (who may constitute the vast majority) think that they ought to know it and that Demosthenes' account must be accurate because everyone else knows the facts. Demosthenes then reports that Euaion killed Boiotus at a banquet because he received one blow. He then explains that Euaion was provoked not so much by the blow but because of the insolence (*hybris*) with which he was struck (21.71–72). Then, after comparing his own situation with Euaion's (21.73–74), he claims that many jurors were sympathetic to Euaion, "for I hear that he was convicted by only one vote. . . . Let us assume then that it was like this, that those who voted for conviction did so not because he defended himself but because he defended himself in such a way that he killed, whereas those who voted for acquittal granted him even this excessive retaliation because of the *hybris* inflicted on his person" (Dem. 21.75). It is clear from this account that although Euaion may have killed Boiotus at a banquet, everything else Demosthenes reports is very likely his own fabrication. We have no idea whether it bears any resemblance to what actually happened. The account is skillfully constructed, however, and some in the audience may have accepted it as accurate.

Future precedents, which are more common, follow a different strategy. In these, the speaker urges the jurors to consider the effect of their verdict in the present case on similar cases in the future. The common form of argument is that because the defendant is clearly guilty, if he is acquitted, people will not hesitate to commit the same crime in the future, knowing that they will not be punished; on the other hand, if the defendant is convicted, this will deter others from committing the same crime in the future.[21]

Harris proposes several other ways in which precedent worked in Athenian courts, noting in particular the citation of documents.[22] He concludes, "This examination of arguments based on precedents has shown that litigants believed that the courts should be dedicated to achieving consistency in their application of the laws."[23] This may be true, but it does not help us assess the degree to which the courts actually did achieve consistency. In Athens, past and future precedents were both subject to considerable rhetorical manipulation for the strategic purpose of supporting the speaker's case. But even if loose precedents did produce an expectation of consistency, this sort of citation of precedent by litigants could not have produced the same degree of consistency among outcomes that a strict rule of precedent we rely on today is able to achieve.

In sum, because we do not know the outcome of most Athenian trials, it is impossible to assess the consistency of verdicts with any certainty. The

---

21. Rubinstein (2007:362n5) lists forty-six such arguments in the forensic speeches. See also chapter 7, with note 10, where some examples are given.

22. Harris 2013c:267–273.

23. Ibid.:273.

impression we get, however, is that although Athenian litigation was probably less consistent and predictable than it is today, when the facts were clear, the courts probably rendered fairly consistent verdicts.

The second consideration raised by Bingham that requires discussion is "law not discretion" (principle 2), which I will discuss together with "the exercise of power" (principle 4), since both concern the power of individuals to make arbitrary legal decisions. Bingham explains the first of these as follows: "questions of legal right and liability should ordinarily be resolved by application of the law and not the exercise of discretion"; he explains the second as "ministers and public officers at all levels must exercise the powers conferred on them in good faith, fairly, for the purpose for which the powers were conferred, without exceeding the limits of such powers and not unreasonably." Bingham's main concerns are that the discretion allowed to both government officials and judges should be clearly defined and relatively limited, so that decisions are made for their intended purpose and not arbitrarily; decisions should also be subject to legal challenge.

To begin with, Bingham's concern about "laws not discretion" was more easily satisfied in Athens than in just about any other legal system, for the simple reason that the power of Athenian officials, and thus their ability to affect legal decision making, was strictly limited. Any decisions they made could be reviewed and challenged not only in their accountability hearing (*euthynai*) at the end of their year in office but also in various other ways during their tenure in office.[24] Athenian jurors, on the other hand, were not subject to control by officials, and did not face an accountability hearing at the end of their term. They had complete control over the verdict and could act completely arbitrarily if they wished. But the jurors' discretion was clearly limited by their oath that they would judge according to the laws and decrees of the city and, if necessary, according to their most just understanding; they also had sworn to judge in accordance with the accusation in the case. Additionally, the large size of Athenian juries, with jurors having little or no opportunity for collaboration, meant that an occasional arbitrary decision by a juror would have been unlikely to affect the verdict.[25] To be sure, nothing absolutely prevented jurors from acting arbitrarily, but we have no evidence that they regularly did so.

Bingham's third consideration, procedural fairness, is perhaps the most subjective of his principles. Indeed, he notes that "fairness is a constantly

---

24. See Hansen 1991:220–222.

25. The seating arrangement of the jurors was randomly determined by lot (see *Ath. Pol.* 63–66), and with no time allotted for deliberation before the votes were cast, a single juror could at most discuss the case only with the few jurors seated very near him.

evolving process" and shows how English criminal law has evolved over the last two centuries to be, as he sees it, more fair.[26] Even today, criminal proceedings often fall short of true fairness, especially when the financial resources available to the prosecution and the defense differ widely. The Athenians certainly took steps to promote fairness in judicial procedure,[27] though they never prohibited the use of a logographer, which must have given rich litigants an advantage over their poorer adversaries similar to the advantage the rich have today. In the end, it is not easy to assess just how fair Athenian judicial procedures were in comparison to our own, but it is hard to point to any factor that would seem to make either of the legal systems significantly more fair than the other.

Overall, then, with regard to what are perhaps the most universally agreed features of the rule of law—the existence of a fixed, knowable set of laws to which all were subject and a clear, well-established process for adjudicating claims brought under these laws in a fair and just way—the rule of law was certainly achieved in Athens. A large set of substantive rules provided the framework for their judicial system, and a number of procedural rules allowed relatively easy (and cheap) access to the courts and a fair playing field for litigation, with equal time allowed for each speaker and the pretrial disclosure of each side's arguments and of all the evidence each side would introduce during the trial. The Athenians also strictly observed, to an extent rarely achieved even today, the principle that all people, no matter how rich or powerful, were subject to the law.

On the other hand, the Athenians appear regularly to have violated the principle of keeping extraneous, nonlegal considerations out of the decision-making process, if this principle is understood in the same terms as it generally is today. Such matters as the litigants' characters, their previous conduct, and their (and their ancestors') public service are so often discussed in the forensic speeches that it is impossible to think that these had no effect on the jurors' decisions. As I argued above, however, the Athenians themselves had a broader and more flexible concept of legal relevance than we do. In particular, they considered more of the background and context of a case to be relevant than we would allow, and as part of that context they also allowed litigants to discuss their own and their opponent's character and their previous conduct, including their public service, to a far greater extent than we would consider proper. For them, both background and character contributed to the contextualization of a dispute, adding to the likelihood that

26. Bingham 2010:90–109.

27. See, for example, Thür 2008.

someone did or did not do what was alleged in the accusation.[28] And as we have already noted, because there was almost no forensic science at the time, in assessing the facts of the case, the Athenians were largely dependent on likelihood, which was the highest standard of certainty it was possible to achieve. Contextualization was also important in assessing the justice of a case, because justice depends on the full context of the case, not just on the relatively narrow set of facts that (in our law) are considered legally relevant.

For the Athenians, then, adhering to the rule of law was completely consistent with allowing legal decision making to be influenced by a broad array of considerations that we do not allow in our own law. Two of these considerations, moreover, justice and public interest, were important not only in that they may have been part of the broader context of a case but also because in themselves they were seen as fundamental objectives of the legal system along with the rule of law. We might think that these three objectives are in conflict, but because for the Athenians all laws were both just and in the public interest, the three objectives—rule of law, justice, and public interest—were fully consistent with, and indeed supportive of, one another.

We may conclude, then, that not only did the Athenians believe in the rule of law as an important goal, but their legal system also to a large degree achieved this goal in practice, as long as one understands the concept of the rule of law as they did, as broader, more flexible, and more openly responsive to the requirements of justice and the needs of the community than the rule of law is for us.[29] Despite these differences, however, most features of the rule of law that we value today also formed part of the Athenians' concept of the rule of law.

We can say, then, that Athenian law had three main objectives, which, as they saw it, were fully compatible with one another: justice, public benefit, and the rule of law. For us, these objectives are often incompatible. In particular, our view of the rule of law generally precludes any attempt to ensure that every verdict is either just or beneficial to society as a whole; for the most part, we are only interested in whether it is fully in accord with the law. But it was not difficult for the Athenians to hold all three objectives simultaneously, because they had a substantially broader and more flexible understanding of the rule of law and a strong commitment to ensuring that

28. For contextualization, see Lanni 2006, esp. 46–53 on background information and 59–64 on character.

29. Cf. Cohen 2005a:235: "The Athenian understanding of . . . the rule of law in important ways differed fundamentally from our own."

their legal system continued to be an integral part of their democratic political system.

Another, perhaps better, way to understand the Athenian view would be to say that Athenian law had just one main objective: to ensure the rule of law in the full Athenian democratic sense. The three goals—law, justice, public interest—were conceptually separable, but their democratic ideology treated the three as inseparable in practice. For the Athenians, a judgment that was in accord with the laws was a judgment that was also just and in the public interest. As the speaker of Dem. 25.26 puts it, "The laws want what is just (*to dikaion*) and fine (*to kalon*) and advantageous (*to sympheron*)."

The rule of law is always a work in progress; some features are always observed to a greater degree than others. Thus, the answer to the question, did the Athenians observe the rule of law, is yes, to a large extent. They adhered to the rule of law as they understood it, but (like all societies) they never achieved perfect adherence.

CHAPTER 9

THE SUCCESS OF DEMOCRATIC LAW

I began this book by outlining the basic structure of Athens's democratic government and its democratic legal system, and then considered the implications of putting both of these under the full control of the *dēmos*, the citizen body, which enacted laws and sat in judgment over prosecutions of those who violated these laws. The *dēmos* was answerable to no higher personal authority in any of these roles; however, they did subordinate themselves to the higher authority of the laws, including a number of mostly unwritten procedural rules, which limited the complete freedom to act that they had in theory. I also noted the criticism this has given rise to in modern times (as well as in antiquity); particularly troubling to many has been the absence of a legal profession, which some scholars consider essential to the very definition of law.[1]

My main purpose in writing this book has been to try to understand how such a legal system controlled entirely by the *dēmos* could achieve anything resembling the rule of law. Although the forensic pleadings themselves, in their narratives and arguments, often seem quite familiar, Athenian litigation procedures have a number of features that either are absent from our legal system today or play a role that we try hard to minimize, often because they are thought to work against achieving the rule of law.[2] My aim has been to try to understand how these features, often considered "marginal" today, worked and what effect they had on the ability of the Athenian legal

1. See, for example, Watson 1985 and Gagarin 1985–1986.

2. I omitted several other such features of Athenian law because they have been well treated by others and do not directly affect the main argument of this book. These include the various extra-judicial means of enforcing community norms or resolving disputes, such as gossip or community shaming (for which see Hunter 1994 and Forsdyke 2012: esp. 144–170). I also omit any discussion of indirect ways in which forensic discourse helped enforce norms and maintain order in the community, which are well treated by Lanni 2016.

system to achieve outcomes that were fair and consistent with the laws of the city or, in other words, to what extent and in what ways (if any) did the Athenians achieve the rule of law?

After briefly describing the basic features of Athens's government and legal system, I began by examining ways in which Athenian litigation was a performance. Performance, to be sure, has a role in litigation today, since most good trial lawyers today are also good performers, especially in jury trials. But performance per se is frowned on; judges generally try to keep it to a minimum, and unwritten rules of decorum warn that the worst thing that can happen to a trial is that it becomes a "circus," a competition between performers. Athens put no such restrictions on performance, which played a large role in litigation from the earliest times, as is evident in the trial scene depicted on Achilles' shield in the *Iliad*. Homer portrays this trial as a performance with ritual features, in which litigants, judges, and an audience of community members all play a role. This audience, moreover, not only shapes the performances by its responses to the performers, it also shapes the final judgment.

In Athenian law, the litigants were the only performers, but as in all performances, theirs was shaped by their audience. Feedback from this audience significantly affected the litigants' performances, and they learned to anticipate their audience's response to their pleadings and to adjust their arguments accordingly. Trial lawyers today also pay close attention to the reactions of jurors and may adjust their pleading accordingly, but because the Athenian audience, consisting of the large jury and also other onlookers, came much closer to representing the entire community than does a modern jury, the verdict in an Athenian trial was much more likely to have the approval of the entire community than it does today. Furthermore, the performative nature of litigation contributed to making Athenian pleadings more rhetorical. Although gestures and other forms of expression may have played some role, the litigants' main means of performing was by speaking; a heavy emphasis on rhetorical skill was the natural result.

The next feature I examined, the negotiation of settlements out of court, also contained some special forms that helped make Athenian litigation more rhetorical. In many ways, negotiations in Athens were similar to the pretrial negotiations (including plea bargaining) that are common today, but the Athenians developed three special forms of negotiation relating to swearing an oath, interrogating a slave under torture, and requesting a witness's testimony, the purpose of which was more to gain a rhetorical advantage than to arrive at a mutually satisfactory resolution of the dispute.

Rules that seem to have existed at the earliest stages of law in Greece specified that evidence obtained by an oath or by interrogation under torture could not be formally introduced in court unless both sides in the case had agreed to accept the results of the oath or the interrogation. And because both sides almost never agreed to this, the main reason why a litigant proposed an oath or interrogation under torture was to gain rhetorical advantage, often by accusing the other party of not wishing to know the truth. Similarly, although witnesses could not be compelled to testify, the testimony of a witness was sometimes requested in court even though the witness had already declined to testify. In all these cases, when a litigant made a request that was denied, it had no legal effect on the case, but it allowed the litigant to make a rhetorical point. These sorts of negotiations thus contributed to making forensic pleadings more rhetorical.

I turned next to rhetoric, which, like performance, is generally restricted to a limited role in litigation today but played a major role in Athenian litigation. In Athens, rhetoric was an essential means of both establishing the facts of the case and determining the relevant laws by explaining the meaning of statutes and their application to the case at hand. I argued that the primitive state of forensic science meant that in most cases few if any hard facts were established, with the result that the litigants' rhetoric, and in particular the stories they told, necessarily became the primary means by which the jury learned what had happened. Moreover, because the opposing litigants' stories almost always diverged in some respects, and often differed widely, the jurors had to exercise their own judgment, guided primarily by the two pleadings they had just heard, to decide for themselves the truth of what happened.[3]

Similarly, in determining the legal issues, the jury would sometimes have heard the text of one or more laws that the litigants asked the clerk to read out to the court, but the meaning of these laws and their possible application to the case they were judging may have required further explanation. Some jurors might have encountered some of these same statutes in earlier cases, but most would still need some guidance, which could only come from the two litigants. And other statutes could be introduced by litigants without their texts being read out in court, so that unless a juror knew the precise text already (which cannot have happened often), they would have to rely entirely on the litigants for both the text of these laws and their possible application to the case at hand.

The importance of rhetoric then led us to ask in chapter 5 whether Athenian law provided any controls that would have restricted the freedom of litigants in speaking about anything they wished or of jurors in judging by whatever criteria they wished. First, we saw that the oath sworn by all ju-

3. *Hē alētheia tōn prachthentōn*; cf. Ant. 3.4.1–2 (cited in chapter 4, at note 24).

rors required that they judge cases according to "the laws and the decrees of the Athenian people." Athens had a good many written statutes, but even if these needed further interpretation, their texts would have exercised some control over the litigants' pleadings, because the jurors' own common-sense understanding of the laws would have restricted the litigants' leeway in interpreting them.

Equally important was the "rule of relevance," which required litigants to stick to the issue, together with the corresponding clause in the judicial oath requiring jurors to judge a case according to the issue; and the issue for each case was determined by the plaintiff's written accusation, which he had considerable freedom in composing. This accusation was read out at the beginning of each trial, and in the absence of an authoritative judge (in today's sense) who might rule on the relevance of an argument, it was up to the audience, the jurors and bystanders, to ensure that the litigants stuck to the issue. They did this primarily by raising a hubbub or uproar (*thorybos*) when litigants strayed from the issue. I concluded that, although the Athenians had a broader and more flexible understanding of relevance than we do today, litigants generally observed the rule of relevance, sometimes explaining why a line of argument was, in fact, relevant even if it might not appear to be.

The breadth and flexibility of the Athenians' understanding of relevance led me to consider two other factors that were important in Athenian litigation but have little or no place in litigation today, justice and public benefit. These were accepted as proper considerations in any litigation, even if they were not directly relevant to the specific issues of the case, because they were intrinsic to the entire Athenian legal system, litigation and legislation alike. Today we may consider justice an overall goal of our legal system, but except in extreme cases, we are reluctant to admit considerations of justice into the judgment of individual cases. In Athens, by contrast, litigants treat all laws as just and invoke justice almost as often as they invoke law, often in ways that suggest that the two are virtually interchangeable. Jurors also swore to judge according to their "most just understanding" as well as according to the laws. And because, for the Athenians, whatever was lawful was just, litigants' arguments about achieving justice were accepted in the same way as their arguments about obeying or enforcing the law. Considerations of justice are thus not uncommon in court pleadings, and we must assume that they could have some influence on a jury's decision.[4]

Similarly, the Athenians' acceptance of public benefit as a proper consid-

4. Just how much justice resulted from the Athenian legal system (or from any legal system) is impossible to determine, even if one could agree about a definition of justice that could be unambiguously applied in every case.

eration in legal cases was a consequence of their deliberate creation of a legal system that would be fully democratic in the sense of putting complete control of the system in the hands of the people. They also were committed to enacting only laws that served the public interest. It was thus natural for them to assume that not only would the system as a whole benefit the community, but so, too, would all individual laws and the outcomes of every trial. Consequently, they allowed litigants to raise considerations of public benefit in their pleadings, even when they were not strictly relevant, though in such cases public service was usually raised only briefly, as an additional factor at the end of their pleading.

In chapter 8, I came to the question with which I began: to what extent, or in what ways, did the Athenians achieve the rule of law? I concluded that in several respects they clearly observed the rule of law: they generally achieved the orderly and peaceful regulation of their society according to a set of authoritative rules and procedures, and they made all persons, no matter how rich or powerful, subject to the law. Beyond this, we must understand that material differences between classical Athens and today meant that hard evidence was rarely available to help jurors judge a case; therefore, they had to rely primarily on a standard of likelihood in determining guilt and innocence. This helps explain why their concept of relevance was necessarily broader and more flexible than our own. If one is judging likelihood, then the background and context for the events in question become important and relevant factors, meaning that the entire lives of both litigants are potentially relevant to the case. Thus, a number of factors that we would exclude today from litigation because they are not directly relevant to the central issue were accepted as relevant by the Athenians for good reasons. Their broader understanding of relevance, therefore, not only did nothing to diminish their adherence to the rule of law but was arguably necessary if they were to be able to achieve the rule of law to the greatest extent possible.

Ultimately, the key to understanding how the Athenian legal system worked and why it largely adhered to the rule of law lies in understanding its democratic nature. This begins by understanding democracy as the Athenians did—a government system that was run by the people and truly served the interests of the people. Democratic law in this political system thus meant, in the first place, a legal system in which litigation was entirely in the hands of ordinary citizens. Bury and other modern critics cited in the introduction and chapter 1 are right to see the potential dangers in such a system: eloquent litigants cleverly playing on the prejudices and emotions of uneducated jurors, who had to decide cases without any guidance by legal experts, could easily have resulted in verdicts that had nothing to do with law or justice. But this view of Athenian law fails to consider the many other features that prevented it from succumbing to this and other dangers.

In the first place, Bury and other critics have been overly influenced by the parody of a juror presented in Aristophanes' *Wasps* as ignorant, biased, and self-serving. As discussed in chapter 2, however, juries were probably reasonably representative of an average collection of Athenians. Although not professionally trained, they had to be at least thirty years old, and many would have had experience serving on the Council or in one or more of the other annual offices, and many would also have previously served on juries. There is no reason to think that they routinely violated their oath or that their decisions were largely the result of prejudice and emotion.

Second, in keeping with the Greeks' long-standing belief in the importance of written laws, they enacted a large set of laws that were written and displayed in public. One of the earliest historical events in Athenian memory was the enactment (ca. 621) of Draco's homicide law. Their first large-scale set of laws was enacted not long afterward by Solon (ca. 594). The Athenian Assembly, open to all citizens who wished to attend, continued to enact new laws after that, and at the end of the fifth century, the entire body of laws that had accumulated up to that time was examined, conflicting or overlapping laws were removed, and the remaining laws were all re-inscribed and displayed in the agora. The short-lived oligarchic revolutions in 411 and 404/3 taught the Athenians to appreciate their democracy, but also to understand the danger of uncontrolled majority rule, and led them to devise new rules and procedures, resulting in a more controlled, systematic process by which the Assembly enacted new laws—laws that would be just and in the public interest.

In addition, the Athenians created an oath, which they administered to all jurors, in which they swore in the first place to judge according to these laws. None of these measures guaranteed that verdicts would be in accordance with the law (no system can guarantee this), but they established the expectation that they would be. They also made clear to the Athenians that the laws were the foundation of their democracy, and that the citizens' management of their political and legal systems had to be based on these laws, and litigants in court regularly repeated these points in their pleadings.

Additional clauses in the juror's oath supplemented the requirement to judge according to the law in important ways. First, because it was not always clear which law or laws (if any) applied to a case, or exactly what an applicable law might mean, jurors were also required to swear that if there was no law—and presumably if the law was not clear or if it was not clear which law or laws applied to the case—they would then use "their most just opinion." This clause brought the element of justice into every case, although in fact, because all laws were assumed to be just, the element of justice was already implicit in the requirement that jurors judge according to the laws.

Further measures were also taken to ensure procedural fairness, and some of these were also specified in the juror's oath. The most important of these was a clause in the oath that jurors should judge concerning the issue at hand, that is, the accusation specified by the prosecution in the case. To impose this requirement, the issue in each case had to be made clear, so the accusation was posted at the entrance to the court and was read out at the beginning of the trial. Litigants were also required to stick to this issue; they may have had to swear an oath that they would do so, but in any case the so-called rule of relevance was well known and widely acknowledged.

Another clause in the oath required that jurors listen to both the prosecution and the defense similarly, that is, impartially. In addition to this basic element of procedural justice, the Athenians also tried to ensure procedural fairness by giving equal time to both litigants and by requiring that all documentary evidence be presented at a pretrial hearing so that both sides could be prepared to discuss this, and only this, evidence. As with judging according to the laws, nothing can guarantee that the actual procedure in any case is completely fair, but these measures would have done much to ensure a fair procedure in most cases. To be sure, the law could not eliminate all inequities. A litigant who could not afford a logographer may have been at a disadvantage if his opponent could afford one, or if his opponent was a better speaker. But the quality of legal representation today can also vary considerably, resulting in at least as much inequity in this regard.

In sum, the Athenians devised many means to prevent their democratic legal system from delivering the kind of arbitrary and capricious verdicts that Bury and others criticize, and they did everything they could, given the material conditions of the time, to ensure that verdicts would accord with the law and with justice. At the same time, they were also concerned that their democratic legal system benefit the *dēmos*, and so public interest was a consideration in every legal case. It was never the sole consideration in a case, however, and if it was cited, it was always as an additional consideration and was usually mentioned only toward the end of a litigant's pleading, and litigants never suggested that there might be a conflict between public interest and law or justice. As an objective of their legal system, however, public interest was probably not on the same level with law and justice, since (unlike them) it is not included in the juror's oath.[5]

The Athenians also took other steps to ensure that their legal system served the public interest, making the system easily accessible to all, even

5. Wallace's assertion (2006:430) that "in Athens' courtrooms as elsewhere, the welfare of the community was paramount" goes too far in implying that public interest overrode all other considerations; see also Cartledge, cited in chapter 7, note 14. In court, public interest worked together with law and justice; none of these was paramount.

those with few resources. Laws were relatively short and clearly written, with little technical language, and they were displayed in public where they could be consulted by all. The procedure for bringing complaints was relatively simple and inexpensive, allowing ordinary citizens to take their grievances to court with relative ease. If this produced an abundance of litigation, most Athenians do not appear to have been troubled by this. Jurors also received a small payment for every day they served, so the legal system provided a subsistence wage for some of the poorest citizens.

On the other hand, the ease of prosecution combined with the vagueness of many statutes and the considerable degree of freedom that plaintiffs had in composing a specific accusation meant that if a man had personal enemies and they wished to find something to accuse him of, they could often do so, even if he had led a generally upstanding life. In that case, however, his generally upstanding life might provide at least a little help in his defense.

Because the Athenians considered their legal system to be part of their political system, and in some respects the most important part, the idea of an autonomous legal system isolated from the rest of the government would have made no sense to them, and we have no evidence that they ever considered such a possibility. Not even Plato and Aristotle ever considered the possibility of a truly autonomous law, although both preferred a more authoritarian legal system with some involvement of experts as judges.

Within the context of Athenian participatory democracy, however, the Athenian legal system, tailored as it was to fit the needs of their political system, functioned well. It could only work for a relatively small community with a large degree of citizen involvement, however, and therefore it could not be transferred to and implemented in other, larger communities, as Roman law was. Its influence on other Greek poleis, however, was substantial, especially during the Hellenistic period. And for the Athenians themselves, their legal system was well suited to their relatively small polis community, and its results were generally in accordance with the laws, with justice, and with the public good. In this way it undoubtedly served their needs better than a legal system like Roman law (or modern Western law) would have. Athenian law was the right legal system for Athens.

BIBLIOGRAPHY

Adamidis, Vasileios. 2017. *Character Evidence in the Courts of Classical Athens: Rhetoric, Relevance and the Rule of Law*. Abingdon, UK.

Alwine, Andrew T. 2015. *Enmity and Feuding in Classical Athens*. Austin.

Amsterdam, Anthony G., and Jerome Bruner. 2000. *Minding the Law: How Courts Rely on Storytelling, and How Their Stories Change the Ways We Understand the Law—and Ourselves*. Cambridge, MA.

Apostolakis, Kostas E. 2007. "Tragic Patterns in Forensic Speeches: Antiphon 1 *Against the Stepmother*." *Classica et Mediaevalia* 58:179–192.

Asper, Markus. Forthcoming. "Thinking in Cases: Ancient Greek and Imperial Chinese Case Narratives." In *Ancient Case Studies After John Forrester*, ed. Markus Asper. Berlin.

Bauman, Richard. 1977. *Verbal Art as Performance*. Prospect Heights, IL.

———. 1986. *Story, Performance, and Event: Contextual Studies of Oral Narrative*. Cambridge.

Bearzot, Cinzia, Mirko Canevaro, Tristano Gargiulo, and Elisabetta Poddighe, eds. 2018. *Athenaion Politeiai tra storia, politica e sociologia: Aristotele e Pseudo-Senofonte*. Milan.

Beauchet, Ludovic, 1897. *Histoire du droit privé de la République athénienne*. Paris.

Benforado, Adam. 2015. *Unfair: The New Science of Criminal Injustice*. New York.

Benveniste, Émile. 1973. *Indo-European Language and Society*. Coral Gables, FL. (Translation of *Le vocabulaire des institutions Indo-Européennes*. Paris, 1969.)

Bergman, Paul. 1989. *Trial Advocacy in a Nutshell*. 2nd ed. St. Paul, MN.

Bers, Victor. 1985. "Dikastic *thorubos*." In *Crux: Essays Presented to G. E. M. de Ste. Croix on His 75th Birthday*, edited by P. Cartledge and F. D. Harvey, 1–15. Exeter.

Bingham, Tom. 2010. *The Rule of Law*. London.

Blanshard, Alastair. 2004a. "The Birth of the Law-Court: Putting Ancient and Modern Forensic Rhetoric in Its Place." In *Oratory in Action*, ed. Michael Edwards and Christopher Reid, 11–32. Manchester, UK.

———. 2004b. "What Counts as the *Demos*? Some Notes on the Relationship between the Jury and 'The People' in Classical Athens." *Phoenix* 58:28–48.

———. 2014. "The Permeable Spaces of the Athenian Law-Court." In *Space, Place, and Landscape in Ancient Greek Literature and Culture*, ed. Kate Gilhuly and Nancy Worman, 240–275. Cambridge.

Bohannan, Paul. 1957. *Justice and Judgment among the Tiv*. Oxford.

Bonner, Robert J. 1905. *Evidence in Athenian Courts*. Chicago.

Brunschwig, Jacques. 1996. "Rule and Exception: On the Aristotelian Theory of Equity." In *Rationality in Greek Thought*, ed. Michael Frede and Gisela Striker, 115–155. Oxford.

Burke, Edmund M. 2019. "Athenian State Finances." In Martin, ed., 2019:143–153.

Burnett, D. Graham. 2001. *A Trial by Jury*. New York.

Bury, John B. 1900. *A History of Greece to the Death of Alexander the Great*. Oxford. (Revised by Russell Meiggs. Oxford, 1975).

Calhoun, George M. 1944. *Introduction to Greek Legal Science*. Oxford.

Campbell, Tom. 2008. "Justice." In Cane and Conaghan, eds., 2008:660–662.

Cane, Peter, and Joanne Conaghan, eds. 2008. *The New Oxford Companion to Law*. Oxford.

Canevaro, Mirko. 2013a. *The Documents in the Attic Orators: Laws and Decrees in the Public Speeches of the Demosthenic Corpus*. Oxford.

———. 2013b. "*Nomothesia* in Classical Athens: What Sources Should We Believe?" *Classical Quarterly* 63:139–160.

———. 2016. *Demostene, "Contro Leptine": Introduzione, Traduzione e Commento Storico*. Berlin.

———. 2019. "Law and Justice." In Martin, ed., 2019:73–85.

Canevaro, Mirko, Andrew Erskine, Benjamin Gray, and Josiah Ober, eds. 2018. *Ancient Greek History and Contemporary Social Science*. Edinburgh.

Cantarella, Eva. 2002. "Dispute Settlement in Homer: Once Again on the Shield of Achilles." In *Mélanges en l'honneur Panayotis D. Dimakis: Droits antiques et société*, ed. Sophie Adam, et al., 147–165. Athens.

———. 2005. "Violence privée et procès." In *La violence dans les mondes grec et romain: Actes du colloque international (Paris, 2–4 mai 2002)*, ed. Jean-Marie Bertrand, 339–347. Paris.

———, ed. 2007. *Symposion 2005*. Vienna.

Carawan, Edwin. 1983. "*Erotesis*: Interrogation in the Courts of Fourth-Century Athens." *Greek, Roman, and Byzantine Studies* 24:209–226.

———, ed. 2007. *The Attic Orators*. Oxford.

Carey, Christopher. 1994a. "'Artless' Proofs in Aristotle and the Orators." *Bulletin of the Institute of Classical Studies* 39:95–106. Reprinted in Carawan, ed., 2007:229–246.

———. 1994b. "Legal Space in Classical Athens." *Greece & Rome* 41:172–186.

———. 1995. "The Witness's *Exomosia* in the Athenian Courts." *Classical Quarterly* 45:114–119.

———. 1998. "The Shape of Athenian Laws." *Classical Quarterly* 48:93–109.

———. 2000. *Democracy in Classical Athens*. London.

Carter, L. B. 1986. *The Quiet Athenian*. Oxford.

Cartledge, Paul. 2016. *Democracy: A Life*. Oxford.

Cartledge, Paul, Paul Millett, and Stephen Todd, eds. 1990. *Nomos: Essays in Athenian Law, Politics and Society*. Cambridge.

Carugati, Federica, and Barry R. Weingast. 2018. "Rethinking Mass and Elite: Decision-Making in the Athenian Law-Courts." In Canevaro et al., eds., 2018:157–183.

Christ, Matthew R. 1990. "Liturgy Avoidance and Antidosis in Classical Athens." *Transactions of the American Philological Association* 120:147–169.

———. 1998. *The Litigious Athenian*. Baltimore.

Cohen, David. 1991. "Demosthenes' *Against Meidias* and Athenian Litigation." In *Symposion 1990*, ed. Michael Gagarin, 155–164. Cologne.

———. 1995. *Law, Violence and Community in Classical Athens*. Cambridge.

———. 2005a. "Crime, Punishment, and the Rule of Law in Classical Athens." In Gagarin and Cohen, eds., 2005:211–235.

———. 2005b. "Introduction." In Gagarin and Cohen, eds., 2005:1–26.

———. 2005c. "Theories of Punishment." In Gagarin and Cohen, eds., 2005:170–190.

———. 2015. "Tyranny or the Rule of Law? Democratic Participation in Legal Institutions in Athens." In Hammer, ed., 2015:167–178.

Cohen, Edward E. 2016. "Transformation of the Athenian Economy: Maritime Finance and Maritime Law." In Tiersch 2016:207–222.

Conley, John M., and William M. O'Barr. 1990. *Rules Versus Relationships: The Ethnography of Legal Discourse.* Chicago.

Cronin, James F. 1939. "The Athenian Juror and Emotional Pleas." *Classical Journal* 34:471–479.

Davies, John. 2016. "Athens after 404: A Battleground of Contradictory Visions." In Tiersch 2016:385–394.

Davies, Wendy, and Paul Fouracre, eds. 1986. *The Settlement of Disputes in Early Medieval Europe.* Cambridge.

De Brauw, Michael. 2001–2002. "'Listen to the Laws Themselves': Citations of Laws and Portrayal of Character in Attic Oratory." *Classical Journal* 97:161–176.

Edwards, Mike. 2013. "*Hypokritēs* in Action: Delivery in Greek Rhetoric." In Kremmydas, Powell, and Rubinstein, eds., 2013:15–25.

Finley, Moses I. 1973. *Democracy Ancient and Modern.* New Brunswick, NJ.

Forsdyke, Sara. 2012. *Slaves Tell Tales: And Other Episodes in the Politics of Popular Culture in Ancient Greece.* Princeton.

———. 2018. "Ancient and Modern Conceptions of the Rule of Law." In Canevaro et al., eds., 2018:184–212.

Foxhall, Lin, and Andrew Lewis, eds. 1996. *Greek Law in Its Political Setting: Justifications Not Justice.* Oxford.

Gabrielsen, Vincent. 1987. "The *Antidosis* Procedure in Classical Athens." *Classica et Mediaevalia* 38:7–38.

Gagarin, Michael. 1975. "The Vote of Athena." *American Journal of Philology* 96:121–127.

———. 1979. "The Athenian Law against *Hybris*." In *Arktouros: Hellenic Studies presented to Bernard M. W. Knox on the Occasion of His 65th Birthday*, edited by Glen W. Bowersock, Walter Burkert, and Michael C. J. Putnam, 229–236. Berlin.

———. 1981. *Drakon and Early Athenian Homicide Law.* New Haven, CT.

———. 1983. "Antilochus' Strategy: The Chariot Race in *Iliad* 23." *Classical Philology* 78:35–39.

———. 1985–1986. Review of Watson 1985. In *Classical Journal* 81:173–175.

———. 1986. *Early Greek Law.* Berkeley.

———. 1992. "The Poetry of Justice: Hesiod and the Origins of Greek Law." *Ramus* 21:61–78.

———. 1996. "The Torture of Slaves in Athenian Law." *Classical Philology* 91:1–18.

———. 1997. "Oaths and Oath-Challenges in Greek Law." In *Symposion 1995*, edited by Gerhard Thür and Julie Vélissaropoulos-Karakostas, 125–134. Cologne.

———, ed. 1998–2017. *The Oratory of Classical Greece.* 15 vols. Austin.

———. 2003. "Telling Stories in Athenian Law." *Transactions of the American Philological Association* 133:197–207.

———. 2004. "The Rule of Law in Gortyn." In Harris and Rubinstein, eds., 2004: 173–183.

———. 2007a. "From Oral Law to Written Laws: Draco's Law and Its Homeric Roots." In Cantarella, ed., 2007:3–17.

———. 2007b. "Litigants' Oaths in Athenian Law." In Sommerstein and Fletcher, eds., 2007:39–47.

———. 2008. *Writing Greek Law*. Cambridge.

———. 2012. "Law, Politics and the Question of Relevance in the Case *On the Crown*." *Classical Antiquity* 31:293–314.

———. 2014. "Rhetoric as a Source of Law in Athens." In *Symposion 2013*, edited by Michael Gagarin and Adriaan Lanni, 131–144. Vienna.

———. 2017. "Rhetoric and Law." In MacDonald 2017:43–52.

———. 2018a. "Abuse Is in the Eye of the Beholder." In *Use and Abuse of the Law in the Athenian Courts*, edited by Chris Carey, Ifigeneia Giannadaki, and Brenda Griffith-Williams, 17–31. Leiden.

———. 2018b. "Challenges in Athenian Law: Going beyond Oaths and *Basanos* to Proposals." In *Symposion 2017*, edited by Gerhard Thür, Uri Yiftach, and Rachel Zelnick-Abramovitz, 165–177. Vienna.

———. 2018c. "Hyperides against Athenogenes and the Athenian Law on Agreements." In Perlman, ed., 2018:35–53.

———. 2019. "Court Procedures and Arbitration." In Martin, ed., 2019:87–99.

Gagarin, Michael, and David Cohen, eds. 2005. *The Cambridge Companion to Ancient Greek Law*. Cambridge.

Gagarin, Michael, and Paula Perlman. 2016. *The Laws of Ancient Crete c. 650–400 BCE*. Oxford.

Gilbert, Gustav. 1893. *Handbuch der griechischen Staatsalterthümer*. 2nd ed. Leipzig.

———. 1895. *The Constitutional Antiquities of Sparta and Athens*. London.

Goldhill, Simon. 1999. "Programme Notes." In Goldhill and Osborne 1999:1–19.

Goldhill, Simon, and Robin Osborne, eds. 1999. *Performance Culture and Athenian Democracy*. Cambridge.

Goodrich, Peter. 1998. "Law by Other Means." *Cardozo Studies in Law and Literature* 10:111–116.

Gordon, Robert W. 2016. "Legal Storytelling as a Variety of Legal Realism." In *The New Legal Realism*, Vol. 1*: Translating Law-and-Society for Today's Legal Practice*, ed. Elizabeth Mertz, Stewart Macaulay, and Thomas W. Mitchell, 169–179. Cambridge.

Gowder, Paul. 2014. "Democracy, Solidarity, and the Rule of Law: Lessons from Athens." *Buffalo Law Review* 62(1):1–67.

Griffith-Williams, Brenda. 2013. "Violence in Court: Law and Rhetoric in Athenian and English Assault Cases." *Greece and Rome* 60:89–100.

———. 2016. "Rational and Emotional Persuasion in Athenian Inheritance Cases." In *Emotion and Persuasion in Classical Antiquity*, ed. Ed Sanders and Matthew Johncock, 41–55. Stuttgart.

Grote, George. 1846–1856. *A History of Greece from the Earliest Period to the Close of the Generation Contemporary with Alexander the Great*. 12 vols. London.

Hall, Edith. 1995. "Lawcourt Dramas: The Power of Performance in Greek Forensic Oratory." *Bulletin of the Institute of Classical Studies* 40:39–58.

———. 2006. *The Theatrical Cast of Athens: Interactions between Ancient Greek Drama and Society*. Oxford.

Hammer, Dean, ed. 2015. *A Companion to Greek Democracy and the Roman Republic*. Chichester, UK.

Hansen, Mogens Herman. 1983. "The Athenian 'Politicians,' 403–322 B.C." *Greek, Roman, and Byzantine Studies* 24:33–55.

———. 1985. "Athenian Nomothesia." *Greek, Roman, and Byzantine Studies* 26:345–371.

———. 1986. *Demography and Democracy: The Number of Athenian Citizens in the Fourth Century B.C.* Herning, Denmark.

———. 1991. *The Athenian Democracy in the Age of Demosthenes.* Oxford.

———. 2006. *Studies in the Population of Aigina, Athens and Eretria.* Copenhagen.

———, ed. 2010. *Démocratie athénienne—Démocratie moderne: Tradition et influences.* Geneva.

Harris, Edward M. 1990. "Did the Athenians Regard Seduction as a Worse Crime Than Rape?" *Classical Quarterly* 40:370–377.

———. 1994. "Law and Oratory." In *Persuasion: Greek Rhetoric in Action*, edited by Ian Worthington, 130–150. London.

———. 1995. *Aeschines and Athenian Politics.* New York.

———. 1999. "The Penalty for Frivolous Prosecutions in Athenian Law." *Dike* 2:123–142. Reprinted in Harris 2006a: 405–422.

———. 2000. "Open Texture in Athenian Law." *Dike* 3:27–79.

———. 2006a. *Democracy and the Rule of Law in Classical Athens: Essays on Law, Society, and Politics.* Cambridge.

———. 2006b. "A Response to Robert Wallace." In Rupprecht ed. 2006:67–72.

———. 2006c. "The Rule of Law in Athenian Democracy: Reflections on the Judicial Oath." *Dike* 9:157–181.

———. 2006d. "Solon and the Spirit of the Laws in Archaic and Classical Greece." In *Solon of Athens: New Historical and Philological Approaches*, edited by Josine H. Block and André P. M. H. Lardinois, 290–318. Leiden.

———. 2007. "Did the Athenian Courts Attempt to Achieve Consistency? Oral Tradition and Written Records in the Athenian Administration of Justice." In *Politics of Orality*, edited by Craig Cooper, 343–370. Leiden.

———, trans. 2008. *Demosthenes, Speeches 20–22.* Austin TX.

———. 2013a. "How Strictly Did the Athenian Courts Apply the Law? The Role of *Epieikeia.*" *Bulletin of the Institute of Classical Studies* 56:27–48.

———. 2013b. "The Plaint in Athenian Law and Legal Procedure." In *Archives and Archival Documents in Ancient Societies*, edited by Michele Faraguna, 143–162. Trieste.

———. 2013c. *The Rule of Law in Action in Democratic Athens.* New York.

———. 2016. "From Democracy to the Rule of Law? Constitutional Change in Athens during the Fifth and Fourth Centuries BCE." In Tiersch 2016:73–87.

———, trans. 2018a. *Demosthenes, Speeches 23–26.* Austin TX.

———. 2018b. "Trials, Private Arbitration, and Public Arbitration in Classical Athens or the Background to [Arist.] *Ath. Pol.* 53, 1–7." In C. Bearzot et al., eds., 2018: 213–230.

Harris, Edward M., and Lene Rubinstein, eds. 2004. *The Law and the Courts in Ancient Greece.* London.

Harris, William V. 1989. *Ancient Literacy.* Cambridge, MA.

Harrison, A. R. W. 1971. *The Law of Athens.* Vol. 2: *Procedure.* Oxford.

Hart, H. L. A. 1994. *The Concept of Law.* 2nd ed. Oxford.

Harter-Uibopuu, Kaja. 2002. "Ancient Greek Approaches toward Alternative Dispute Resolution." *Willamette Journal of International Law and Dispute Resolution* 10:47–69.

Harvey, David. 1990. "The Sykophant and Sykophancy: Vexatious Redefinition?" In Cartledge, Millett, and Todd, eds., 1990:103–121.

Headlam, J. W. 1893. "On the πρόκλησις εἰς βάσανον in Attic Law." *Classical Review* 7:1–5.

Herman, Gabriel. 1994. "How Violent Was Athenian Society?" In *Ritual, Finance, Politics: Athenian Democratic Accounts Presented to David Lewis*, edited by Robin Osborne and Simon Hornblower, 99–117. Oxford.

———. 2006. *Morality and Behaviour in Democratic Athens: A Social History*. Cambridge.

Hesk, Jon. 1999. "The Rhetoric of Anti-Rhetoric in Athenian Oratory." In Goldhill and Osborne, eds., 1999:201–230.

Hohfeld, Wesley Newcomb. 1919. *Fundamental Legal Conceptions as Applied in Judicial Reasoning and Other Legal Essays*. New Haven, CT.

Hunter, Virginia J. 1994. *Policing Athens: Social Control in the Attic Lawsuits, 420–320 B.C.* Princeton, NJ.

Ismard, Paulin. 2017. *Democracy's Slaves: A Political History of Ancient Greece*. Cambridge, MA. Translation of *La démocratie contre les experts: Les esclaves publics en Grèce ancienne*. Paris, 2015.

Johnstone, Steven. 1999. *Disputes and Democracy: The Consequences of Litigation in Athens*. Austin, TX.

Jones, A. H. M. 1957. *Athenian Democracy*. Oxford.

Kapparis, Konstantinos A. 1999. *Apollodoros "Against Neaira" [D. 59]*. Berlin.

———. 2018. *Athenian Law and Society*. Abingdon, UK.

Kleinfeld, Joshua, et al. 2017. "Democratizing Criminal Justice Symposium." Special issue, *Northwestern University Law Review* 111(6).

Konstan, David. 2000. "Pity and the Law in Greek Theory and Practice." *Dike* 3:125–145.

Kremmydas, Christos. 2012. *Commentary on Demosthenes Against Leptines*. Oxford.

Kremmydas, Christos, Jonathan Powell, and Lene Rubinstein, eds. 2013. *Profession and Performance: Aspects of Oratory in the Greco-Roman World. Bulletin of the Institute of Classical Studies: Supplement 123*. London.

Kroll, John H. 1972. *Athenian Bronze Allotment Plates*. Cambridge, MA.

Langdon, Merle K. 2015. "Herders' Graffiti." In Matthaiou and Papazarkadas, eds., 2015:49–58.

Lanni, Adriaan M. 1997. "Spectator Sport or Serious Politics? οἱ περιεστηκότες and the Athenian Lawcourts." *Journal of Hellenic Studies* 117:183–189.

———. 1999. "Precedent and Legal Reasoning in Classical Athenian Courts: A Noble Lie?" *American Journal of Legal History* 43:27–51.

———. 2004. "Arguing from 'Precedent': Modern Perspectives on Athenian Practice." In Harris and Rubinstein, eds., 2004:159–171.

———. 2006. *Law and Justice in the Courts of Classical Athens*. Cambridge.

———. 2010. "Judicial Review and the Athenian 'Constitution.'" In Hansen, ed., 2010:235–276.

———. 2013. "Law and Democracy in Classical Athens." In *The Greek Polis and the Invention of Democracy: A Politico-cultural Transformation and Its Interpretations*, edited by Johann P. Arnason, Kurt A. Raaflaub, and Peter Wagner. 163–180. Chichester, UK.

———. 2016. *Law and Order in Ancient Athens*. Cambridge.

———. 2018. "The Role of the Complaint (*graphe/enklema*) in the Athenian Legal System." In *Symposion 2017*, edited by Gerhard Thür, Uri Yiftach, and Rachel Zelnick-Abramovitz, 185–202. Vienna.

Lanni, Adriaan, and Robert W. Wallace. 2018. "Introduction." In Perlman, ed., 2018: 1–9.

Lassiter, Christo. 1996. "TV or Not TV—That Is the Question." *Journal of Criminal Law and Criminology* 86(3):928–1001.

Laws, Sir John. 2013. "The Rhetoric of the Common Law." In Kremmydas, Powell, and Rubinstein, eds., 2013:111–117.

Lipsius, Justus Herman. 1905–1915. *Das attische Recht und Rechtsverfahren*. Leipzig.

MacCormick, Neil. 2005. *Rhetoric and the Rule of Law: A Theory of Legal Reasoning*. Oxford.

MacDonald, Michael J. 2017. *The Oxford Handbook of Rhetorical Studies*. Oxford.

MacDowell, Douglas M. 1975. "Law-Making at Athens in the Fourth Century B.C." *Journal of Hellenic Studies* 95:62–74.

———. 1978. *The Law in Classical Athens*. London.

———. 1990, ed. *Demosthenes* Against Meidias *(Oration 21)*. Introduction, translation, and commentary. Oxford.

———. 2000. *Demosthenes on the False Embassy (Oration 19)*. Introduction and commentary. Oxford.

———. 2010. "Aristophanes and Athenian Law." In *Law and Drama in Ancient Greece*, edited by Edward M. Harris, Delfim F. Leão, and Peter J. Rhodes, 147–157. London.

Martin, Gunther. 2008. "The Witness's *Exomosia* in Athens." *Classical Quarterly* 58: 56–68.

———, ed. 2019. *The Oxford Handbook of Demosthenes*. Oxford.

Matthaiou, Angelos P., and Nikolaos Papazarkadas, eds. 2015. *ΑΞΩΝ: Studies in Honor of Ronald S. Stroud*. Athens.

Menken, H. L. 1995. *A Second Menken Chrestomathy*. New York.

Mertz, Elizabeth. 2007. *The Language of Law School: Learning to "Think Like a Lawyer."* Oxford.

Miller, Fred D. 2009. "Origins of Rights in Ancient Political Thought." In *The Cambridge Companion to Ancient Political Thought*, edited by Stephen Salkever, 301–330. Cambridge.

Mirhady, David C. 1991. "The Oath-Challenge in Athens." *Classical Quarterly* 41:78–83.

———. 1996. "Torture and Rhetoric in Athens." *Journal of Hellenic Studies* 116:119–131.

———. 2007. "The Dikasts' Oath and the Question of Fact." In Sommerstein and Fletcher, eds., 2007:48–59.

Missiou, Anna. 2011. *Literacy and Democracy in Fifth-Century Athens*. Cambridge.

Navarre, Octave, and Pierre Orsini. 1957. *Démosthène: Plaidoyers Politiques*. Vol. 1. Paris.

Ober, Josiah. 1989. *Mass and Elite in Democratic Athens: Rhetoric, Ideology, and the Power of the People*. Princeton, NJ.

O'Connell, Peter A. 2017. *The Rhetoric of Seeing in Attic Forensic Oratory*. Austin, TX.

Omitowoju, Roseanne. 2002. *Rape and the Politics of Consent in Classical Athens*. Cambridge.

O'Neil, James L. 2001. "Was the Athenian *Gnome Dikaiotate* a Principle of Equity?" *Antichthon* 35:20–29.

Osborne, Robin. 1985. "Law in Action in Classical Athens." *Journal of Hellenic Studies* 105:40–58.

———. 1990. "Vexatious Litigation in Classical Athens: Sykophancy and the Sykophant." In Cartledge, Millett, and Todd, eds., 1990:83–102. Cambridge.

Osborne, Robin, and Peter J. Rhodes, eds. 2017. *Greek Historical Inscriptions 478–404 BC*. Oxford.

Ostwald, Martin. 1986. *From Popular Sovereignty to the Sovereignty of Law: Law, Society, and Politics in Fifth-Century Athens*. Berkeley, CA.

Palmer, L. R. 1950. "The Indo-European Origins of Greek Justice." *Transactions of the Philological Society* 49:149–168.

Pébarthe, Christophe. 2006. *Cité, démocratie et écriture: Histoire de l'alphabétisation d'Athènes à l'époque classique*. Paris.

Perlman, Paula, ed. 2018. *Ancient Greek Law in the 21st Century*. Austin, TX.

Phillips, David D. 2009. "Hyperides 3 and the Athenian Law of Contracts." *Transactions of the American Philological Association* 139:89–122.

———. 2017. "Assumption of Risk in Athenian Law." In *Ancient Law, Ancient Society*, edited by Dennis P. Kehoe and Thomas A. J. McGinn, 46–65. Ann Arbor, MI.

Porter, John R. 1997. "Adultery by the Book: Lysias 1 (*On the Murder of Eratosthenes*) and Comic *Diegesis*." *Echos du Monde Classique* 40, n.s. 16:421–453.

Pritchard, David M. 2015. *Public Spending and Democracy in Classical Athens*. Austin, TX.

Rhodes, Peter J. 1981. *A Commentary on the Aristotelian* Athenaion Politeia. Oxford.

———. 1991. "The Athenian Code of Laws, 410–399 BC." *Journal of Hellenic Studies* 111:87–100.

———. 1995. "Judicial Procedures in Fourth-Century Athens: Improvement or Simply Change?" In *Die athenische Demokratie im 4. Jahrhundert v. Chr.*, edited by Walter Eder, 303–319. Stuttgart.

———. 2004. "Keeping to the Point." In Harris and Rubinstein, eds., 2004:137–158.

———. 2016. "Fourth-Century Appointments in Athens." In Tiersch, ed., 2016:109–119.

———, ed. 2017. *The Athenian Constitution, Written in the School of Aristotle*. Liverpool.

———. 2018. "What Is a Constitution?" In C. Bearzot et al., eds., 2018:21–31.

Roberts, Jennifer Tolbert. 1982. *Accountability in Athenian Government*. Madison, WI.

———. 1994. *Athens on Trial: The Antidemocratic Tradition in Western Thought*. Princeton, NJ.

Robertson, Noel. 1990. "The Laws of Athens, 410–399 BC: The Evidence for Review and Publication." *Journal of Hellenic Studies* 110:43–75.

Roebuck, Derek. 2001. *Ancient Greek Arbitration*. Oxford.

Roisman, Joseph. 2003. "The Rhetoric of Courage in the Athenian Orators." In *Studies in Manliness and Courage in Classical Antiquity*, edited by Ralph M. Rosen and Ineke Sluiter, 127–143. Leiden.

———. 2005. *The Rhetoric of Manhood: Masculinity in the Attic Orators*. Berkeley, CA.

———. 2006. *The Rhetoric of Conspiracy in Ancient Athens*. Berkeley, CA.

Ross, Alf. 1958. *On Law and Justice*. London.

Rubinstein, Lene. 2000. *Litigation and Cooperation: Supporting Speakers in the Courts of Classical Athens*. Historia Einzelschrift 147. Stuttgart.

———. 2003. "Stirring Up Dicastic Anger." In *Law, Rhetoric, and Comedy in Classical Athens: Essays in Honour of Douglas M. MacDowell*, edited by D. L. Cairns and R. A. Knox, 187–203. Swansea, UK.

———. 2007. "Arguments from Precedent in Attic Oratory." In Carawan, ed., 2007: 359–371.

———. 2014. "Evoking Anger through Pity: Portraits of the Vulnerable and Defenceless in Attic Oratory." In *Unveiling Emotions II: Emotions in Greece and Rome: Texts, Images, Material Culture*, edited by Angelos Chaniotis and Pierre Ducrey, 135–165. Stuttgart.

Rupprecht, Hans-Albert, ed. 2006. *Symposion 2003*. Vienna.

Scafuro, Adele C. 1997. *The Forensic Stage: Settling Disputes in Graeco-Roman New Comedy*. Cambridge.

———, trans. 2011. *Demosthenes, Speeches 39–49*. Austin, TX.

———. 2015. "The Economics of the Athenian Court System." In Matthaiou and Papazarkadas, eds., 2015:363–392.

Scheppele, Kim Lane. 1989. "Legal Storytelling." *Michigan Law Review* 87:2073–2098.

Schiappa, Edward. 2003. *Protagoras and Logos: A Study in Greek Philosophy and Rhetoric*. 2nd ed. Columbia, SC.

Schrager, Sam. 1999. *The Trial Lawyer's Art*. Philadelphia.

Serafim, Andreas. 2017. *Attic Oratory and Performance*. London.

Sickinger, James P. 1999. *Public Records and Archives in Classical Athens*. Chapel Hill, NC.

———. 2007. "Rhetoric and the Law." In *A Companion to Greek Rhetoric*, edited by Ian Worthington, 286–302. Oxford.

Simpson, A. W. Brian. 1995. *Leading Cases in the Common Law*. Oxford.

Smith, Taffiny L. 1997. "The Distortion of Criminal Trials through Televised Proceedings." *Law and Psychology Review* 21:257–269.

Sommerstein, Alan H., and Judith Fletcher, eds. 2007. *Horkos: The Oath in Greek Society*. Exeter, UK.

Stroud, Ronald S. 1968. *Drakon's Law on Homicide*. Berkeley, CA.

———. 1974. "An Athenian Law on Silver Coinage." *Hesperia* 43:157–188 (with plates 25–27).

———. 1998. *The Athenian Grain-Tax Law of 374/3 B.C.* Princeton, NJ.

Sundahl, Mark J. 2009. "The Living Constitution of Ancient Athens: A Comparative Perspective on the Originalism Debate." *John Marshall Law Review* 42:463–504.

Szegedy-Maszak, Andrew. 1978. "Legends of the Greek Lawgivers." *Greek, Roman, and Byzantine Studies* 19:199–209.

Talamanca, Mario. 1979. "Dikazein e krinein nelle testimonianze greche più antiche." In *Symposion 1974*, edited by A. Biscardi, 103–135. Cologne.

Tandy, David W. 2015. "Production, Trade, and Consumption in Greek Democracy." In Hammer, ed., 2015:349–367.

Taylor, Claire. 2007. "From the Whole Citizen Body? The Sociology of Election and Lot in the Athenian Democracy." *Hesperia* 76:323–345.

———. 2016. "Social Dynamics in Fourth-Century Athens: Poverty and Standards of Living." In Tiersch, ed., 2016:261–277.

Tellegen-Couperus, Olga, and Jan Willem Tellegen. 2013. "*Artes Urbanae*: Roman Law and Rhetoric." In *New Frontiers: Law and Society in the Roman World*, edited by Paul J. du Plessis, 31–50. Edinburgh.

Thomas, Rosalind. 2016. "Performance, Audience Participation and the Dynamics of the Fourth-Century Assembly and Jury-Courts of Athens." In Tiersch, ed., 2016:89–107. Stuttgart.

Thür, Gerhard. 1970. "Zum dikázein bei Homer." *Zeitschrift der Savigny Stiftung* 87: 426–444.

———. 1977. *Beweisführung vor den Schwurgerichtshöfen Athens: die Proklesis zur Basanos*. Österreichischen Akademie der Wissenschaften, Sitzungsberichte 310. Vienna.

———. 1996. "Oaths and Dispute Settlement in Ancient Greek Law." In Foxhall and Lewis, eds., 1996:57–72.

———. 2005. "The Role of the Witness in Athenian Law." In Gagarin and Cohen, eds., 2005:146–169.

———. 2007. "Das Prinzip der Fairness im attischen Prozess: Gedanken zu Echinos und Enklema." In Cantarella, ed., 2007:131–150.

———. 2008. "The Principle of Fairness in Athenian Legal Procedure: Thoughts on the Echinos and Enklema." *Dike* 11:51–73. Translation of Thür 2007.

———. 2013. "The Statute on *homologein* in Hyperides' Speech *Against Athenogenes*." *Dike* 16:1–10.

———. 2015. "Transaction Costs in Athenian Law." In *Law and Transaction Costs in the Ancient Economy*, edited by Dennis P. Kehoe, David M. Ratzan, and Uri Yiftach, 36–50. Ann Arbor, MI.

———. 2018. "Formal Proposals in Athenian Law." In *Symposion 2017*, edited by Gerhard Thür, Uri Yiftach, and Rachel Zelnick-Abramovitz, 179–184. Vienna.

Tiersch, Claudia, ed. 2016. *Die Athenische Demokratie im 4. Jahrhundert: Zwischen Modernisierung und Tradition*. Stuttgart.

Todd, Stephen C. 1993. *The Shape of Athenian Law*. Oxford.

———. 1996. "*Lysias against Nikomachos*: The Fate of the Expert in Athenian Law." In Foxhall and Lewis, eds., 1996:33–56. Oxford.

———. 1998. "The Rhetoric of Enmity in the Attic Orators." In *Kosmos: Essays in Order, Conflict, and Community in Classical Athens*, edited by Paul Cartledge, Paul Millett, and Sitta Von Reden, 162–169. Cambridge.

———, trans. 2000. *Lysias*. Austin.

———. 2005a. "Law and Oratory at Athens." In Gagarin and Cohen, eds., 2005:97–111.

———. 2005b. "Law, Theatre, Rhetoric and Democracy in Classical Athens." *European Review of History* 12:63–79.

———. 2007. *A Commentary on Lysias: Speeches 1–11*. Oxford.

Wallace, Robert W. 1994. "Private Lives and Public Enemies: Freedom of Thought in Classical Athens." In *Athenian Identity and Civic Ideology*, edited by Alan L. Boegehold and Adele C. Scafuro, 127–155. Baltimore, MD.

———. 2006a. "Law and Rhetoric: Community Justice in Athenian Courts." In *A Companion to the Classical Greek World*, edited by Konrad H. Kinzl, 416–431. Malden, MA.

———. 2006b. "Withdrawing *Graphai* in Ancient Athens—A Case Study in 'Sycophancy' and Legal Idiosyncrasies." In Rupprecht, ed., 2006:57–66.

———. 2009a. "Charismatic Leaders." In *A Companion to Archaic Greece*, edited by Kurt A. Raaflaub and Hans van Wees, 411–426. Chichester, UK.

———. 2009b. "Personal Freedom in Greek Democracies, Republican Rome, and Modern Liberal States." In *A Companion to Greek and Roman Political Thought*, edited by Ryan K. Balot, 164–177. Chichester, UK.

———. 2015. *Reconstructing Damon: Music, Wisdom Teaching, and Politics in Perikles' Athens*. Oxford.

———. 2016. "Equality, the Dēmos, and Law in Archaic Greece." In *Symposion 2015*, edited by Delfim F. Leão and Gerhard Thür, 1–13. Vienna.

———. 2018a. "Administering Justice in Ancient Athens: Framework and Core Principles." In Perlman, ed., 2018:10–24.

———. 2018b. "Legal Complaints, Relevance in Court Speeches, and Community Welfare: Response to Adriaan Lanni." In *Symposion 2017*, edited by Gerhard Thür, Uri Yiftach, and Rachel Zelnick-Abramovitz, 203–209. Vienna.

Watson, Alan. 1985. *The Evolution of Law*. Baltimore, MD.

Westbrook, Raymond. 2010. "The Early History of Law: A Theoretical Essay." *Zeitschrift der Savigny Stiftung* 127:1–13.

Whibley, Leonard, ed. 1905. *A Companion to Greek Studies*. New York.

Whitehead, David. 2000. *Hypereides: The Forensic Speeches*: Introduction, translation, and commentary. Oxford.

Wohl, Victoria. 2010. *Law's Cosmos: Juridical Discourse in Athenian Forensic Oratory*. Cambridge.

Wolff, Hans Julius. 1946. "The Origin of Judicial Litigation among the Greeks." *Traditio* 4:31–87.

Worthington, Ian. 1991. "Greek Oratory, Revision of Speeches, and the Problem of Historical Reliability." *Classica et Mediaevalia* 42:55–74.

Worthington, Sarah. 2008. "Equity as a System of Law." In Cane and Conaghan, eds., 2008:408–409.

Wyse, William. 1905. "Law." In *A Companion to Greek Studies*, edited by Leonard Whibley, 377–402. New York.

Yunis, Harvey. 2005. "The Rhetoric of Law in Fourth-Century Athens." In Gagarin and Cohen, eds., 2005:191–207.

———. 2017. "Plato's Rhetoric in Theory and Practice." In MacDonald, ed., 2017: 121–131.

INDEX OF ANCIENT TEXTS

GENERAL INDEX